Not-So-Nuclear Families

Not-So-Nuclear Families

Class, Gender, and Networks of Care

KAREN V. HANSEN

RUTGERS UNIVERSITY PRESS
New Brunswick, New Jersey, and London

Library of Congress Cataloging-in-Publication Data

Hansen, Karen V.
    Not-so-nuclear families : class, gender, and networks of care / Karen V. Hansen.
        p.   cm.
Includes bibliographical references (p.   ) and index.
    ISBN 0-8135-3500-X (hardcover : alk. paper)—ISBN 0-8135-3501-8 (pbk. : alk. paper)
    1. Family—United States.   2. Social networks—United States.   3. Social classes—United States.   I. Title.
    HQ536.H3188 2004
    306.85'0973—dc22

                                                                              2004007532

A British Cataloging-in-Publication record for this book is available from the British Library

To Benjy and Evan

Contents

List of Tables and Figures *ix*
Preface and Acknowledgments *xi*

Chapter 1   Networks of Interdependence in an Age of Independence   *1*

Part I   Profiles of Four Networks of Interdependence

Chapter 2   The Cranes: An Absorbent Safety Net   *25*

Chapter 3   The Aldriches: A Family Foundation   *47*

Chapter 4   The Duvall-Brennans: A Loose Association of Advisors   *72*

Chapter 5   The Beckers: A Warm Web of People   *98*

Part II   Constructing and Maintaining Networks

Chapter 6   Staging Networks: Inclusion and Exclusion   *127*

Chapter 7   The Tangle of Reciprocity   *155*

Chapter 8   Men, Women, and the Gender of Caregiving   *182*

Conclusion   *209*

Appendix   *219*
Notes   *221*
Bibliography   *241*
Index   *255*

List of Tables and Figures

Tables

1.1 Characteristics of Adult Members of Networks of Care 18
1.2 Gender and Marital Status of Network Anchors and Members 19
2.1 Crane Network 26
3.1 Aldrich Network 48
4.1 Duvall-Brennan Network 73
5.1 Becker Network 100
8.1 Men in the Networks of Care 183

Figures

7.1 Continuum of Reciprocity 158
7.2 Reciprocity Relationships in Nelson's Single-Mother Community 159
7.3 Reciprocity Relationships in Sahlins' Kin-Based Societies 160

Preface and Acknowledgments

The project I describe in this book, with its emphasis on both family and class, is rooted in my own life history.[1] Well before I began studying families across class, I had ample opportunity to accumulate insights—and prejudices.

At eighteen, I left my white working-class home in northern California to enter a privileged university environment in Southern California.[2] I had just graduated from a high school located literally on the other side of the tracks from the middle-class neighborhood. At my high school, race was the operative identity and social divider. Class distinctions were slight; virtually all the students were poor or working class.

In my first few months at the University of California, however, everyone on the campus seemed wealthy. At every turn, I ran smack up against class privilege. I felt nothing short of shock when I discovered my new classmates were no smarter than my friends back at home who were working on the Hewlett Packard assembly line, or who had joined the air force to reduce their chances of being sent to Vietnam. My boyfriend at the time, like many others who were smart and industrious, worked in a cannery during the summer so he could attend community college during the academic year.

At the University of California I attended, the prejudices I had developed against middle-class kids were confirmed. From my perspective, they had it easy; they had been admitted to this elite university because their parents were rich. They inherited the privileges of their middle-class status. They had grown up with the expectation they would go to college, and their parents had the know-how to help them. While not less deserving than my friends back home, they were certainly no more deserving, either.

This wasn't my first exposure to structural inequality, but it was a life-altering one. My experience made a sociologist of me. I recall writing a paper in an introductory sociology class about "passing" in the middle-class university context. Thanks to my blonde hair and blue eyes, and a school dress code that emphasized flip-flops and shorts, I looked much like most of my campus peers. Even a superficial probe, however, would reveal my class differences. The t-shirts, shorts, and jeans in my dorm room closet did not hide a back row of formalwear, as those in the other girls' closets did.[3]

I was able to survive more successfully academically than I did socially. But I had no clue how a research-oriented university operated. What was a teaching assistant? What were professors doing that kept them from meeting with students except for two hours a week? Gradually, I came to better understand both the university and my place in it. The sociology I studied offered me tools for analyzing structural inequality; the history courses gave it a context. Through classes on race, stratification, women's history, social anthropology, and gender, I came to see myself from a structural perspective.

Family Feasting

My university education enriched an understanding of my social location that had begun taking shape much earlier, sitting at the dinner table at home. When I was a child, dinnertime often had the aura of a special event. It was not just my love affair with food that made it so, but the gratitude my family expressed over our good fortune in having meat, potatoes, vegetables, and, God bless us, a tasty dessert of some kind. My parents knew what it was like to go hungry. So when my father would begin dinner by asking, with a big smile, "I wonder what the poor people are doing?" we always laughed. The question was funny, of course, because *we* were the poor people. "Oh, Daddy!" my nieces and I would protest, giggling.[4] How could anyone describe our feast as a meal of the poor? Never mind that the salad was made of iceberg lettuce or that the green beans were canned. Never mind that the rotation from meatloaf to hamburger to pork chops was a short one. We loved what we had. We ate our dinners and celebrated our bounty. The joke was on those people who thought we were poor, but for whom poverty meant only deprivation and suffering.[5]

My parents had grown up in the hinterlands of western Canada, where a well-fed family was but a poor harvest from starvation. In April 1945, ten years before I was born, they left Alberta to move to a more prosperous and more urban region of northern California. They left behind their extended kin and family homesteads and brought with them their two children (my older sister and brother). Entitlement was not a sensibility my Norwegian and Danish grandparents cultivated in my parents, who adopted the righteousness of the belief that people get what they deserve. No begging, no special treatment, no favors. No asking, even, in most cases. If you worked hard, you would be rewarded; if you did not, you would suffer accordingly. My parents complemented this inherited ideology with a radical egalitarianism. As we were growing up, they reminded my older sister and brother and me that we were no better than anybody else. No worse, but no better.

My parents' education ended with the eighth grade. This was a respectable achievement for the children of rural Scandinavian immigrants, but it was not sufficient to ensure success in the States. When my father began to pursue the American dream by taking a correspondence course in real estate (determined to rise above his lot as a logging truck driver and a mechanic), he relied on my mother's strengths in reading and spelling to supplement his math skills. Their teamwork paid off. He completed the course and began a new career. His business successes and failures both prompted moves; our family relocated to one small community after another. My mother counted thirty-five moves in thirty-seven years. All the while, she entered and exited the paid labor force. She always said the best job she ever held was as a meat wrapper in a butcher shop. In what eventually became a long history of low-wage work, this was her only stint as a union member.

My sister and brother, twenty and eighteen years my senior, respectively, came of age in the 1950s. In spite of their bright intellects and personalities, they did not have the opportunities I would have a generation later. Their experiences served as cautionary tales for me. At fifteen my sister eloped and divulged her secret only when she became pregnant. With a young child, she abandoned schooling and began a life-long up-and-down journey of family devotion and hard work.

My big brother had a clearer sense of how to work the U.S. system effectively. As a boy, he had more options. He signed up for the navy right out of high school, like so many working-class boys who viewed the military as one of the few viable paths to a future. Once out of the navy, he attended night school and got a college degree to become an elementary school teacher. He left home soon after I was born, so I did not see him very much while I was growing up. But he would show up once or twice a year, like a beacon lighting the way, evangelizing the true path: education.

When I was nine and my father was forty-eight, my father had a heart attack that left him physically and mentally diminished. His upward striving had robbed him of his health. Simply maintaining his economic position became a losing struggle. He resorted to taking jobs as a handyman and a hotel night clerk. Periodically despondent, he would threaten to give up and go on the dreaded "welfare." Without knowing specifically what welfare was, I understood that it represented a final indignity, a lowly place to which my father would stoop only in great desperation: the end of the line. We never did apply for welfare, but the possibility lurked in the shadows of our family life, the ultimate insult to my father's manhood. When I was sixteen, the only child still at home, my father died. The apartment building he and my mother had been managing jointly required a couple, so my mother lost her job. She found a smaller building to manage and we survived.

Neither of my parents valued education of itself, and neither could understand why I loved school as I did. They honored the hard work that intellectual achievement required, however. And both my parents liked to read. My mother, in fact, *loved* to read, especially historical romance novels. As she aged and the fat paperbacks got too heavy, she would cut their spines, dividing them into halves or quarters so they would be easier to hold. That did not limit her enjoyment, but it did complicate trading a grocery bag full of novels with her friends, because the component parts of the books would sometimes get mixed up. For her, books were not sacred. They were a medium of escape, a vehicle for freedom. She could flee to a faraway land, a place happy and sexy, for the cost of a novel (ten cents at our local Goodwill thrift store). A place riddled with tragedy, but filled with women whose suffering paid off in the end.

Ironically, my mother did not take the same pleasure in my reading she took in her own.[6] She resented the depth of my escape and withdrawal. With my nose in a book, I seemed to her both antisocial and self-indulgent. I am thankful that my brother and his wife, also a schoolteacher, cheered on my academic pursuits from afar, as did a series of passionate and committed teachers over the years. My mother complained that reading led me to shirk my household responsibilities. I held fiercely to my reading—to all my schooling activities—in part because I had discovered that scholarly accomplishments could lead me to another life, a class away from the hardships my parents had faced. As Mary Childers has said about her own childhood, living in poverty creates deprivation, but it also helps "create some conditions for freedom, inspiration, and resilience."[7] I found inspiration in academic achievement, adult encouragement, and social analysis.

If I became a sociologist as a result of attending the university, I morphed into an anthropologist after joining the family of my life partner, Andrew. He and I met in the unlikely context of the San Francisco Socialist School. When I went back east to meet the many members of his extended Boston Brahmin family, I came up against the most stark class differences I had yet encountered. This family's ancestors first viewed North America from Plymouth Rock, not Ellis Island. Over the centuries, the clan has included merchants, inventors, writers, poets, mill owners, and government officials. Family members educated in elite private schools of the Northeast have served the country in many wars, and a couple of generations also worked directly for U.S. presidents.

When I walked into the family's Big House in Massachusetts, I felt as if I had entered a foreign country. Once staffed by a coterie of servants who kept the coal furnaces stoked, the laundry clean, and the meals coming, the hundred-plus-year-old house is now too unwieldy and energy inefficient to be used as anything other than a summer retreat. It is full of family ghosts, tragic memories, remnants of adventurous lives, and lots of laughter.

I knew immediately that this was not an environment in which I could "pass." Members of my family had worked as domestic servants; they did not employ them. We valued land as peasants who cultivated it, not as lords who accumulated it. My only recourse was to be different. So when I did not know the proper attire for dinner, I had to make up for it in dinner conversation.

Profoundly unlike my family of origin, but much like my political family of choice, Andrew's family was composed of intellectuals interested in politics and international affairs. Sitting down to dinner involved feasting on provocative ideas, as well as on good food. I recall one night being seated next to one of his many charming cousins. An hour into the meal, after discussing feminism, Emma Goldman, and the perils of the current Republican administration, he turned to me and delightedly asked, "Where did you *come* from?" Where, indeed. Luckily, Andrew's family is one that respects, indeed valorizes, eccentricity. As we talked and ate, laughed and argued, I found my place at this very different dinner table.

In the sea of difference, I was surprised, as well, by the similarities I discovered between my family of origin and the upper-class clan who inhabited the Big House. Andrew's family, like my own, placed great stock in kinship. And the Big House, like my grandparents' farm in Alberta, acted as a favorite gathering place for everyone—grandchildren, uncles, aunts, nieces, nephews, cousins, and the children of all. Collectively, this group, like my own extended family, delighted in spending time together, telling each other stories, and sharing food.

Once I began reading about upper-class families, I discovered that the literature confirmed some of the parallels I had observed between upper-class and working-class families. These shared characteristics include the valuation of kinship ties; fertility patterns (families at either end of the spectrum tend to have more children than those in the middle class); and the reliance on available family resources (for example, using connections to obtain a job).[8] In the United States, extended kinship ties typically are taken as a marker of working-class or immigrant status. And yet E. Digby Baltzell, a sociologist who studies the upper class, points to the importance of extended kinship in upper-class life that parallels its significance in the working classes: "The core of any upper class is, of course, the family, especially the extended or consanguine variety, which includes not only parents and children but also grandparents, extended cousinages, and ancestors."[9]

The Fruitfulness of Class Comparisons

My class history has taught me that comparisons across class always yield surprises and can provide a goldmine of insights. Thus, the research I have undertaken, including the project discussed in this book, uses class as an essential analytic tool. From my perspective, understanding contemporary families is possible only by understanding class, and vice versa. I have no interest in joining the "conspiracy of silence" about class that masks those at the top and bottom of the economic spectrum.[10] A thoroughgoing class analysis must include an examination of the full range of economic positions.

In the United States, class and race are often intertwined in lived reality and in scholarly thinking. Demographically, African Americans, Hispanics, and American Indians are not distributed proportionately across the economic spectrum. Instead, they are concentrated in lower income sectors. This clustering has led the general public and the academy to lose sight of the fact that in this country, the majority of poor people are white.[11] Similarly, both scholars and average citizens ignore the fact that many of the poor are employed. They are not poor because they do not work; they are poor because they have low-paying jobs. Poverty, a needless tragedy in a prosperous nation, should not be tolerated in the United States. Nor should poverty be allowed to act as the sole contrast to middle-class prosperity or hardship. The difficulty of adequately defining class and the ongoing debates about the wisdom of applying class labels should not blind scholars to the importance of class distinctions. To paraphrase W. I. Thomas, such distinctions are real in their consequences, even when definitional boundaries remain blurry. In a society that venerates the middle class but accepts a huge concentration of wealth among a small percentage of the population, the lack of attention to the effects of profound inequality between families strikes me as a glaring oversight.[12]

Systematic comparisons across class put the undifferentiated middle classes in relief and highlight their uniqueness. Freeing social analysis from a framework that unquestioningly treats the middle classes as normative provides opportunities for new understandings of family practices, including the construction of networks.

My experience living in different class locations has shaped my ability to recruit interview subjects; for this study I mobilized my own networks of affiliation, occupation, and familial connection. These life experiences also enhance my chances for gaining subjects' trust and respect and for establishing empathy as I conduct interviews.[13] Perhaps most important, though, my background as an "insider" and an "outsider" with respect to several class locations has given me a chance to experience firsthand the far-reaching effects of social stratification.[14] From my vantage point, a study of networks of care could be meaningful only if it built upon class comparisons as a central axis of analysis. Ever since first reading Carol Stack's book *All Our Kin*, I have mused, pondered, and puzzled about domestic networks and their intersections with class and race. Lillian Rubin's *Worlds of Pain* holds comparable power in shaping my early interest in the academic study of working-class families. Both authors treat their subjects with respect and grant them their rightful dignity. Their work has set an agenda in family scholarship for analyzing race and class for the past thirty years.

After exploring the permeability of household boundaries in nineteenth-century working-class communities, in the mid–1990s I began researching the intersections of class, networks, and families, using the archives at the Henry A. Murray Research Center at Radcliffe College. Arlie Hochschild convinced me it was worth my time to study the present, not just the past, and, along with Barrie Thorne, invited me to come to the Berkeley Center for Working Families at the University of California, Berkeley. While at the center in 1999 and 2000, I grounded the network concept in a comparative research project focused on the care available for school-age children. The Alfred P. Sloan Foundation generously funded my position as an associate senior researcher. The Berkeley Center, under the codirectorship of Arlie and Barrie, created a lively intellectual community, sponsoring weekly colloquia and offering endless good-natured debate. That forum provided a creative, safe space for airing my early analysis. The chief organizational genius of the center, Bonnie Kwan, helped make it work as a bureaucracy as well as a community. I also received able research assistance from two graduate students, Cherrie Jo Pascoe and Roberta Espinoza.

Without the forthright honesty and generous time of those who agreed to be interviewed, I would not have a book. I thank them all profusely.

I am blessed with many friends and colleagues who have gone out of their way numerous times to read chapters of the book. Three people read the book in its entirety, some chapters multiple times; I want to especially thank Anita Ilta Garey and Debra Osnowitz for their time and their thoughtful comments, and for compassionately and critically envisioning the manuscript with me. Kristi Long has thrown herself into the project of the book with an astute editor's eye. Anita Garey has come to know the subjects in this book as well as I do and has played center on my A team, which also includes Andrew Bundy, Alice Friedman, and Arlie Hochschild. These remarkable people have been willing to talk with me endlessly, go with me on exhausting walks, and make me laugh in the process. Penny Cherns has likewise made herself available to spin hare-brained schemes and ponder the implications of my analysis.

Others read carefully one or more chapters in various stages of the book's preparation: Stephanie Bryson, Andrew Bundy, Mary Bundy, Mary Childers, Twilla Derington, Mignon Duffy, Claude Fischer, Karla Hackstaff, Kay Jenkins, Ronda Keesler, Annette Lareau, Peggy Nelson, Susan Ostrander, Ilene Philipson, Jane Manley, Dhooleka Raj, and Nicholas Townsend. Bonnie DiMatteo helped me find my voice, and Kathy Mooney and Bobbe Needham have stepped in to make my voice more clear and powerful.

Back at Brandeis, I would survive much less effectively as a professor and as a writer without the witty charm and able skills of Judy Hanley, who runs the Sociology Department thoughtfully and makes the impossible possible. Elaine Brooks kept me mindful of graduate program needs while I was preoccupied with the book. In addition, two programs at Brandeis have funded partners in research over the past two years who have proven invaluable. The Student-Scholar Research Program at the Brandeis Women's Studies Research Center has enabled me to hire and mentor two undergraduates who ran to the library at a moment's notice, made endless photocopies, and good naturedly helped: Sara Horowitz and Leah Sykes. A new program in the Women's Studies Program on campus has designed a similar setup with graduate students, the Grad-Faculty Partnership Program. In the summer of 2003, I had the good fortune to be the faculty partner of Rosemary Casler, whose reading of the manuscript and meticulousness with my bibliography inspired great confidence, as well as appreciation. The accomplished and helpful reference staff at Goldfarb Library at Brandeis made their work and mine much easier. And Mignon Duffy, census maven, combed U.S. Census Bureau statistics to check the accuracy of my reporting and interpretation.

My own not-so-nuclear family has endured living with a crowd of forty extra personalities and a book in the making for the past four years. Without their tolerance, support, and love, I could not have made it. With an abundance of gratitude and appreciation, I thank Benjy and Evan, who gave substance and meaning to the topic of care, and Andrew Bundy, who is the anchor in my life.

Not-So-Nuclear Families

Networks of Interdependence in an Age of Independence

Chapter 1

WHEN I ASKED Robert Holcomb, an unmarried father of a six-year-old, "Who helps you care for your son when he visits you?" Robert replied, "Me."[1] Robert views himself as self-reliant, and he leads a full and active life, despite the challenges posed by his paraplegia. Through sheer determination and force of will, he has become independent in most of his daily activities. But I could see that Robert was confined to a wheelchair, and I knew that he did not drive. I also knew that his son lives in a town two hours away. So I probed, "Just you?" He nodded, and nodded again, in response to my questioning. Still, after a pause, a more complicated story unfolded. "I should back up here, when I said that," Robert amended, and then began to describe the dimensions of his support system. He lives with his sister, her husband, and their children. When he needs to pick up his son, his best friend from childhood drives him to the boy's home. This elaboration reveals the interdependent relationships that enable Robert to think of himself as independent. He is not a man who lacks appreciation for others, but from his point of view, he has beaten the odds. Without strength of character, something no one could give him, he would not be alive, let alone be a vigorous, involved father.

Although Robert's physical challenges are unusual, his attitudes about his capabilities are not. The impulse to describe oneself as a can-do, go-it-alone, self-sufficient parent is a typical one. Many, perhaps most, Americans would describe their actions in several realms, including child rearing, in similar terms. Laws in the United States mandate parents' responsibility for and authority over their children. Cultural expectations are no less compelling. American families are assumed to be small, self-reliant units headed by a breadwinning father and cared for by a stay-at-home mother. And yet, over half of all households in the United States with young children have two employed parents.[2] Do parents go it alone? How do working parents, especially, care for their children? How do they mobilize the help they need? And what enables them to think they are independent when they actually receive a lot of support?

In *Not-So-Nuclear Families*, I probe these questions by investigating the lives of working parents and the networks they construct to help them care for their children. My book chronicles the conflicts, hardships, and triumphs of four families and their networks as they navigate the ideology that mandates that parents, mothers in particular, rear children on their own, in the face of a reality that requires that they rely on the help of others.

Employed parents in the United States face a household labor shortage that some have labeled a "crisis of care."[3] Sweeping economic and social changes in the twentieth century altered the landscape for all families, of all races/ethnicities, and classes. The shift from a manufacturing to a service economy has undermined the male wage rate and pushed more and more wives and mothers into paid employment.[4] Women, historically the chief providers of child care, are increasingly unavailable. The number of mothers in the labor force has risen steadily for decades.[5] What's more, the number of mothers who work full time has increased *fivefold* over the last half century. By 1999, there were 24.6 million school children (63.8 percent of all school-age children) with mothers who were in paid employment.[6]

With so many mothers in the labor force, families must scramble to find child care. Because neighbors, friends, and relatives are as likely as parents to be working, the number of responsible adults with sufficient time available to attend to the needs of school-age children appears to fall far short of the demand. The widespread conception in the culture, and in academic disciplines such as sociology, is that with the depleted ranks of kin and neighbors, the caretakers historically called on to care for children are no longer available. In both popular culture and scholarly research, entrenched assumptions about the "proper" configuration of families with children continue to preserve the power of the ideology of small and independent families.

Caregivers may appear to be disappearing, but children are not. Here is the puzzle: If more mothers are employed, if both men and women are working longer hours (as they are in several economic sectors), and if there have been few significant family-friendly structural transformations in the workplace or state-initiated policies that mandate support for working parents trying to raise children, who then is caring for school-age youngsters in the United States?[7]

Although the national focus is on developing after- and before-school options for school-age children, parents in fact rely much more frequently on informal care. And kin are the mainstay of that informal care. According to U.S. census data for 1999, "other relatives" continue to be the *most common* type of caregivers for grade-school children.[8]

Not-So-Nuclear Families investigates the clash between belief and practice: the ideology of family independence versus the *practice of interdependence*. This research challenges the widespread assumption that nuclear families raise children without help. And by focusing on white families, assumed to be categorically middle class and nuclear, it challenges the mythology that the United States is a classless society and that middle-class families are disconnected, self-sufficient entities. I find that parents consciously and creatively construct networks of interdependence. They regularly and intentionally tap people beyond their immediate family for aid in the care of their children. I examine the connections among parents, children, and caregivers to illuminate the complex process of creating and sustaining care networks. I show how the networks operate, describing what their members trade and how they conceive of the rights and responsibilities of kinship, children, and reciprocity.

The book's focus on the care networks of four families in different class locations (working class, middle class, professional middle class, and upper class) permits me to explore class-based similarities and differences in the arrangements the families make. Although these networks are not offered as typical of their members' class positions, they allow a close examination of how structural transformations unfold on a micro level. Studying them closely results in a detailed understanding of the ways economic and social locations shape what people expect;[9] what they see as possible given their circumstances; and how they make sense of extrahousehold involvements in their efforts to rear children. In several class locations, these parents see their situation as structured by a set of trade-offs: time on the job versus time with family; time with a spouse versus time with the children; reliance on kin versus self-reliance; receiving help versus incurring obligation; exhaustion versus unmet tasks. Consequences follow from each decision about a trade-off, and parents have to determine for themselves the value on each side of the equation.

In this book, I explore how the patchwork of parents' caretaking arrangements actually functions.[10] When the care occurs outside formal institutions such as schools and day-care centers, to whom do parents turn? And on what grounds? On what principles do the care relationships operate? How do adults and children negotiate needs, and on what terms? Subjects of this research hold a wide range of opinions about child rearing, of philosophies of community and kin involvement, and of attitudes about what children need. Virtually none, however, find it easy to forge and sustain networks of care. In this book, I attempt to see parents' options and decisions from their perspective and to trace empathetically the paths they take to find their way through an ever-changing maze of child-rearing predicaments.

The Power of Ideology in Everyday Life

Why, given the strong empirical evidence to the contrary, are U.S. families assumed to be nuclear in their structure and in their practice? The focus on nuclear household units emphasizes a small insular group that consists of parents and children, a "social nucleus."[11] This emphasis amounts to an ideology of the small and independent family that not only shapes conceptions held by the general public, but also influences sociologists whose work examines the household and ignores relationships outside it. The ideology of the nuclear family has roots in historical and contemporary evidence of household structure and is augmented by a sociological fascination with families as opposed to kinship (the latter is deemed the provenance of anthropologists). It rests, as well, on certain U.S. beliefs and traditions, including the breadwinner family that Dorothy Smith calls the "Standard North American Family" (SNAF);[12] the doctrine of privacy in defining families and households; and individualism. In making sense of these sometimes conflicting sets of ideas, people develop expectations about what families and kin should do.

The ideology of the Standard North American Family assumes a heterosexual, two-parent model.[13] Although children are not a necessary component of a Standard North American Family, when they are present, family households constitute the primary site of child rearing. Also implicit in this ideological code is the idea that children continue the legacy of the family materially, culturally, religiously, and, except in cases of adoption, genetically. Therefore, the logic goes, parents have a vested interest in their children's welfare and general well-being.

The male-breadwinner nuclear family has historically been available only to men who could earn a family wage (meaning, primarily, white middle-class men and working-class men in unionized industries). This family structure, moreover, is characterized by an unyielding gender division of labor. Despite its significant problems, this family structure did provide a clear means of caring for children. At the turn of the millennium, however, even that benefit is no longer viable. As families across the economic spectrum search for alternative strategies to make child rearing and family life feasible, white middle-class families are restructuring kin relationships, following the path of African Americans, immigrants, and members of the working class.[14] Historically, families in these groups have relied at least in part on income and resources generated by women. Because of economic need, they have acted independently of the culturally dominant preference for mothers to stay home to rear their children.[15] At the same time, these groups have tended to adopt "attitudes, values, and beliefs that give primacy to the family over the individual," the extended family in particular, a practice known as "familism."[16] Middle-class and Anglo-American families have tended to present themselves as less familistic in their values. The image of the privileged middle-class family connotes self-reliance, implying that it does not engage in networks. The power of this image has contributed to middle-class white families perceiving themselves as neither asking for nor receiving help from extended kin, even when this image contradicts their lived experience.

The ideology of the small and independent family is also rooted in a belief in the privacy of the family, a notion that arises from the historical role of private property in legally defining the family.[17] As with other ideologies, ideas about how private a family should be have changed over time and vary with economic position and cultural orientation.[18] Equating family life with the private sphere has granted the household a great deal of autonomy in negotiating interpersonal relations and in child-rearing practices. Moreover, since the household is seen as a bounded entity, privacy rights trump outside interference, whether the source be neighborhood gossips or government regulations.[19]

Complementing the doctrine of privacy is the American belief in individualism and self-sufficiency. Sociologist Claude Fischer defines individualism as "the principle that gives priority to the individual over the group or institution."[20] Indeed, mainstream U.S. culture celebrates the individual and views both success and failure as the result of individual endeavor.[21] This ideology is incorporated into family life in complex, sometimes contradictory, ways because child bearing and rearing require interdependence. But, since children undergo a long period of dependency (how long varies by culture and class), the internal household practice of interdependence counters the hegemonic ideology of individualism. And it is precisely those activities that create the financial dependence of the women who do them. In the United States, people generally believe that families are independent entities but that within any given family, the members are interdependent.[22] Outside the family, however, mainstream U.S. culture stigmatizes dependence as implying weakness, laziness, and incapacity in all but very young children.[23]

Yet parents need help and often seek it. Although the dominant ideology casts the nuclear family as the sole province of child rearing, people other than parents necessarily are involved in children's lives at virtually every developmental stage. For a variety of reasons, the culturally preferred caretaker—the mother—often cannot be the primary caregiver twenty-four hours a day. Nonetheless, "there is a 'moral imperative' that [mothers] continue to provide continuous care for their children."[24] The ideology of intensive mothering—"emotionally demanding, financially draining, labor consuming child rearing"[25]—shapes the cultural expectations not only for middle-class parents, but for working-class parents as well.[26] When the mother is unavailable and the father (commonly the next-in-line caregiver) cannot arrange to care for the children, most parents prefer extended family members to substitute for them.[27] In the United States today, this preference for kin is increasingly difficult to satisfy; kin cannot guarantee help. Parents are left to meet the needs of their children in a context of contradictory expectations and assorted impediments and opportunities.

The logic and obligations of kinship do not help a person whose kin are unavailable, dysfunctional, far away, disapproving, or disaffected.[28] Some people reject their family of origin or extended kin, or are rejected by them, long before they have or think about having children.[29] In the absence of sufficient kin, parents may turn to formal institutions (e.g., schools, child-care centers, after-school programs, religious institutions, recreational activities) and informal networks of interdependence (neighbors and friends).[30]

Still, the ideology and terminology of kinship loom large. Even people who reject or dismiss their biological kin seem to embrace the idea that families are important.[31] Thus the social logic that kin *should* help rear children surfaces, regardless of how individuals define their kin. Questions remain, however. Which kin help care for children? Whether by biological or social definitions, who constitutes kin?[32] How do people in general and the courts in particular set boundaries around who counts as kin?[33] What are the capacities of kin? Not all kin ties are active. Kin may not be geographically close, physically able, or emotionally capable.[34] And although kinship obligations may explain some relatives' motivation to help rear their nieces, nephews, grandchildren, or cousins, they do not explain how that motivation is mobilized.

Perspectives on kinship, networks, and child rearing are profoundly influenced by gender ideology as well. Conceiving of gender as a social construction (as opposed to a biologically assigned identity) helps explain historical fluctuations in men's and women's practices and in culturally bound definitions of appropriate male and female behavior. The construction of gender unfolds in the context of a racial/ethnic- and class-stratified division of labor in society that is shaped by what Gayle Rubin calls the sex/gender system.[35] For the past two centuries at least, the tasks of child rearing and caregiving have been assigned primarily, although not exclusively, to women.[36] Without trying to specify precisely how individuals come to acquire or enact certain gendered behaviors, I would argue that their behavior is influenced by culturally constructed notions of what is appropriate for good mothers or good fathers or good people to do vis-à-vis children. Most pertinent here is Arlie Hochschild's concept of gender strategies. A gender strategy is "a plan of action through which a person tries to solve problems at hand, given the cultural notions of gender at play."[37] In *Not-So-Nuclear Families*, women interpret those cultural notions and strategize to mobilize help from the fathers of their children, friends, neighbors, and extended kin to care for their children. Located at the structural nexus of domestic work, child rearing, and paid labor, they nonetheless exercise some discretion about how they act on and interpret their situations. Men strategize to be involved in the lives of their children, nieces, nephews, and grandchildren and, importantly, to support the women who are mothers. They do so from their historical place as family providers, thus needing consciously to break with dominant patterns of behavior. Both men and women rely disproportionately on women as network members, perhaps through a belief that women make better child-care providers and are more readily available to help others.

Most Americans believe the country is composed largely of middle-class people. Unless they are on welfare or fabulously rich and famous, people are assumed to be middle class.[38] This mythology about a middle-class society blurs the very real divisions and inequities that exist.[39] In fact, wealth and income disparities have always existed but have been widening since the 1970s. Demographic data reveal clear evidence of larger concentrations of wealth at the top, creating greater disparities between the top and the bottom quintiles of the population.[40] These "new inequalities" not only have affected those at the bottom but also have placed a greater burden on families in the middle, those who worry about slipping down the economic ladder.[41] Katherine Newman reports that "Americans earning in the middle of the wage scale saw their earnings decline since 1989, after adjustment for inflation."[42] And, according to the Center on Budget and Policy Priorities: "The average income of the middle fifth of families fell by $710 between the late 1970s and the mid–1990s, from $41,430 to $40,720."[43] That drop occurred in the wake of families adding a second wage earner to shore up household earnings. So even with wives and mothers working, family income has declined over the past two decades. Among all groups, these economic inequalities have profound direct and indirect consequences for families, for expectations about what families should do, and for the ways families rear their children. Differences in resources (most particularly in income and wealth, time, and people) often lie obscured in white families who are presumed to be middle class, yet shape the networks parents assemble to help them rear their children.

The Crux of the Family Labor Shortage

As many studies document, two demographic trends in particular have affected, and continue to affect, child-rearing practices: the rising proportion of mothers, particularly mothers of young children, in the paid labor force; and the growth in the proportion of employed mothers who work full time.[44]

In the immediate aftermath of World War II, following a wartime escalation of women's entry into paid employment, women were ideologically and structurally encouraged to head back to the home.[45] However, after a brief postwar drop, the number of women in the labor force steadily increased through the 1990s.[46] By 2000, married and formerly married women with children were more likely to work than those without children. In 1958, 3,033,654 children ages six to eleven had mothers who were employed full time.[47] In 1999, there were 17,307,000 children ages five to fourteen with full-time working mothers.[48] The magnitude of the increase in the number of children with working mothers is staggering in its social consequences.

The increase of women in the paid labor force has not been accompanied by structural transformations in the workplace or by policies instituted by the state that would create family-supportive conditions for rearing children.[49] The paid employment of women decreases the amount of time they are available to be involved in child rearing, helping others care for their children, kin keeping, and doing other kinds of community work.[50] Especially hard hit have been poor and working-class communities that rely on the activism and presence of women, many of whom have been pressed into paid employment as a result of the 1990s welfare "reform."[51]

Work, which determines the contours of much of an employed parent's day, and schooling, which centrally organizes children's time, shape and mediate the legal and moral responsibilities of parents to provide food, clothing, and shelter for their children. The workplace assumes workers are independent wage earners who can entirely devote themselves to the job at hand, and who have families at home to take care of them.[52] Neither assumption is valid for most employed women. While women have increased their numbers in professional and managerial occupations, they continue to be concentrated in the female-dominated occupational categories of clerical and service work.[53] Not coincidentally, women in the workplace generally have fewer benefits and less flexibility in their jobs than men have. Moreover, as Jody Heymann points out, "while working women are disproportionately responsible for caring for children, the elderly and disabled adults, they face significantly greater work-related barriers to providing that care than men do."[54] Families' efforts to adapt to inflexible structures result in mothers getting less sleep; fathers doing more child care; children taking care of themselves; and relatives, neighbors, or friends helping out.

The structure schools impose is, like that of the workplace, large and inflexible. The school day averages about six hours, ending at various times in the early to midafternoon. Trying to close the care gap using day care is expensive and often not comprehensive.[55] For children in elementary school, there are a growing number of "out of school time" care options provided at school sites, but the quality, staffing, cost, and availability of such programs vary widely.[56]

Overall, the structures of work and school combine to make providing care for school-age children an ongoing challenge for employed parents. No matter how well organized, no matter how reliable, no matter how hardworking, these parents have difficulty making sure their children are supervised during the care gap. As one of the uncles in my study points out, "There're times when you have little kids and you're just totally frazzled. And, you know, there's just a zillion things to do, and you can't be a zillion places at once or doing a thousand things, so you gotta ask for help." This is one reason networks become so important.

The acute need for a network of care among all classes of families seems particular to the gendered organization of labor in a specific historical moment.[57] When mothers are expected to take the primary responsibility for rearing children, and those mothers work for wages, they need help. One woman reports that working has pressed her to engage in give-and-take relationships: "Because I work, I've had to rely on others." Women of color, immigrant women, and working-class women have always had such a need. Now women of the middle classes share that need.[58] They are experiencing a keen family labor shortage that networks help alleviate.

Care for School-age Children

Nostalgic for an idealized family life, some scholars and a sector of the public imagine a time, often focusing on the fifties, when more relatives supported parents in rearing their children.[59] Census data confirm that, indeed, "other relatives" were the most common category of caretaker for schoolchildren of full-time working mothers in the fifties. In 1958, individuals in this category— including older siblings aged thirteen to eighteen, grandparents, and extended kin (but not fathers)—accounted for 39.8 percent of the caretakers of children with full-time working mothers.[60] Interestingly, however, in 1999, "other relatives" cared for 40.6 percent of the school-age children whose mothers worked full time.[61] The widespread perception that fewer people help their extended kin in child rearing is simply not supported by the data. To the contrary, kin continue to step forward as important players in the lives of children.[62]

What *is* very different between 1958 and 1999 is that, with the huge increase in the number of children whose mothers work part-time and full time, the absolute demand for care has skyrocketed. While the proportion of families that enlists relatives has remained relatively constant, the need for caretakers of children has ballooned, and it has done so across the economic spectrum. At the turn of the twenty-first century, more day-care centers and after-school programs exist than ever before, and they are commonly used if available.[63] But nowhere does the supply meet the demand. This gap in care has put pressure on kinship systems that were already overextended.[64]

Employed mothers historically have relied on a patchwork of caregivers, where multiple people fill in various time slots. Reliance on multiple caregivers enables parents to insure their children have adult supervision even in those small gaps between formal arrangements. This interstitial coverage can make a critical difference, regardless of the number of hours a caregiver provides. A mere five to ten hours per week can be indispensable to the economic arrangements of a family and the well-being of a child. Child-care providers can supplement institutional care and yet make the crucial difference in whether a parent can work, or whether a child is safe.

Family Reliance on Networks

Networks make a difference, usually positive, sometimes negative, in people's lives.[65] Researchers have reached different conclusions, however, about who relies on kin networks more—Euro-Americans or people of color, members of the working class or those of the middle class—and why.[66] The debate on this question has persisted, in part, because of research design. Many network studies either "examine poverty populations in isolation" or have not been designed with sufficient comparability to enable scholars to disentangle race and class effects.[67] Studies that compare a working-class Latino neighborhood to a middle-class Anglo one, for instance, cannot shed much light on the relative importance of either race/ethnicity or class. After conducting an extensive study of kin networks herself, Anne Roschelle recommends that "scholars must begin to examine the different types of network participation engaged in by different groups under different circumstances."[68] Accordingly, some scholars are beginning to devise successful strategies for parsing the race/ethnic variation and class dimensions in domestic networks.[69] Ironically, because native-born Euro-Americans have been assumed not to have kin networks, they have not been studied as a parallel subpopulation.[70] This oversight, along with my desire to compare networks across class, motivated me to begin my research with white parents.

Recent research based on national surveys has investigated the impact of differential resources on network formation. Large-scale quantitative studies show that those in the middle class are more likely to have networks than the poor or those in the working class.[71] This research finds that the more economic and educational resources a family has to draw upon, the more it helps others and receives help in turn.[72] These findings contradict those of earlier, qualitative, ethnographic studies that found domestic networks to be the province of poor, working-class, and immigrant communities. While most of the earlier studies were not comparative, subsequent theory and research built on the assumption that networks were a product of necessity in the U.S. context, and social scientists continued to interpret their findings in that vein. As a result, families were assumed to participate in networks of support only if they could not purchase what they needed, making them deviant according to the Standard North American Family ideal.

Notably, interpretations of the value of and motivation for building networks have flip-flopped with the more recent quantitative results. The emergent interpretation is that families with more resources are better equipped to participate in a network; in effect, they have more to contribute, especially when compared to poorer families who risk their own well-being by sharing and participating in a network. Having been discovered, the connectedness of middle-class families is now taken to be a marker of health and vibrancy and a measure of these families' success. No longer are extended domestic networks treated as pathological, aberrant phenomena that need to be explained. Rather, such networks are deemed a normative asset for the middle class and are associated with relative privilege. The end result, however, is that poor, working-class, and racial/ethnic communities continue to be seen as aberrant, but now by a new norm, one for which previously they had been the standard-bearers.

Sociologists have searched for both structural and cultural reasons to explain the dramatic shift in the kinds of families now identified as building and relying upon networks.[73] Some argue that the shift in findings could reflect a genuine inversion of the resources available to families.[74] That is, the change may be the result of social and economic processes that have impoverished the basic landscape of poor, working-class, and/or African American communities.[75] This includes the transformation to a postindustrial economy, which has reduced the number of manufacturing jobs in general, but especially in inner cities.[76] It also has pulled more women into the paid labor force. And, as Roschelle aptly points out, the eighties hit poor and working-class families particularly hard.[77] Crack cocaine invaded poor neighborhoods, and the federal government implemented policies that widened wealth and income gaps by reforming tax legislation, dismantling affirmative action, and busting unions. In sum, the profound structural changes over the past three decades offer a compelling, although partial, explanation of shifts over time in various groups' use of networks.

Another explanation for the reversal in findings about network involvement looks to differences in methodological approach. The earlier studies tended to be largely ethnographic, while some of the more recent studies use large quantitative data sets that are representative of the U.S. population as a whole.[78] Large multivariate studies are good at counting things that can be measured. Ethnographic studies examine interstices among people that surveys cannot capture.

Another way to think about the increase in middle-class families' reliance on networks is that they have greater labor-power needs than they had thirty years ago and therefore create networks to help them rear children and do kin work. I would argue that structural shifts have created harsher conditions in middle-class communities, as well as in working-class ones, and that middle-class families are clambering to assemble networks out of necessity. The greater contemporary precariousness of middle-class families stems both from employment insecurity and longer work hours, and from a shortage of kin workers. Family households have been able to hold their ground financially only because the wages women earn by going into the labor force are added to the household coffer.[79] But some families then have fewer people resources and less time to engage in family activities.[80] The parallel decline in resources within poor communities may push people below a threshold level of comfort, making it impossible for them to share child care and other commodities as readily as they did before the economic restructuring.

Studying Interdependent Networks that Care for Children

I focus my attention on networks of differing social and economic resources. How do those in the structural middle find help? How do their strategies differ from those at the bottom? From those at the top? What similarities do they share?

I examine a specific kind of interdependent network—a network of care, that is, one organized to help parents care for their children while they are on the job and the children are not in school. How do parents cover that weekly gap between work and school that the Annie E. Casey Foundation estimates to be as high as twenty-to-twenty-five hours?[81] The help provided ranges from practical hands-on care, those activities that some researchers frame as *care for*, to advice and emotional support, which they label *care about*.[82] I illustrate how parents in several economic locations construct informal networks of interdependence to substitute for and supplement institutions that cover the gap in after-school and before-school care.[83]

I begin by identifying white parents in different class positions. The homogeneity of race/ethnicity across the cases enables me to explore similarities and differences across class location. That comparability also allows me to focus attention on the ways white families define their care assets and deficits and how they mobilize their differential resources to address these issues.

My goal of understanding the *internal processes* of networks seems best accomplished through qualitative, open-ended interviews. I seek to understand why parents rely on particular people, how they feel about this interdependence, what they trade, and what they think they have gained and lost in the process. Rather than interview independent individuals, I chose to study connected individuals who are part of a parent's network of care. My method— to approach each network as a case study—is motivated by my desire to analyze particular networks in their entirety and to get a fuller picture, from multiple vantage points, of approaches to caring for children and to supporting parents. Each of the four case studies thus focuses on a network, a web of people, rather than on a collection of separate individuals. While the particulars of the cases are idiosyncratic rather than representative in some kind of statistical sense, by delving into the network dynamics, I am able to probe the interpretations and meanings people assign to their involvements and interactions with other people. The cases include people who struggle with the contradictions of their circumstances—trying to raise their children responsibly while trying to earn a living, engaging others to help them in those inevitable yet impossible moments when the care puzzle pieces fail to come together. It is less their particular decisions that interest me, and more their deliberations, the patterns of their interactions, and the ways that others respond to them.

Large-scale surveys of patterns of exchange analyze the *structures* of networks, rather than the *processes* of mobilizing them.[84] They focus on the size, composition, and density of networks, on those things that can be measured or counted—money, material goods, and concrete favors. Other aspects of network relationships, such as support or advice, are difficult to assign value to and, other researchers have found, harder to assess and track.[85] While useful, the survey approach fails to provide sufficient insight into the internal dynamics of a network. A random, nationally representative sample that produces statistically generalizable findings may miss the very essence of networks—

that is, their overlapping circles of interdependency—and may methodologically tilt findings toward a more disconnected portrait of the world. However, looking at a network from multiple participants' points of view can be done only through intensive study. Because perception and subjectivity are part of an ongoing construction and negotiation of network relations, they are best studied using an interpretive, qualitative analysis.

I began by recruiting four network "anchors," the individuals at the center of each child-rearing project. I prefer "anchor" to "focal person" or "ego," terms more commonly used in network studies, because I believe "anchor" better captures the essence of this person's network activity. A "focal person" suggests one at the center, but it does not convey that individual's *agency*; and "ego," which has been used extensively in network studies, seems an inappropriately individualistic term for a person whose role is fundamentally interactive. In contrast, "anchor" reflects the centrality of the parent in assembling a crew of helpers and securing them to the children.[86] "Anchor" also connotes stability, security, and weight. It communicates an important analytic point: The center of the network is the anchor, not the child. The network anchors I recruited shared several characteristics. They all (1) had children between the ages of five and twelve; (2) had a partner in rearing their children; and (3) were employed.[87]

In the comparative tradition of network studies, this investigation includes one network each from four economic locations: working class, middle class, professional middle class, and upper class.[88] By including an upper-class case, my research design extends the class categories beyond the construct of working class versus middle class commonly found in comparative research.[89] In stratifying my sample by class, I am trying to understand the ways that economic conditions shape people's lives, the needs of their children, people's perceptions of the needs of their children, and hence the contours of their networks. I define class location as a product of several economic and social forces, including a person's current occupation and job history, education, and wealth, with particular attention to home ownership, in addition to income.[90] In conceiving of class as a complex relationship of economic and social dimensions, I posit that experiences and ideologies are shaped by class location. I am interested in the contingencies of class, that is, occurrences or dynamics connected to class but not determined by it. Class contingencies shape and reflect a particular "constellation of resources," as Anita Ilta Garey puts it. Garey's notion of resource constellations broadens the concept of assets beyond the narrowly conceived categories of income or education. She identifies racial/ethnic privilege, neighborhood context, relationship status, transportation options, family size and ages of children, and physical health as different aspects of one's constellation of resources, and therefore one's social capital.[91] I recognize all these dimensions as shaping ideas and practice, although in this research, I focus most particularly on the time, money, and people to which networks have access in varying degrees.

At the end of my first interview with each anchor, I asked her or him to enumerate those who helped rear her or his children. I respected the list constructed by the anchor and the boundaries placed by the anchor around whom to include and exclude. By openly asking who made up the network, I was able to explore the anchor's on-the-ground definition of a network of care. The lists the anchors generated included both primary and secondary caregivers: neighbors, grandmothers, friends, uncles, aunts, babysitters, and nannies. The network participants ranged from those involved in daily interactions with the children (including providing transportation or direct supervision) to those who live outside the geographic orbit of daily life, but who contribute invaluable advice and emotional support.[92] Over a nine-month period, I interviewed *all* the participants named by the anchors, asking each about his or her role as a giver of care and a recipient of care, advice, or favors. I also asked the network members about the tending of their own children, if they had them, and about their childhood experiences as recipients and providers of care.[93] The network participants' lives are ever changing and my portraits are necessarily provisional. After interviewing the adults, I interviewed all the anchors' school-age children. Speaking with the children gave me an opportunity for a final visit to the anchors' households and provided insight into the children's specific needs and capacities. In addition, I interviewed three people whose lives touched the anchors in tangential ways, but who were not identified as network members. In total, across all four networks, I interviewed forty individuals.

There are several advantages to profiling an entire network rather than disparate individuals. First, my approach allowed repeated contacts with each network and provided glimpses of its issues at different moments in time. So, for example, as the health crisis of the mother of the working-class anchor evolved, the network needs and activities shifted. I interviewed the anchor three times. In addition, since she acted as the interview broker and family scheduler, I saw and spoke to her when I made arrangements to interview her mother, her grandmother, her close friend, and her son. And each time I interviewed a participant in this network, I also talked briefly to the anchor. Each of these contacts gave me the opportunity to get a snapshot of the network as the health crisis unfolded.

A second advantage of approaching the network as a case study is that I was able to observe one system of caregiving from several different vantage points. By building in triangulation, the research design transcends self-reports, which in network studies are especially limiting. For example, the working-class father told me he was deeply involved with his six-year-old son, yet he had never married his son's mother and lived one hundred miles away. The respect for him expressed by the boy's grandmother gave this father's account more gravity. His self-description was also strengthened by the boy's mother, who said that she turned to him for advice and support in child rearing. And, finally, the boy himself made it clear that he idolized his father. These separate accounts combined to give me greater confidence in the validity of the father's self-report.

Last, the network approach enhanced my ability to solicit disclosure. The personal-contact structure of recruitment made it easier to establish rapport and build trust during my initial interview with each anchor. The anchor's introduction to the other network members in turn helped establish my credibility and created opportunities for open communication. When I arrived for interviews, people generally already knew something about me and the study.[94]

THE RESEARCH SITE

I conducted the interviews for the book in northern California between 1999 and 2000. Northern California has long been a frontier of family change, and hence a compelling site for social science research.[95] In the late twentieth century, as at other times in history, California's economy cyclically flourished and languished; the state often led the nation in economic trends and in the postindustrial organization of work. Moreover, the social trends that accompanied these economic transformations created what Judith Stacey in *Brave New Families* calls "postmodern family conditions" and a great deal of "family turbulence."

California's demographic profile is not representative of the United States as a whole, but exhibits similarities along important dimensions. For example, the state's percentage of people divorced and percentage of households headed by women are comparable to those nationwide. Racially and ethnically, California is home to a diverse population and has proportionately more residents of Hispanic origin (32.4 percent versus 12.5 percent in United States as a whole) and of Asian origin (10.9 percent versus 3.6 percent in the United States as a whole).[96] The state's labor force is racially stratified, and that racial stratification shapes the distribution of resources—housing and schooling in particular.[97] Labor-market characteristics and resource-allocation patterns have real consequences for informal networks because proximity plays a key role in who is sought as a participant in an informal network.

CHARACTERISTICS OF THE NETWORKS AND NETWORK MEMBERS
Of the four networks I investigate, three are anchored by women and one has co-anchors, a man and a woman, who jointly coordinate the care of their children. All the anchors are in their forties, while network members range from their twenties to their seventies. The networks range in size from four to eight members. Of the forty people I interviewed, thirty-one are active members of the main networks—ten are men and twenty-one are women (see Table 1.1). In addition, I conducted interviews with three adults who have contact with the anchor, but who only occasionally participate in network activities. Six interview subjects are children—three boys and three girls.

With the important exception of one African American woman in the working-class network, all active members in the four networks identify themselves as white. Many people mentioned having hired child-care providers who were from Third World countries, including Ghana and Guatemala, but during the study period, all informal care providers in three of the four networks were white. Racial/ethnic similarity acts subtly and overtly as a sorting mechanism—as do class and child-rearing values—in the construction of networks (see the discussion in Chapter 6, "Staging Networks: Inclusion and Exclusion"). Network members largely share the class status of the anchor, with the exception of the nanny and the babysitter in the upper-class network, who were both middle class. Anchors solicit help from network members in part because these helpers have an approach to child rearing that is the same as or compatible with the anchors'. These values and practices are shaped, but not determined, by class and culture. Subjects identified a range of religious observances—from Catholic, Jewish, evangelical Christian, and Unitarian to "nothing." But even in observant families, religion did not provide an overt set of values on the basis of which anchors explicitly included or excluded potential network members.

The network members' household structures differ. Among the central anchors, two live in married, nuclear household families; one in a three-generation household headed by a woman; and one in a separated family whose children shuttle between two homes, one headed by the father and the other headed by the mother. An even broader range of structures exists across the rest of the network participants. Most live in two-parent heterosexual households with children; some live alone; and several live with partners, adult siblings, or roommates. Slightly over half (55 percent) of the network members are married or living with a partner; the remainder are separated, divorced, widowed, or never married (see Table 1.2). A few have lesbian relationships. All the networks have fathers who are involved, although their participation varies from on-site coparenting and co-anchoring to "helping out" with the

Table 1.1
Characteristics of Adult Members of Networks of Care

Main Network	Name	Age	Miles from Anchor	Marital Status	Employment Status	# Kids < 5 years	# Kids 5–12 years	# Kids 13–18 years
CRANE	Patricia	40s	—	Single	Part-time	—	1	—
	Ben	30s	0	Divorced	Full time	1	—	—
	Fran	60s	0	Divorced	Unemployed –disability	—	—	—
	Tracy	20s	0	Divorced	Full time	—	4	—
	Robert	40s	100	Divorced	Part-time, nonmarket, disability	—	1	—
BECKER	Dina	40s	—	Married	Full time	—	2	—
	Mark	40s	—	Married	Full time	—	2	—
	Susan	60s	2	Married	Full time, nonmarket	—	—	—
	Peter	70s	2	Married	Part-time, nonmarket	—	—	—
	Kent	30s	4	Single	Full time	—	—	—
	Shannon	30s	6	Single	Full time	—	—	—
	Caitlin	30s	20	Married	Part-time	2	—	—
	Michaela	30s	4	Single	Full time	—	—	—
	Ryan	20s	4	Single	Full time	—	—	—
DUVALL-BRENNAN	Maggie	40s	—	Married	Full time	1	1	—
	Jack	40s	—	Married	Full time	1	1	—
	Tom	50s	15	Domestic partnered	Full time	—	—	—
	Teresa	40s	15	Domestic partnered	Full time	—	—	—
	Byron	30s	5	Married	Full time	1	1	—
	Rebecca	30s	5	Married	Full time	1	1	—
	Ruth	40s	5	Single	Full time	—	—	—
	Brenda	30s	10	Married	80% time	—	2	—
	Lucia	30s	15	Married	Full time	1	2	—
	Amanda	50s	3000	Divorced	Full time	—	—	—
ALDRICH	Sarah	40s	—	Separated	Full time	—	1	1
	April	30s	10	Single	Full time	—	—	—
	Jane	60s	1	Married	Full time, nonmarket	—	—	—
	Lydia	40s	2	Married	Full time	—	1	2
	Alex	40s	2	Separated	Full time	—	1	1
	Kate	40s	10	Married	Part-time	—	1	1
	Aidan	30s	15	Married	Full time	—	—	—

children, and from daily contact to weekend and summer visits. Two fathers are married to the mother-anchors, one is separated, and one lives separately and was never married to the mother.

The anchors have established a variety of primary child-care arrangements; these systems are seldom fully sufficient, so the networks of care provide es-

Table 1.2
Gender and Marital Status of Network Anchors and Members

	Female		Male		
Network	Married/ Partnered	Single**	Married/ Partnered	Single	Total
Crane	0*	3	0	2	5
Becker	3	2	2	2	9
Duvall-Brennan	5	2	3	0	10
Aldrich	4	2	0	1	7
Total	12	9	5	5	31

* Figures do not include children or peripheral members of the network.
** Never married, divorced, separated, or widowed.

sential backup. The working-class anchor relies primarily on kin; the middle-class anchor and her husband use a swing-shift system supplemented by kin; the professional middle-class anchors turn to institutional care for their children; and the upper-class anchor employs a full-time, live-out nanny. These arrangements do not reflect the entire range of child-care options in the United States, nor are they necessarily the most common types of child care within each class location.[98] They do, however, represent a range of strategies and constructed choices that are class linked. The factors that shape who cares for children of employed women include household structure, hours of employment, number and ages of children, race/ethnicity, marital status of the woman, access to kin, and degree of economic disadvantage.[99]

Economic circumstances fundamentally shape the resources available to anchors and network members. The anchors hold jobs in different places in the stratified economic system. All are employed, as are the majority of the adult members of the networks. Network members work in jobs that reflect a range of positions in the labor market: low-wage, part-time work occasionally replaced by welfare; freelance self-employment; full-time-plus lawyering; "family friendly" teaching; nonpaid volunteer work; flexible shift work; and bartering within the underground economy.

Brief Overview of the Book

Not-So-Nuclear Families is organized into two main sections. The first profiles the study's four networks, and the second focuses on the process of developing and sustaining networks. Approaching the networks as case studies acknowledges the importance of the interconnectedness of the interview subjects and their multiple, overlapping, and sometimes independent relationships with each other. Each exchange within a network, each interaction, is based on subjects' histories with one another. Previous interactions, feelings, and perceptions of obligation underlie the present and condition the future. The profiles of the Crane, Aldrich, Duvall-Brennan, and Becker networks, presented in Chapters 2 through 5, examine the intersections of the biography of the anchor and his or her family history, the context within which the anchor is now trying to rear children, and the social structures that frame work, partnership, friendship, and parenting. In the tradition of C. Wright Mills, I place the anchors in their social, familial, and economic contexts, understanding that they rear their children in situations that are circumscribed by conditions largely beyond their control.[100] As Debra Van Ausdale and Joe Feagin put it: "The importance of the social connection, context, and mind cannot be exaggerated." Invoking Karl Marx, they remind us that "society does not consist of individuals; it expresses the *sum of connections and relationships* in which individuals find themselves."[101] Subjects act on their choices as they see them, but social and economic structures narrow their fields of vision, as well as locate them within an economic hierarchy.

In addition to mapping the anchor's collective life, each profile details the lives of the individual network members, whose contribution to the rearing of children of elementary-school age brings them together in overlapping circles. Most of the network members have networks of their own to help them care for elders, rear children, and live their everyday lives. When relevant, I describe these networks and the challenges they help their anchors meet. Chapters 2 through 5 each end with a description of the features distinctive to the profiled network and an analysis of how those features are linked to the network's class location, constellation of resources, and other overarching themes of the study.

The case studies begin with the powerful example of the working-class network, the Cranes, as a means of decentering middle-class family norms. The upper-class case, the Aldriches, follows. While the two networks operate in distinct economic universes, their juxtaposition highlights some of their unexpected similarities. The third profile presents the Duvall-Brennans, the professional middle-class network that feels acutely the strain of competing work-family demands. The challenge of piecing together an effective network marks the Duvall-Brennans as a negative case, contrasting with the vibrancy of the first two. The middle-class Becker network, as wealthy in people as the Aldriches are in material resources, constitutes the fourth case. The only network made up entirely of kin, the Beckers cast a decidedly positive spin on the benefits of resolute network involvement.

The second section of the book explores the gendered, not-so-nuclear practices of people in the study—how they develop and sustain their commitments to one another. Anchors deliberately screen and recruit people to help them, developing networks of interdependence. Chapter 6, "Staging Networks: Inclusion and Exclusion," analyzes the processes, which I call "staging," involved in assembling networks. Staging includes identifying and screening potential network members, recruiting them, and engaging them, all in preparation for mobilizing them to help with child care at some later date. The acts of including some people and excluding others are core aspects of staging. Chapter 6 specifies the dimensions of the staging process, exploring the issues of kinship and friendship, intentional proximity, specialization and expertise, and shared child-rearing values. It closes with a look at the forces of exclusion—how anchors act as gatekeepers of their networks and how some individuals opt out of network obligations.[102]

Without reciprocity, these networks could not exist, let alone thrive. The reciprocal dynamic essentially holds them together. The motivation to help rear other people's children stems from a sense of kinship obligation, the hook of reciprocal relations, a fondness for children, or all of these. How that motivation is activated is the subject of Chapter 7, "The Tangle of Reciprocity," which explores the social logics of mobilization and the negotiation of needs and desires within the networks. Perceptions of value prove fundamental to the social construction of fairness and balance, those essentials that sanction networks. Network members navigate structural constraints, assessing each other's commitments, needs, intentions, and capacities in light of their own. To obligation and a sense of responsibility, respondents add relational rewards. They incorporate joy, pleasure, appreciation, and other emotions in their calculations of value and worth, in their economy of gratitude.

Chapter 8, "Men, Women, and the Gender of Caregiving," moves beyond an examination of the gendered division of labor in networks to explore the meanings and value that men and women assign to male involvement in the networks and in children's lives. Although past research documents extensively the centrality of women in domestic and kin networks and the marginality of men, this study finds men indispensable to the operational success of the networks in which they participate. During the past generation, people have come to expect fathers to be involved in the lives of their children, in addition to being breadwinners. This chapter explores the ways that men in the networks contribute—not just fathers, but also grandfathers and uncles. Aware of the family-labor shortage, they volunteer and are recruited into the networks of care to provide emotional support, logistical help, and general relief to the children's mothers.

In the "Conclusion," I return to the question of how to interpret the practice of interdependence in a culture that celebrates independence. By considering in tandem the accounts of subjects from different social locations, this chapter highlights the unforeseen strengths of the networks, whose maintenance requires endless sets of trade-offs. Kinship culture and class contingencies shape the abundance or scarcity of resources in the networks. Some networks are robust and pliable; others are thin and brittle. Regardless of size or elasticity, however, each provides an invaluable safety net to working parents. The conclusion points to key social policies that can bolster family life and facilitate networks of care.

The stories of the people interviewed for this book offer a way to understand the particulars of the labor shortage that hampers working families. They emerge out of a long and sometimes invisible history and insist upon recognition. Collectively, the accounts challenge long-held myths about white families in the United States that, in practice, are not so nuclear.

Part I

Profiles of Four Networks of Interdependence

Chapter 2   The Cranes

An Absorbent Safety Net

FAMILY DOMINATES THE milieu in which the Cranes' lives unfold, providing a major point of reference and inspiration. Six-year-old Robbie Crane has an angelic face, with huge eyes and long, thick eyelashes. To his single mother, Patricia Crane, his biological father, Robert Holcomb Sr., and his maternal grandmother, Fran Crane, Robbie seems a gift from God. "There's a purpose for him being here," Fran told me with conviction. "I have no idea what it is. I felt that from the minute he was born." On biological grounds alone, Robbie's existence is surprising. Before she became pregnant with her son, Patricia had been told that she was no longer capable of having children. Moreover, Robbie is his father's only biological child, even though, according to Fran, Robert's sexual practices over the years might well have resulted in children. It is more than the mystery of Robbie's conception that make this child seem unusual to his family, though. As an example of Robbie's unique qualities, Fran and Robert independently recounted the same story. Fran described the evening that Patricia's best friend's mother died: "Robbie was there at her house when she passed away. And he was outside in the backyard, and he came in and told them that an angel came and got—he called her Grandma—that an angel came and got Grandma. And they went and checked and she was dead."

Raising Robbie—keeping him safe and cared for—is a responsibility shared across a network of adults, most, but not all, of whom are members of his extended family. Robbie's parents each take a deep interest in their son and are friendly with one another, but they are not married and they do not live together. Robert's home is located about a two-hour drive south in the town where both he and Patricia grew up. Despite this physical distance, Robert is

Table 2.1
Crane Network

Anchor	Patricia Crane
Children	Robbie, 6 Brendan, 19
Anchor's Occupation	Cleaner at a truck stop Driver for a car auction
Class Location	Working class
Family Culture	Family resilience Absorbing people in need Ethic of aid
Child-care Strategy	Kin (grandmother) coverage, plus neighbor/friend babysits
Network Members	• Fran Crane, Patricia's mother • Ben Crane, Patricia's brother • Tracy Johnson, friend/neighbor • Robert Holcomb, Robbie's father

an active participant in Robbie's life, an important parenting partner to Patricia, and a significant member of the Crane network of care. The rest of the network Patricia relies on to help her raise her son consists of her mother, Fran, her younger brother, Ben Crane, and her next-door neighbor, Tracy Johnson. (See Table 2.1 for a list of the members and key characteristics of the Crane network.) When Patricia is working, Ben picks up Robbie from the school bus stop and takes him across town to where his great-grandmother Louise lives. There, Fran looks after him until Patricia is off work and simultaneously keeps an eye on her mother, Louise, who is nearly ninety and increasingly debilitated by Alzheimer's disease. Several times a week, Ben steps in while Patricia works the 2:00 to 8:00 P.M. shift. Tracy watches Robbie one morning per week and occasionally during the afternoon. For her part, Patricia provides Fran with food and shelter, Ben with emotional support and meals, and Tracy with time off from her responsibilities as a working single mother with four children.

This network of interdependence struggles with the limitations of its financial resources and its vulnerability to health crises. Although Patricia is employed (she works two jobs—as a member of a sanitary maintenance crew at a truck stop and as a driver at a car auction), she sometimes needs to suspend paid employment in order to provide care for others in her network. During those periods, government support systems (such as Social Security and disability insurance), however inadequate, function as a safety net. Similarly, on the few occasions when none of the regular members of the Crane network is available to watch Robbie, Patricia turns to a human safety net of friends and neighbors. The resident manager at her apartment complex, for example, is a willing backup caregiver.

Overall, the Crane network illustrates the centrality of kin as care providers. The Cranes demonstrate that networks centered around care for children typically involve the exchange of many things besides child care, and involve caring for individuals of different ages, not just children. Patricia's friendship with and reliance on her neighbor Tracy, moreover, highlights how nonfamily members recruited to fill gaps left by inadequate or absent kin may come to be embraced as part of the network. Finally, the Cranes' responses to open-ended interview questions point to the importance of shared values and broad agreement among network members about how to care for children. For the people in this network, family comes first, sometimes as a resource to tap for support, sometimes as a site of multiple needs that members take turns to meet, and sometimes as both. Network members acknowledge specific obligations and responsibilities toward one another, and all share the expectation that the assistance they give will be repaid in some way, at some future time. As this chapter will show, this reciprocity, however uneven it may be in the short term, helps the individual members in the longer term, as they go about trying to meet the challenges of their daily lives.

Second Chances on the South Side

When I interviewed Patricia Crane for the first time, we sat in the living room of her one-bedroom apartment at the Hacienda Apartments, a complex that sits along a wide, intermittently busy boulevard in the city of Oakfield, California.[1] The street is dotted with fast-food joints, empty lots, and gas stations. The area does not look terribly run down, but neither does it feel like a neighborhood. The Hacienda Apartments consist of several single-level buildings— about fifty units in all—arranged in a horseshoe pattern. The complex was built in the 1920s to provide housing for the area's many agricultural workers; it offers one-room studios, a few kitchenettes (studios with refrigerators and stoves), and some one-bedroom units. Lee Ramsey, the apartment manager, dismisses the apartments' graceful white arches and red-tiled roofs, saying that its Mission adobe-style exterior is more appropriate for a town in the California foothills than for Oakfield, which is located in the state's heavily agricultural Central Valley.

A few large valley-oak trees shade the complex's internal yard, along with numerous eucalyptus and several walnut trees. Bright yellow flowers planted at the trees' base add a welcome splash of color. On hot days, tenants sit out in front of their apartments, casually observing the activities in the buildings' common space. Lee tries to place families with children in units near the green patch of lawn in one corner of the interior horseshoe, so the children will have someplace to play. The patch is inviting, shaded by a commanding walnut tree, but it is no more than a twenty-by-twenty-foot square. A white picket border, about eighteen inches high, marks the area off from the driveway. The manager's unit stands in the soft center of the horseshoe. Its fenced yard (easily three times as big as the play area for the children) is home to two dogs and a cat. Outside the perimeter of the apartment complex, but symbolically in its center, facing the street, is a liquor store.

Lee Ramsey has been managing the Hacienda Apartments for the past three years. As a result of her hard work, the drug and prostitution traffic for which the complex had been notorious is gone. She explains that the Hacienda Apartments now function as a small community, safer for the elderly, families with children, anyone whose life situation might make them vulnerable: "Yeah, we keep an eye out, because we go to food banks, and every now and then you get a good supply of rice and beans and noodles. And it's like, okay—who just moved in with nothing? And you help out when you can. When you have an extra piece of furniture—we can furnish a place in a matter of days. . . . You do what you can." Noting with pride that those who move into the building now are a "better" group of people, Lee says, "I look at this as a place [for people] to stop and regroup for a second chance."

Patricia Crane, her mother, Fran, and her thirty-two-year-old brother, Ben, are just such people. Patricia and Robbie relocated to Oakfield two years earlier, from a town in the coastal county of Santa Cruz. Ben moved about the same time, following his sister's lead. Patricia wanted to be near Fran, who had recently moved and whose health was beginning to fail; Oakfield's much lower rents were also a draw. On the other hand, the city's heavily agricultural economy does not support wage rates as high as those Patricia and Ben had earned in the Santa Cruz area, where both worked in an electronics factory. Patricia, Robbie, Fran, and Ben moved to the Hacienda Apartments five months ago. The mix of units there fits the Crane family's needs. Patricia has a one-bedroom apartment, but the bedroom is for Fran. Patricia sleeps on the couch in the living room, with Robbie on the floor beside her.[2] Until recently, Tracy, the only nonfamily member of the Crane network, and her children lived in the apartment right next door. Ben rents a studio a few doors away, explaining that he does not need "a kitchen in my place, because we have a kitchen over here. So it's cheaper. It's cheaper that way, you know. I just give [Patricia] the grocery money every now and then." With the kitchen in her unit serving as everyone's home base, Patricia's role as network anchor has a physical as well as psychological reality.

Patricia Crane, Anchor

I can hear the sound of the television as Patricia opens the door to usher me into her apartment for our first interview session. She is an extremely thin woman in her early forties. She stands about five feet, five inches tall, with shoulder-length brown hair, dark eyes, and a sallow skin tone that hints of ill health. Although she has quit smoking, the apartment still smells faintly of stale cigarette smoke. The living room is small, about ten feet by ten feet. A large brown-and-beige plaid couch dominates the left side of the room, the television and a set of bookshelves are straight ahead, and an overstuffed chair is squeezed into an alcove on the right. Just beyond the couch is a door that leads into the bathroom. The kitchen is visible through a doorway to the right of the television. There is a window over the kitchen sink that provides a view of the street. The bedroom, tucked off the kitchen, cannot be seen from the living room.

We sit down and I explain the study and the informed-consent procedures. After signing the forms, Patricia turns the television to mute, much to my relief. I have been silently wondering how well my tape recorder could capture her voice if competing with the TV. In response to my open-ended questions, Patricia tells me about herself and about the complex caretaking system she relies on to keep Robbie safe while she is at work.

The only girl in a family of five children, Patricia grew up in the San Joaquin Valley and lived there most of her life. She describes her stepfather as "pretty stern" and says that her brothers were "raised by the belt." She, however, was never beaten. She has happy memories of summers spent in the mountains with her grandparents. She would bunk together with her siblings and her cousins in a cabin. The children would hunt for frogs and lizards to give their grandfather, who would then make "lizard stew," the Crane family equivalent of stone soup. Her family belonged to the Salvation Army church, which she still attends. When I ask if she identifies with any particular ethnic group, Patricia says "white." Later, she mentions that her biological father was part Choctaw Indian, although how much a part she does not know.

She joined the Job Corps before she finished high school, acquiring job training and, later, her general equivalency diploma (GED). Patricia has held many kinds of low-wage positions, including waitress, warehouse worker, cleaning person, and electronics assembly-line worker. Like her mother and her grandmother, she also has been an agricultural laborer in the lettuce-packing sheds near her hometown. Patricia has never done clerical work. She explains that it does not suit her; she does not like sitting behind a desk. She tells me without hesitation that the job she liked best was her position in an electronics factory in the Santa Cruz area: it required that she use her brain as well as her body, and it paid "good money." One start-up company she worked for conducted a lot of experiments; Patricia discovered that she enjoyed the experience of helping to shape a product. That kind of job does not exist in Oakfield, however, so she cannot earn the same level of wages or gain a similar degree of job satisfaction.

When she was twenty-two, Patricia became a mother. Just after she gave birth to her first son, Brendan, she took guardianship of Ben, her youngest brother: "I had Ben since he's been eleven years old. I had custody of him, because he got too much for Mom to handle. You know, he was getting in too much trouble. So I went to court [at her mother's request], and I got custody of him. So I had Ben and my oldest son at the same time. . . . I had to, or else he was going to CYA [California Youth Authority]. It was either he goes, or comes with me. So I said, 'Come with me, and we'll work it out.' And we did." In conjunction with the court and her mother, Patricia took responsibility for Ben as he struggled to find his way. This established a lifelong pattern of closeness between the siblings in the context of their extended family.

Ben was occasionally responsible for his sister's baby son while she was at work. He developed a strong brotherly relationship with Brendan over the years, and a still stronger mother-son kind of relationship with Patricia. Sometimes this arrangement succeeded, other times not. Eventually, Ben was taken out of Patricia's care. He dropped out of high school, spent time in juvenile detention, and drifted.

Brendan, now nineteen, was also a challenge. Patricia had help from her mother in rearing Brendan, but still found him difficult to manage.[3] His father, largely absent from Brendan's life, was formerly in the bail-bond business. Currently, he is in prison, serving time for stabbing a neighbor. As a teenager, Brendan went to live with his father. This change in his home life seemed to do him no good. His troubles worsened; he was arrested for burglary and then sent to an honor camp. He ran away from the camp, got caught, and was slammed into jail.

Although there are times when Patricia does not hear from Brendan and does not know where he is, she tries to help her son when she can. Not long ago, learning he was in serious trouble with the law, she took immediate action on his behalf:

And they was gonna Three Strike him.[4] But I, I—me and his lawyer—went to the Three Strike board, and he only got seven and a half years instead of twenty-five years to life. . . . So they three striked him and was gonna send him to prison for life. Yeah, I didn't even know about that until my aunt had read in the [newspaper] an article about Brendan. About my son! And she called me, and I says, "What's he doing in jail?" I don't know nothing about this! And she goes, "Yes, he's in jail." And so I got ahold of him out there, and that's when I got this lawyer and we started fighting for him.

The state prison where Brendan is serving his term is several hours' drive from Oakfield. Patricia is worried about her son; she has not yet been officially approved for a visit.[5] Just this morning, though, she had received a phone call from Brendan. "He sounds fine," she tells me, adding, "as okay as he can be in there."

When Patricia turns to the topic of her child-care arrangements, I learn that her elaborate system of care is in jeopardy. Her mother, Fran, is in the hospital, battling lung cancer. A fatigue born of worry shows on Patricia's face. Leaning forward from the couch, taut with determination, she describes the shifting circumstances brought on by her mother's health crisis:

Now it's gonna be put on me to take care of my mom. So I'm gonna have to work that out with my work schedule. . . . The social worker up there at the hospital was talking to me about just not going back to work right now, and Social Security will pay me, I guess. They'll pay me to stay here and take care of Mom. So yeah, that's what we're looking into now. . . . I've gotta have oxygen here and all kinds of other things for her, so it's gonna be a pretty major turnaround for me. I'm used to being out working, and I've gotta stay home now. It's gonna drive me nuts. [Laughs.]

One month later, I return to interview Patricia a second time. In the interim, Fran has come home from the hospital, weak and on oxygen. She is temporarily living with Sherry, her half-sister, in the same house with their mother, Louise. Because Sherry's house is on the other side of town from the Hacienda Apartments, Patricia's day has an entirely different shape. Now, she drops Robbie off at the school bus stop in the morning and then drives thirty minutes across town to her Aunt Sherry's house. She makes sure that both her mother and her granny get their medications and meals. Then, she drives back to her side of town to pick up Robbie in the afternoon. This routine has required that Patricia quit her jobs at the truck stop and at the car auction.[6]

I am puzzled that Patricia does not include Aunt Sherry in her network. Patricia's explanation is that she relies on Sherry for advice about education and learning, but not hands-on care, although she does help on occasion. For instance, Sherry has a computer in her home and has purchased several programs appropriate to kindergarteners and first-graders, specifically for Robbie to use. I comment about the difficulties imposed by job constraints, since I know Aunt Sherry to be employed full time.[7] When I interview Fran Crane she explains further. Sherry, her half-sister, simply cannot take on care responsibilities like those involved in caring for their mother, because, never having had to take responsibility as a child, she does not know how. As the youngest in the family, Sherry was always "spoiled," according to Fran.

At the close of the interview, when I ask if there is anything else I should know about her system of care, the response Patricia offers is distressing, though predictable in a country where poor people are not guaranteed adequate health care. She talks about health insurance and her lack of it. Without insurance, every doctor's appointment or medical procedure becomes an out-of-pocket expense for her. When Robbie gets sick, Patricia is forced to weigh her son's health against her limited financial resources. It is an impossibly painful calculation. "Especially when he gets hurt. I'm sitting here—should I take him to the doctor's or shouldn't I? You know? All the time, I take him to the doctor's anyway. That's the only thing that I think is unfair." The lack of affordable health care also takes its toll on Patricia's own health. She simply forgoes medical attention she cannot afford. To add insult to injury, the State of California holds her responsible for paying a two-thousand-dollar medical bill that resulted from care given to Brendan at the honor camp, after he had been beaten by other boys there.

The Crane Network Members

FRAN CRANE

Until her hospitalization, Fran Crane, Patricia's sixty-two-year-old mother, had been the linchpin of the care network for Robbie. When I first interviewed Fran, several months after she had come home from the hospital, she was still hooked up to an industrial-sized oxygen tank as she sat in Patricia's living room. Raspy voiced and sometimes angry sounding, she has a no-nonsense, forthright manner of speaking that is similar to Patricia's. In her sixties, Fran is about Patricia's height, but softer around the edges. She has gray permed hair, big glasses, and slightly foggy eyes. Her wrinkled face looks tired and sick. And, indeed, she is both. Just the day before, her radiologist had told her that her lung cancer seemed to be spreading. She and Patricia fear that this cancer might be the same fast-metastasizing type that had killed one of Fran's sisters. But, they have not given up hope, because, as Ben puts it, his mother is "a tough lady."

Fran is a middle child. She grew up with five brothers and sisters. Her biological father divorced her mother and later died in an auto accident (Fran was fifteen at the time). In telling me about her history, Fran describes herself as "the black sheep" of her family of origin, always feeling like the outsider, not belonging. But her sense of obligation nevertheless keeps her deeply tied to the remaining members. She sees and cares for her mother, Louise, every day, despite a longstanding resentment that Fran forthrightly describes as hatred. She believes this feeling is mutual, given her mother's response to a direct question Fran posed: "I even asked my mother one time,'What did I ever do to you?' Because I was a straight-A student. I was the only, only one of her kids that really done good in school. Well, Sherry done good in school, but out of all the older ones, you know. And I asked her, 'What did I ever do to you to make you hate me so much?' Now, this is just about three or four years ago that I asked that. And she just looked up at me and said, 'You asked for it.'"

Because I found it difficult to understand how Fran could so vehemently dislike her mother and at the same time be willing to provide daily care for her, even as she battled her own cancer, I turned to Louise for information. At eighty-nine, Fran's mother seems surprisingly young, in part because she has a lot of energy and in part because of the impishness implied by her dyed red hair. Red perhaps overstates the case, since an inch or two of her roots are solid white; however, her intention is red, and her spirit matches her chosen hair color. She has a reputation within the family for being a skilled driver: She passed her first driver's license test using her brother's GMC flatbed truck with a double clutch. In keeping with her independent nature and her migratory life, she drove vehicles of all kinds—vans, recreational vehicles, cabs, even ambulances—and continued to drive a car until she turned eighty-seven.

From Louise, I learned that Fran's place in her family was shaped in important ways by her parents' circumstances. Like the Joads in *The Grapes of Wrath*, John Steinbeck's account of a family's quest for survival during the Great Depression, Louise and her new family migrated to California during the 1930s, in search of work. [8] Louise had grown up on a farm in Oklahoma, one of nine children. Her mother died when she was twelve; she was raised by her father and five of her brothers. She married as a teenager and gave birth to her first three children before she was twenty. Devastated by the Great

Depression of the 1930s, she and her young husband sought a better way of life by moving west, first to New Mexico, and then to California.

To help support her expanding family—she had five children by the time she was in her early twenties—Louise spent countless hours working in the lettuce fields and packing sheds in the Salinas Valley. She tells me it was "Hard work, . . . and muddy. Muddy. Our faces would look like freckles from the mud. But I liked, liked working it." For a time, her father-in-law helped mind the children while she was in the fields and her husband, Fran's father, was working as a truck driver. Louise had one more child before the marriage ended in divorce. Two children died young—one at four months, and one at age nine, in a fire. She married a second time and had two more children (one of whom is Patricia's aunt, Sherry). Louise claims it was not until her third marriage, however, that she found happiness. She now has a vast number of grandchildren, great-grandchildren, and even a few great-great-grandchildren. She is uncertain of their exact number: "I haven't counted them lately. They're hatching."

Fran corrects some of the more self-congratulatory aspects of her mother's account of the past. She notes, acidly: "We raised our own selves. My mother was never home for us kids. And we raised Sherry. Us older kids raised Sherry and [her brother], the two younger kids. And we raised our own self. My older sister that's dead now, . . . they was like my mama." Fran's relationship with Louise seems never to have been an easy one. She reports that she always felt picked on and unappreciated. She manages her current daily caretaking of her mother by setting firm boundaries with Louise about how she treats her. Fran says she could not survive being with her mother constantly: "I couldn't have her—Lordy, Lord! She'd be in the hospital or I would. . . . I couldn't live with her. You know, . . . because she gets too bossy."9

A couple of times, Fran mentions dying. She does not sound remorseful or melodramatic, just matter-of-fact. She worries about what her son, Ben, will do when she dies. She says he follows her everywhere and would, if he could, follow her into her grave. She is grateful that he can rely on Patricia. "He'll just hang onto Patricia is what he'll do." Fortunately, though, within two months of the interview, Fran's condition improves sufficiently to allow her to be taken off oxygen. She starts smoking again.

In June, for Fran's visits back to the Hacienda Apartments, Patricia asked Lee Ramsey if she could install an air conditioner in the apartment. The intensity of the Central Valley heat (in July and August, temperatures climb to over ninety degrees most days) made breathing harder for Fran. The property owners refused the request. They have a vested interest in limiting the amount of electricity consumed: The monthly rent on the units at the complex includes utilities. Lee, as the representative of the owners, reasoned that since the hot weather would not continue indefinitely, Fran should just wait it out. There were no other options. Such is the indignity of living with insufficient resources.

BEN CRANE

In terms of time spent with Robbie, Patricia's brother Ben's contribution is second only to Fran's. He picks up and drops off; he drives; he supervises; he plays with Robbie. Physically, Ben is Patricia's mirror opposite: He is tall, well over six feet, and robust, with fair hair and blue eyes. He emanates a healthy glow that comes from the steady exposure to the outdoors he gets in his position as foreman for a tree-cutting service. His shirt, unbuttoned a few buttons, reveals his chest and several necklaces. Ben and Patricia also are strikingly different in temperament. As soon as he speaks, it becomes apparent that Ben is not a man in charge. He seems content to let Patricia organize their lives now, much as she did when he was in her care as a youngster.

Ben has had his share of struggles with substance abuse and has floundered, sometimes, as he has tried to find his way in the world. He recalls how, as a young adult, he was confrontational and difficult to control: "I didn't finish school. I ended up getting in trouble and spending some time in a boy's ranch for a while." For the past year and a half, he has been in rehabilitation at the Salvation Army and is successfully holding on to his sobriety. At the age of thirty-two, he appears to be establishing a positive direction for his life. He does, however, still see himself as the younger brother/son to Patricia—and she concurs, admitting: "I'm always giving him money, and stuff, and making sure he has his lunch in the morning. I make his lunch. And he comes over here and has dinner and stuff. Yeah, he's always gonna be my kid. [Laughs.]" In addition to being an uncle/brother/son in the Crane network, Ben is a single parent with a four-year-old son, Paulie. With custody on the weekends, and sometimes more often, Ben has responsibilities and a need for a care network of his own. He relies on Patricia, Fran, and a close male friend. He feels he is a captive of the welfare system, pressed by the government to pay child support to his former wife, although, according to Ben, she is a drug user. He says that he and Paulie's mother maintain a good relationship, but he is upset by what he sees when he goes to her house (his ex-wife lives in a town nearby) to pick up his son. Ben is concerned for Paulie's well being. Often Patricia steps in as intermediary and picks up Paulie for him. Ben gratefully accepts this help, acknowledging that he has trouble handling interactions involving his former wife.

Ben brings Paulie over to play with Robbie every weekend and, occasionally, he takes both boys on outings such as roller skating. Both Patricia and Ben characterize Ben as the "on-site male role model" for Robbie, but Ben tells me that he is more like a big brother to Robbie than an uncle. This kind of a relationship is not surprising with respect to Ben's bond with Patricia's older son, Brendan, who is only eleven years younger than Ben. With Robbie, however, the gap is a huge twenty-six years, implying a disparity in maturity levels too wide to sustain a viable brother-type relationship.

TRACY JOHNSON

High-energy, chipper, eye-catching Tracy Johnson is a woman with a beaming, bright smile and an engaging, nonchalant warmth. She walks in the door of Patricia's apartment while Patricia and I are exchanging stories about our respective six-year-olds. Tracy sits down and starts talking, all the while taking off her work clothes. It takes me a few minutes to realize who she is—my next interview subject, and one of Patricia's closest friends.

A few months earlier, when I interviewed Patricia for the first time, Tracy and her children were living in the apartment next door. She took care of Robbie one morning a week and, occasionally, in the afternoons. Patricia is white and Tracy is black, but as Tracy puts it, Robbie "blends" with her family. Robbie refers to Tracy as his girlfriend, to everyone's delight. Although she recently started a job at a local warehouse and moved "five minutes away," Tracy still takes care of Robbie when her schedule permits. In describing her ongoing role in Patricia's network, Tracy reveals her understanding of and commitment to reciprocity of care: "When [Patricia] was going through the hospital thing and everything, I was there to pick up her son, take him to school, or whatever. And I needed her to do the same a couple of times. You know, my mom—she left my kids at home, and Patricia had to end up watching them. And I just thank God that Patricia was there."

As a single mother of four—three girls (twins age six and an eleven-year-old) and an eight-year-old boy—Tracy is keenly aware of the importance of a strong, viable network. She relies on her father, her stepmother, her brother, two of her sisters, her boyfriend, and Patricia. If she needs additional help, Tracy has an army of other kin she can tap: She is one of seventeen children (not all her eight sisters and eight brothers live close by, however). Her children's father is conspicuously absent from her network of care. She does not share custody with him. Tracy divorced him when she discovered he fathered a child with another woman. She says she would be happy to have her ex-husband involved with the children, but he does not try to see them often. She credits him with consistently paying child support, however.[10] It is

John, her boyfriend of three years, who acts as a "father figure" to her children. Tracy asserts:

> He would never let any harm come to my children. He's always been there for me, for years. But I've never seen him as a partner. And he was like—when was it? It was August of '98. He says, "Tracy, you need to settle down." He goes, "When are you gonna do that?" And I said, "I don't know." He goes, "Well, why don't you think about settling down with me?" And that's when I just started thinking. I was like, "You fool! You could have had this guy years ago!" And it's wonderful now. I'm kind of happy.

Tracy values John as a perfect male role model for her children. As with other women in Patricia's network, she frequently and emphatically notes the importance of men in children's lives. She is not interested in marrying John, however, nor does she want to share a residence with him. "I like it just the way it is," she explains. "Just the way it is. I have my freedom, my peace, and him."

Tracy characterizes herself as a person who chooses to look on the positive side of things. She interprets her childhood as a cautionary tale—it provides the basis for what she tries to avoid with her own children: "I wouldn't wish that on no kid, to be neglected like I was. And I don't know how I'm so kind and not nasty, evil. [Laughs.] Stingy, greedy. I don't know. I guess it's by the grace of God. But I am a giving person. And I love everything and everybody, and I try never to do anyone wrong. And I would, you know—hope that no one would do me wrong. Or take advantage of me." A very religious Christian, Tracy is nevertheless ecumenical in her approach to worship. "I go to different churches," she says, "and that's because I like different things about different pastors and stuff. You know, I go where the action is, really; . . . if I can find whatever's in my heart that needs to be touched, you know, I'll go." Her faith, and particularly its embodiment in a woman who acts as her spiritual advisor, is an essential source of support. "She's an adviser. She's my mother in the Lord. . . . See, my stepmother doesn't go to church. And my mom, she's a backslider. So I always have to have someone there, close to my heart, that, you know, can understand me, help me out, guide me. Because you know, I'm young—I still need this guidance. [Laughs.] And you know, I tell her everything that goes on with me." She claims that Patricia's attendance at the Salvation Army church does not interfere with their friendship. "You go to your church, praise your God—you can be Buddhist; . . . I don't knock anybody for their religion."

Tracy tries to give more than she receives. Her own network of care encompasses more than her children and Patricia's—it extends beyond the nuclear family into the community. She is acutely aware that some people are less fortunate than she is. She mentions those who are homeless, for example, and those who go hungry. Invoking stories from the Bible, Tracy confidently asserts that the care she gives freely to others will come back to her in a larger sense.

ROBERT HOLCOMB

By the time I called Robbie's father to schedule an interview, I had heard a great deal about him. Both Patricia and her mother clearly admire—in fact, revere—Robert Holcomb. Patricia told me that he has been her best friend since high school. She said that if anything, God forbid, should happen to her, she wanted Robert to have custody of Robbie. Robert lives with his sister's family, approximately two hours south of Oakfield, in the town where both he and Patricia grew up. He and Patricia never married, but they did live together for a time, and they unequivocally share the project of raising Robbie. Robert sees himself, and he is seen by Patricia and the rest of her network, as an engaged and important network member. He spends time with Robbie at least one weekend a month and for longer stretches in the summer. He would like to have custody of Robbie full time, but realizes the value to Robbie of living with his mother and grandmother. Moreover, if he is needed, Robert is willing to help on short notice. Thus, when Fran's hospitalization caused Robbie's behavior at school to deteriorate, Patricia did not hesitate to take Robbie out of school and send him to Robert for ten days. Both parents agree that when Robbie needs more structure and discipline, his father's home is the place to be. Fran envisions a time when Robbie will need to live with his father on a daily basis to be subject to the kind of control a growing boy must have. During our second interview, Patricia mentioned that she is thinking of moving back to her hometown to live with Robert and his family, and bringing not just Robbie, but also her mother, once Fran has regained sufficient strength.

Robert's initial response to my request for an interview was reserved. Sounding skeptical, he warned me that although he had nothing against my study, he would not answer any questions he did not want to answer. After I assured him that I would respect his decisions to answer or not, we set a date and time for the interview.

On the appointed day, I arrive on time and, with briefcase and tape recorder in hand, approach the front door of the welcoming-looking cottage. Robert lives here with his sister, his brother-in-law, and the couple's two-year-old twins. I ring the bell a few times, but no one answers. Meanwhile, a car pulls up next door; the driver looks over at me and scowls. I must look like a social worker or tax collector or some other equally uninvited and unwelcome person. While I stand absently staring at the cottage's still unopened front door, the scowling driver gets out of his car and walks down Robert's driveway, heading toward the garage in back. He returns promptly, asking if I have come to see Robert. When I say yes, he motions me to follow him.

As we near the garage, I can see that it is overflowing with tools and the signs of projects in progress. A man stands in the driveway, working on something propped up against a big table. Just as I say hello, I catch sight of movement behind him, inside the garage, among the piles of tools, pieces of furniture, and workbenches. Focusing, I see a man in a wheelchair. His graying hair flows over his shoulders; his beard hits him midchest. He is shirtless, with an impressive array of tattoos covering his upper body and continuing down over his muscular arms. He is engaged in a project and does not come forth immediately to greet me. I have no doubt, however: This is Robert Holcomb.

When, a few moments later, he wheels around and introduces himself, it is clear that he has been expecting me—as have the other two men in the backyard. I am introduced to the man in the driveway, Robert's brother-in-law, and to the once-scowling man who escorted me down the driveway. He is smiling and seems rather sweet and friendly now. I learn that his name is Leroy. He is one of Robert's best friends from childhood.

Once he is ready to talk, Robert gives me his full attention. The skepticism I heard in his voice on the telephone seems present still. He is not hostile, but neither is he friendly. He has a slight twang and his voice is somewhat muffled by his beard and full moustache. Occasionally, I find his words difficult to decipher—there is never any doubt about his message, though. His meaning comes through clearly and decisively. Almost immediately, I am struck by two things about Robert. One, motorcycle culture shapes his lifestyle. With his tattoos, his garage filled with motorcycle parts, and his tough-guy image, he could easily be taken for a Hell's Angel. Two, Robert commands respect. On the strength of Patricia's and Fran's descriptions of him, I have come to the interview assuming he is doing something right as a father and as a kin member. But, against my best sociological intentions, motorcycle-guy stereotypes win out and I am prepared to find Robbie's father stoic, antifamily, possibly reckless, and probably authoritarian.[11] Instead, as Robert tells me about himself and about his relationship with his son, I discover a man who is wise and deeply philosophical. I find it impossible not to both respect and admire him.

Robert grew up in the Salinas Valley, the son of an agricultural truck driver who operated in the "old school" of parenting, and a clerical worker. His grand-mother took care of him, his brother, and his two sisters while his parents were working. First as a youngster and later as an adult, he worked in the lettuce fields. He eventually became a dock foreman. Agricultural labor is not easy, but Robert says it suited him. He has never enjoyed indoor activities: "You know, I'd rather be out doing leather work or working on a motorcycle or some-thing of that nature. You know, sitting indoors is just not my thing. I enjoy being out. I can't do it. If it's outside, hey, I'll go for it. I don't do indoors good. Never have." He would likely still be part of the area's lettuce industry if it were not for an accident that broke his back in five places and left him with paraplegia. He recounts a critical moment in the aftermath: "I've always prided myself on being a strong-willed person. And I remember the doctors looking at my wife and telling her, 'Well, we don't really know. We can't say at this time.' And that was like a wake-up call for me, I guess. You know. And I just told 'em, 'Hey, I'll be here tomorrow.' I come through the whole thing with no surgery at all." He healed his broken bones and built back his strength. No longer married, he lives independently within a close circle of family and friends.

Robert characterizes himself as a leader. "I'm not a follower, I don't fol-low good at all. You know? I just don't." At the same time, though, he ac-knowledges that he is "a troublemaker," and that he is not necessarily proud of that. Robert makes a point of using his self-knowledge to inform his over-all philosophy of life. He believes in the essential unity of all people and, char-acteristically, gets that idea across very simply: "We're all the same. Doesn't matter." He is similarly thoughtful and direct in his reflections on his role as a father, on the challenges life has presented him, and on human beings as fallible agents in an unpredictable world. In his view, we all make choices in our lives, and we all need to summon the courage to face the consequences of those choices.

For Robert, the relationship he has built with his son transcends all other connections. Simply having Robbie present in his home fills him with joy. It is Robbie who makes it all worthwhile for Robert. His son, he says, "is the driving force of my life."

ROBBIE CRANE

Robbie Crane seems unperturbed by his role as the center of his parents' sepa-rate universes. He is busy being six years old. His favorite thing to do, he tells me, is "play Ring around the Rosies." When his mother adds that Robbie likes to draw, he firmly reasserts his control over the conversation, amending Patricia's statement: "When I have time, when I have time to draw. Like when it's quiet." He loves to pal around with his cousin Paulie. "They're perfect buds," says Patricia, even though they are almost two years apart. When I ask Robbie what kinds of things he does with Paulie, he replies, "Um . . . when he falls down . . . I pick him up." He is similarly protective of his younger cousins, the twins who live at his father's house. He plays with these two-year-olds, "and when they get hurt, I come and help them pick up."

I ask Robbie what he might do if there were an emergency—if, for example, there were a fire, or if his grandmother got hurt. Robbie says he would call his uncle Ben. We also talk about chores and responsibilities. At his mother's, he is responsible for doing his homework and for sweeping the front sidewalk. When he is at his father's, he contributes by doing things "like . . . helping pick up the toys from the twins." When Patricia reminds him that he helps his dad with projects, Robbie cries out in a burst of enthusiasm, "I work on motorcycles!"

LEE RAMSEY

Lee Ramsey, manager of the Hacienda Apartments, is not a regular member of the Crane network, but she provides Patricia with an important form of support. Lee is present at the complex most days, around-the-clock; and she has indicated a willingness to cover in emergencies, should no one else be available. This offer is consistent with Lee's understanding of her job and with her personal values. She views the Hacienda Apartments as a small community and defines her role as part sheriff and part guardian angel, watching out for her tenants. With a laugh, she explains: "Well, you almost have to be. It's your job."

When she first took the job as apartment manager three years ago, Lee summoned the police several times a week. She recalls: "There was a lot of drug dealers. Several hookers. . . . So when we first got there, the noise at night was unreal—the people driving in and out." Fearless, she would walk up to a driver of a car and ask: "Did you know you are in the vicinity of a known drug dealer? And did you know that I am recording your license plate in order to report it to the Drug Watch?" The drivers would screech away. Lee claims she has never been physically threatened, although she now carries pepper mace at the suggestion of her employer. She theorizes that because she's female, people find her less threatening and are less likely to pick a fight with her than with her husband, for example.[12]

She encourages the tenants to look out for one another, to keep multiple "eyes on the street": "Yeah, we have this one lady [Mattie]—she looks out; . . . we've had a lot of older men, older people, in this one area, and she's kept an eye out on them. . . . Or, like the older gentlemen that moved in—make sure they got food. And the food he'd brought from another place was bad, and Mattie saw it and said, 'No.' So it was like she'd done some babysitting for somebody, and they paid her in food. And so with that food, she helped feed this guy." And Lee makes an effort to follow up herself with assistance for residents who seem to need a hand. With her own children grown, Lee works to create a safe environment for her tenants and gets satisfaction in the process.

Family First and a Helping Ethic

For the Cranes, family obligations come first but operate in a culture of helping others. The "family-first" perspective is articulated and regularly tested among the Crane network members. When I asked Patricia Crane if there was any circumstance in which her brother would not help her, she replied, "No. No. Because his family comes first; that's what he says. He's told his boss, 'Anytime I get a phone call, my family comes first.'" Patricia talks about her own employment when her son once got sick:

> Well, I've always tried being in the labor force. But when he was in the hospital for five days, I just took off. I says, "My boy comes first." . . . It's no problem, because I tell them right up front, you know, you know, when they hire me. You know, "My son comes first." You know, like, this incident with my mom, you know? I let my employer know, "I've gotta go to the doctor's. I'm going to the doctor's with my mom all the time. You know, I might be late." And they says, "No problem." You know? And then, when she ended up in the hospital, I called them and they didn't answer. Well, I called them back the next day and they answered. And I told them what had happened, you know? And they says, "No problem. You take off this time, and you come back whenever your mom's better." I've been lucky.

Her friend Tracy Johnson tells about a similar commitment to her family. In fact, she had a disagreement with Patricia about her sense of obligation to her own mother. Even though Tracy was perfectly clear about not wanting her drug-addicted mother around her children, at one point her mother ran out of food and Tracy could not turn her away. Tracy said, "Patricia was like, 'Can't you just tell her no?' And I was like, 'Patricia, no. That's my mom.' It's so hard." For Tracy's inability to turn her mother away, Patricia got angry with her, although she probably would have done the same thing had she been in Tracy's position. Tracy held tight to her sense of responsibility for her mother, even when it conflicted with her obligation to protect her children and her commitment to her friend.

Like many others in the working class, members of the Crane network prefer child-care providers who are related to them.[13] Fran has helped Patricia rear both her children, and the two women are helping Ben with his son. Patricia and Tracy are each other's exception to this child-rearing preference. Reliance on someone outside the family has earned Tracy, especially sharp criticism. Her grandmother, for one, does not mince words:

> She tells me I'm no type of mother to leave my kids. And I do take them sometimes to my best friend, [Jessica]. And I trust her with my life. Because when I moved in around the corner from my dad, what happened? My dad was keeping them. . . . [My grandmother and father] both got sick at the same time, and they couldn't keep my kids. So I needed a babysitter, and I wouldn't go to work. I stayed off work for about a week, and [Jessica] said, "Tracy, I noticed you weren't going to work." And I was like, "Yeah, I know." And she goes, "I know you don't like leaving your kids with anyone, but I watch kids all the time and I will watch your kids for you." And I paid her thirty dollars a week to watch my twins, plus I bought groceries and stuff. And that's the only person I will trust my kids with, outside of family, other than Patricia . . . because I consider her part of my family.

Privileging family does not necessitate excluding friends who have passed the litmus test of trust. (For a discussion of friendship, see Chapter 6). Such inclusions can require one to explain one's behavior, however.

At a more general level, an ethic of helping informs the lives of the Crane network members, extending beyond the confines of their immediate families and beyond child care. Patricia's kitchen, for example, serves as a resource for those who earn her trust or who do not take advantage—in short, anyone she wants to help. In return, others bring groceries, contribute small sums of money, and care for her son, her convalescing mother, or her. Some associations start via happenstance and evolve when one person decides to act unilaterally to extend assistance. Thus, when Fran befriended a woman she met at a Salvation Army bingo game and discovered that her new friend's mother was struggling to care for herself, she drew the mother (dubbed "Grandma") into the safety net of the Cranes. She explains her action this way: "She's just a friend. But if I had somebody out there . . . you know, that needed a friend, I'd hope that somebody would be a friend to 'em and watch out—she don't know nobody, you know? She don't have nobody. And there's those dopey kids. And they're not doing her no good. So somebody needs to watch out for her." Patricia describes Grandma as a bit "nutty," and Fran cheerfully admits that her friend's mother is "a mess": "I don't know how many husbands she's had, but I know she had several of them. And maybe they worked in the fields and stuff, picking fruit and stuff, . . . is what I'm thinking. But that little old lady—she goes out and holds a sign. . . . I drove her over to the Bay Area. You might have seen her over there, because she goes to all those towns over there. And holds a sign up. And now that woman made two or three hundred dollars every day. Every day! People give her money there." I ask if the sign says "Help me" or something like that. "'Need help.' And she's got a little old grandson down there in prison. Every bit of that money goes to him." When Fran went into the hospital, she turned responsibility for Grandma over to Patricia: "I said, 'You watch out for Grandma,' because I think Grandma got out of the hospital maybe the day I went in, because she had [a] gallbladder operation. And the little old lady almost died. And she's eighty-six years old. . . . And I told Patricia to watch out for her and not let the grandkids and kids take advantage of her, you know? Make sure she gets to her doctor's appointments, because they're all dopeheads. . . . I made her—I said, 'You promise me you'll watch out for her.'"

Patricia discovered that all of Grandma's adult children (except the daughter who played bingo with Fran) were drug abusers who visited their mother periodically to steal a few hundred dollars from her if they could. Patricia's reaction to this abuse was, with Lee Ramsey's help, to move Grandma into a studio apartment at the Hacienda complex. Since Grandma's unit has no kitchen, she eats at Patricia's apartment. This Patricia dismisses as inconsequential—Grandma doesn't eat much, mainly eggs and bread—and besides, she has promised her mother she will look after Grandma. In answer to my question of whether Grandma contributes to the groceries, Patricia says, "Oh, she'll give me five dollars occasionally, or something like that." Grandma also spends a great deal of time just sitting in Patricia's living room because, as Patricia explains, "she's not used to living by herself."

Like a sponge gathering moisture into its porous membranes, the Crane network absorbs those around them who need help. The kind of charitable caretaking behavior it exercises is not characteristic of all working-class people. But that such generous behavior does occur in a society bent by individualism, an ideology of independence, and racial and economic stratification is significant. Taking care of Grandma can be trying. "She'll drive you crazy" sometimes, Fran admits. For instance, the woman's obsession with her imprisoned grandson's well-being threatens to push Patricia beyond the limits of her patience one afternoon while I am visiting.

Given Patricia's generosity of time and resources, I ask whether, in return, she ever calls on Grandma for help with Robbie. Her answer is immediate and emphatic: "No!" With children who range from drug addicts to a daughter who is nice but afflicted with a multiple personality disorder,

Grandma has proven herself incompetent at rearing children. Patricia is adamant that Grandma have no involvement with her son. She looks after Grandma, helps her, and feeds her out of a sense of obligation to her own mother, and because, like Fran, Patricia recognizes that someday she herself might need similar assistance.

Uneven Resources and Itinerant Labor Power

Constellations of resources shape all networks of care. While the constellations include a range of assets and deficits, in this analysis, time, money, and people surface as the most significant resources. The constellation of resources for the Cranes is unevenly endowed, abundant in some areas and meager in others, taxing their child-rearing efforts. Members of the network face intermittent unemployment, poverty, and ill health in their caretaking labor force. While the lack of financial resources translates into unsafe neighborhoods and inadequate schooling, their forceful construction of networks of interdependence helps cushion them from some of the harshness of economic insecurity. The Crane network acts as a true safety net for its members and for those it encounters and absorbs. The Cranes have realized economies of scale by living near one another, sharing, and sticking together to fashion a safe and loving environment for the children. Patricia Crane recognizes the interdependent relationships in her network and does not begrudge them. While she is more likely than Robert Holcomb, the father of her child, to acknowledge, unsolicited, the centrality of the safety net, they are equally likely to grant credit and gratitude to those on whom they rely. They have inherited a legacy of family resourcefulness and resiliency, which has stood them well in their resolute capacity to survive personal tragedy and economic downturns.

While they might be short on money, the Cranes have great wealth in people. Although the number of people may be smaller than in other networks, the members who participate exhibit unadulterated, full-bodied commitment. Patricia Crane has assembled a network full of people that can care for Robbie and that care about him. The network has a great capacity to provide hands-on assistance. Labor power is one of the main resources Crane network members supply each other. At a moment's notice, Patricia can "kinscript" someone from her network. Carol Stack and Linda Burton define kinscription as the "rounding up, summoning, or recruiting individuals for kin-work."[14] Consequently, the Crane network is especially vulnerable to attacks on the health of its members. All lack access to adequate health care and no one is financially secure enough to meet the expense of a problem that cannot be alleviated by over-the-counter medicine. Each member seems profoundly aware that her or his relative good fortune in health, housing, and employment could disappear without warning. Homelessness, joblessness, or drug addiction could be but a short step away. Believing that Providence has played a role in their fate for generations, the Cranes gear their behavior to the greater good of all and bless what luck comes their way.

And interestingly, while mutual aid centrally structures the give-and-take dynamic within the network, money exchanges hands on a regular basis. In a cash-poor environment, those few dollars from Grandma can help Patricia buy groceries. And the money Patricia occasionally pays Tracy helps her to meet her bills. The money is exchanged under a basic equality of condition. Whether or not the "commodification" of some of these exchanges alters them in a significant way is a question that remains unanswered.

Participation in the paid labor force for the Crane network members, male and female, is contingent. While they work in jobs no sociologist would label "family friendly"—with low wages and no benefits—the Cranes take the flexibility they need. If a job is too restrictive or clashes with their family needs, they quit, banking on the fact that they can find another, similar job with relative ease. In this sense, they are itinerant workers, committed to labor-market participation, but not to a particular job. They move a great deal; they change jobs several times a year. Despite their need for income, employment does not possess them psychologically in the way it does for middle-class people in the study.

Chapter 3   The Aldriches

A Family Foundation

THE ALDRICH NETWORK, rooted in California history and politics, hails from a profoundly different circumstance than the Cranes (Chapter 2). Sarah Aldrich describes herself as a "woman of means, involved in the community." She grew up in a family that began accumulating great wealth in the nineteenth century and that has wielded influence in education, environmentalism, and politics. After seventeen years of marriage, Sarah separated from her husband, Alex Brolin, about a year and half before I first interviewed her. They have a joint custody arrangement in which the children—Jacob, age eleven, and Kimberly, age fourteen (and outside the formal parameters of my study)—spend half of every week at each parent's home and rotate holiday celebrations. The separation complicates the logistics of child rearing, even though Alex lives only two miles away. Sarah lives in affluent Marin County, in a town where the average selling price of a house in early 2000 was over one million dollars. To facilitate the transitions and to consolidate child care, they employ a full-time nanny, April Miller.

The Aldrich family does not observe a "family-first" ethic regarding care for their children, but rather delegates the primary care of the children to highly skilled child-care workers. Nonetheless, family figures prominently in rearing the children and mobilizing a group to care about them. Sarah shares secondary care with a handful of kin and friends who have passed a high threshold of trust and demonstrated skill and worthiness. Although family members may not be the first called upon in an emergency, the family is a bedrock group of people who can be counted on to listen, to provide backup, and to help. And importantly, the history and legacy of the Aldriches in the

Table 3.1
Aldrich Network

Anchor	Sarah Aldrich
Children	Jacob, 11 Kimberly, 14
Sarah Aldrich's occupation	Philanthropist and trustee
Class Location	Upper class
Family Culture	Public service
Child-care Strategy	Full-time nanny
Network Members	• April Miller, nanny • Alex Brolin, Sarah's husband • Jane Aldrich, Sarah's mother • Lydia Dunn, son's best friend's mother • Kate Farnsworth, Sarah's best friend • Aidan Macleod, babysitter

United States informs the way Sarah Aldrich rears her children and manages her network.

Sarah Aldrich runs her network like the executive director of a family foundation. Her clear-sighted, authoritative approach to assembling and mobilizing her network is evident in her dignified bearing. She has a great deal of confidence in the board of trustees she has assembled. They enable her to carefully divide up and delegate tasks at hand. The board is composed of relative equals but has a self-appointed, unchallenged director. Sarah provides leadership; she has the ultimate authority, and she never doubts or equivocates about that. The trustees feel happy to be on the board and competent to move toward a common goal. Sarah's leadership inspires confidence in them. In staffing the foundation itself, committed to philanthropy and service, Sarah has hired one full-time child-care worker cum right-hand woman, April Miller.[1] She goes to great lengths to provide good pay and positive working conditions.

Sarah's network of care for Jacob includes April; Alex Brolin, her husband, from whom she is separated; Jane Aldrich, her mother; Kate Farnsworth, her best friend; Lydia Dunn, the mother of her son's best friend; and Aidan Macleod, a babysitter who has worked for her once a week for ten years (see Table 3.1). Members of the Aldrich network pick up and drop off children at school, run them to lessons and games, and babysit occasionally; Kate, Sarah's best friend, makes herself available to discuss the challenges and joys of child rearing. Sarah's mother, Jane Aldrich, covers cracks in the transportation and caregiving systems rather than playing center stage, as she works full time at a charitable organization.

For all this help, the glue of the system is April Miller, the live-out nanny who has worked for the family for four years. April is a vivacious thirty-year-old woman who picks the children up from school and shepherds them to their various extracurricular activities—primarily dance for Kimberly and sports for Jacob. She bounces around the house with the children, ponytail flopping, teases them, walks the dog, waters the plants, wraps packages, cuts flowers, plants bulbs, and runs a host of errands, from making dental appointments to shopping for the children's clothes. April said: "I'll do just about everything. My sister teases me and says, 'You know, you're like a wealthy housewife!'"

Most importantly, in the midst of the separation between Alex and Sarah, April manages the transitions back and forth between households. She calls herself the "stuff pony." That term is her way of describing her responsibility for transporting the children and their belongings back and forth between Sarah's and Alex's houses. In part because of her enormous planning responsibilities, and in larger part because of her solid, loving relationship with each of the children, April is indispensable in making this complex shared custody arrangement run smoothly. She anticipates needs in both households and acts as an advocate for the children. For example, on the morning of a day the children shift to Alex's house, April calls Alex to ask what is in the refrigerator and shops for dinner that night and breakfast the next morning. She minimizes the stress of transition and confrontation for all parties involved.

But even a mother with a full-time nanny cannot effortlessly manage all the needs of the children and their care. Sarah reports on their morning routine: "We leave the house at 7:40 and drop Kimberly at ten of eight or so, and then drop Jacob after that at about 8:15." The afternoon pickups are shaped by having older, active, scheduled children. When young, they had a "combination of outside the home daycare and then a person at the house for some amount of time," according to their father. But with a preteen and a teenager with highly scheduled lives, as Sarah puts it, "They need a driver." In line with Annette Lareau's observation about the fate of younger siblings, Jacob's after-school story is shaped by the activities and transportation needs of his older sister.[2] Kimberly has dance lessons six days a week, and Jacob often accompanies whoever takes her to and from her lessons. Jacob also has his own sporting activities. Sarah says: "He has two practices a week at school, and that changes his pickup time," as do his games. Sometimes April picks up, but other times she needs to be in two places at once; that is when Jane and, occasionally now, Alex, since he moved his office closer to home, pick up and transport.

Sarah, proud of her role in helping to design and implement the after-school program at her son's school, discusses an additional institutional component that supports her network: "The other part of my caregiving that you should write down is . . . that the school has after-school care, called Study Hall, . . . so when I can't be involved in the pickups, Jacob can stay there and go to Study Hall. And he has done that this year more than any other year. And then I have a really good friend, . . . Jacob's best friends with . . . her son. . . . And we do tons of 'Can you pick them up? Can you pick them up? Can he go to your house?' And we do a lot of that."

Like many women with inherited wealth, Sarah Aldrich has numerous philanthropic commitments and responsibilities that amount to more than a full-time job.[3] She works as a trustee on boards of several educational and cultural institutions around the state and chairs two of them. As chair of the board of her son's school alone, she spends at least twenty hours a week. Most of Sarah's professional work is nonpaid; the exception is her position as chair of the board of the "family office," a corporate entity that pools investment money from members of the extended family and also organizes collective kin life. Sarah has cut back dramatically on her board work since the separation from her husband in order to be home with the children more. Alex, a developer, also has major board commitments, primarily related to environmental issues.

Like all families with working parents, the Aldriches feel the pinch of inadequate coverage at times—the pull between work, their relationship, and the needs of the children. Sarah Aldrich has effectively set up a network, using her considerable monetary resources and her skills as a dependable friend and a first-rate executive, to rear her children and to ease the tensions of a failing marriage.

A Family Legacy of Wealth and Privilege

Sarah lives in the town where her family moved when she was ten, only five minutes away from her parents, who still live in the house where she grew up. The narrow streets without sidewalks have a slight country feeling; well-shaded cottage-size houses crowd together, occasionally separated by larger estates. The driveway to Sarah's house on the hill is unmarked, the mailbox partly covered by an overgrown vine in a casual but purposely discrete way. The house itself is not visible from the street. As you enter the front door, an enormous modern art painting greets you. The interior of the house boasts expanses of blonde wood, multilevels, and bright, streaming light. To the left and down a few stairs is a spacious, sparkling kitchen accented with a vase of fresh red and white tulips. I walk in and set my briefcase and coat down at the inviting kitchen table. Sarah makes tea and moves us into the dining room that has a commanding round table and two walls of windows framed by bamboo shades. From inside, the house overlooks landscaped grounds, majestic trees, and Mt. Tamalpais, but not other houses.

The neighborhood and home setting influence the needs for child care. Neighbors make no essential contribution to Sarah's network, with the occasional exception of a family at the bottom of the hill that sends their children to the same private elementary school. Occasionally they share dropoff or pickup. Jane Aldrich assesses the qualities of the neighborhood: "In an average, you know, less affluent area, you would have a neighbor you lived right next door to. And maybe, if you had to go somewhere, the neighbor would help out or be there." And: "You see how isolated the homes are, and you don't really know what the people next door are up to." While this particular setting structures privacy in an extreme way, the lack of neighborhood is consistent with the ethos of upper-class life. As Sarah's best friend, Kate Farnsworth, later puts it, growing up in an urban center, she and her brothers and sisters did not play in the neighborhood with other children. They "didn't grow up in that kind of class."

The remoteness of their property has consequences for the children as well. "It's really dark here," Sarah says. "We're up at the top of the hill, and it's just a lot to ask, I think, for kids" to stay by themselves. Therefore she hires a babysitter if she is going to be away in the evenings. April evaluates the house from the point of view of the children: "Sarah lives on that hill. And the kids have never been able to ride their bikes and rollerblade and stuff like that, because it's just a bitch to get up; . . . it's not for kids. That driveway is horrible. And you're away from neighbors and all that kind of stuff." When Jacob was in fifth grade, April said: "'What's going on? Can this child not ride a bike?' Because he never had anywhere to do it." Now that his father lives in a flat neighborhood, he can bike and rollerblade to his heart's content.

Sarah's paternal family history originates in the German Jewish community that immigrated to California in the mid- and late-nineteenth century. The family quickly rose in economic stature, benefiting from the economic boom rippling out from the gold rush. In contrast, Sarah's maternal family arrived on the North American continent on the Mayflower. Her mother, Jane Aldrich, was born an only child to Southern California Republicans, whose roots lay in New England. The life histories of the two parents converged in college. In their adulthood, both became disillusioned with their respective faiths and hence brought up their children outside religious institutions. Sarah said, "No religious training, and no network also; . . . my parents were pretty isolated." It is only in his later years that Sarah's father has returned to an observance of Judaism. Together in that exploration, Sarah and her father have joined a synagogue and attend holiday services. As Jews, Sarah's paternal ancestors were not listed in *Who's Who* or the other gatekeeper of the U.S. upper class, *The Social Register*. These publications, *The Social Register* in particular, have excluded Jews from their pages since they were first published. This exclusion reflected a parallel exclusion of Jews from WASP-defined upper-class society, including private clubs and elite schools, at the turn of the twentieth century.[4] In the face of such discrimination, Jews created their own social and economic institutions.

Alex Brolin's family fits the more conventional definition of upper class, although it had less wealth and power than the Aldriches. Alex's great-grandfather was a Midwestern industrialist who rubbed elbows with the likes of Carnegie. In fact, a group of these big businessmen founded a private club and purchased land together to provide a retreat for hunting, fishing, and family vacations, a practice not unusual for the very wealthy around the turn of the twentieth century.[5] Several generations hence, Alex's father preferred to run small companies rather than multinational conglomerates, but he continued to be appointed to corporate boards and sent his children to elite private schools. Alex's parents belong to a country club, vote Republican, and practice a "Christmas Eve kind of Episcopalian." That is, they attend service for high holy days, such as Christmas Eve, maintain an Episcopalian identity, but invoke its principles and attend church selectively. By Aldrich standards, neither parent is very involved philanthropically, although Alex's mother belongs to the Junior League and his father once served on the board of his school. The Brolin extended family lives all over the United States and historically has lacked the connectivity and sense of identification with the family legacy the Aldrich family has.

Sarah's mother, Jane, shrinks from visibility and the great wealth of the Aldrich family. Her ambivalence led her to minimize reliance on paid domestic help while rearing her four children, and according to Sarah, she made poor choices when she did hire someone. As Sarah puts it, "The caregivers weren't really good." In contrast, Sarah's paternal grandmother lived comfortably with her wealth and position. Sarah finds inspiration in her grandmother Aldrich as a role model: a visible civic leader, a force with which to be reckoned, and a publicly wealthy woman. Jane Aldrich confirms the power of her mother-in-law to influence her children: "Anything she said they took as gospel truth." She constructively used her wealth to assemble a network of workers and friends to care for her grandchildren and herself. Sarah says: "When we visited my grandmother, which was frequently, . . . she had a wonderful maid, Irene, whom we adored, and she watched us a lot. And her niece would come in the summer, sometimes, and watch us. We loved her niece, too."

Aware of her position, Sarah cautiously screens whom she lets into her children's lives. Sarah feels nervous about being exposed by my book as a person with a great deal of wealth. She explains her concern as an inheritance from her father. Sarah refers to the Lindbergh kidnapping of her father's childhood, and then the Patty Hearst case during her own, both of which shape her family's concern about being too public about their wealth. Making oneself known as a person with wealth means possibly being a target of hostility, crime, or simply unwanted solicitations. Discretion about money and philanthropy is part of being upper class.[6]

Sarah and her mother disagree on how much help Sarah needs and gets. From the perspective of Jane Aldrich, the family's wealth and privilege reduce Sarah's need for a network: "Because Sarah has April, there isn't very much I need to do." Sarah disagrees. From her perspective, her mother provides an invaluable foundation. Even with April working full time, Sarah says: "I rely on my mother, and I have for years, to fill in, to do some amount of pickup, sometimes drive to school. . . . I have lots of meetings that start at eight, because I'm on so many boards, and boards are filled with people who work and don't want to meet during the day. They want to meet either at the beginning of their day or the end of their day, which are both times kids also need to be going someplace."

The family wealth affords the children enrichment activities, but compared to the overscheduled children of the middle class, Jacob Brolin's life seems calm and home centered.[7] Like the middle-class children immersed in lessons and athletic training, Kimberly Brolin spends many hours per week training in dance. But unlike the middle-class children, dance is her sole preoccupation. And the exclusive community of which they are a part sets an exorbitant standard of investment in children's activities. Sarah talks about Jacob's sports life and these high expectations: "Last year, he was on his baseball team. He loves baseball, and he wasn't really hitting that well. And he's fairly good. So I was talking to the other moms on the benches, and it turns out all these kids have a trainer. And so I called the trainer up, and he says, 'Oh no, I'm completely booked this year.' So I had to—we got in early for this year, so we'll see." The lessons consume time as well as money, and Jacob and Kimberly find themselves in the car a great deal, going to dance training or Little League practices.

The Aldrich family dynamism exerts a magnetic pull that attracts Alex Brolin as well as the Aldrich descendents. They had a family compound in the mountains, Arcadia Beach, built early in the twentieth century as a place to congregate and to entertain powerful people. Jane Aldrich notes, "It's an ideal place for children," in that it provided a protected area for children to run, play, swim, and hike. Alex waxes eloquent about its impact on him—not just the mountain retreat, but the sense of family that the Aldriches cultivate there. In becoming immersed in Aldrich country, Alex discovered a sense of family absent in his own childhood. He also found political kinsmen in the Aldrich family, equally ardent in their environmentalism. Through the land at Arcadia Beach, the family sustained its legacy and offered a common gathering place for the extended kin.

The family property and the family office combine to create a geographic and financial bedrock for the extended kin. Sarah explains some of the dimensions of the family corporate entity: "We have family committees. We have an investment committee, a direct investment committee, a real estate committee, and a family life committee. So I work with every committee chair to be sure that we have, you know, an active committee process; . . . we have two family meetings a year, over the weekends, [for which] I do the agenda." Within the clan, Sarah exercises influential leadership. She chairs the board of the family office. She feels responsible for her sisters as the eldest of her family of origin. And she organizes extended family events. In effect, Sarah anchors her extended kin as well as her own network.

The solidity of the extended family embrace was shaken when Sarah and Alex separated. Because they had been the heirs apparent to lead the family into the next millennium, the separation had multiple consequences among the family. Jane Aldrich reflects on its impact: "Sarah and Alex have been married so long, and we were all so settled with him. I mean, I was saying, 'They're the ones who will take over our family when we're gone. They'll be the two old ones who will help all the girls with things.' And Alex is a great brother-in-law. So now that's not gonna be the way it was." Aidan Macleod, the occasional babysitter, confirmed this perception of Sarah and Alex as the enduring, rock-solid couple, "together forever." But in a culture where half of all marriages end in divorce, there are no guarantees of long-lasting marriage.[8] Nonetheless, Aidan was "completely shocked" when she found out about the separation.

Aware of the minefields that sprinkle distressed relationships, April Miller had inquired about the quality of Sarah and Alex's partnership when she was initially offered her nanny job. Before she accepted, she asked them for a guarantee: "'You guys have to promise me.' I said, 'I've been in this situation before, and it was a horror show. How's your marriage?' And they were like, 'Believe us, it's perfect! Everything's great!'" April, who has since seen them interact virtually every day, was not surprised. She picks up her account of what she saw several years into her employment: "And then when Sarah said, 'I have something to tell you,' I said, 'Let me finish your sentence. You're gonna get separated.' . . . I could read the writing on the wall. And she was like, 'How'd you know?' And I said, 'I've lived in this house before. It's just two different people. It's a textbook. I can see everything that's about to happen.' And she was like, 'You're right.' I was like, 'Okay, don't let me get in the middle of it.' And they haven't. They totally respected that."

As in any family where people come together and split apart, the separation leaves unresolved relationship rifts in its wake.[9] Jane talks with dismay about the separation: "He was so close to all of us, and still is in many a way, though he's not close to Sarah, so we're all treading carefully around—nothing is natural yet." Even with the joint custody, the separation creates a tug-of-war about where the children will spend holidays. It has had an impact on the extended family involvement on both sides. Alex's parents, who live in the Midwest, have increased their involvement, for example. Jane discusses their involvement in the network of care: "They're much closer to the grandchildren than they have been. When they were first born, Alex's mother said, 'I want to be called Catherine.' And the father said, 'I want to be called Granddad.' . . . She just didn't want to say the word 'grandma.' And they never came to see them for the longest time. . . . I thought, 'Gee, they don't realize how wonderful the children are.'" Ironically, rather than the separation prompting the disintegration of the network, it has motivated people to step up their involvement. In this time of greater need, consistent with studies that show more kin involvement in single-mother-headed households, Sarah and Alex are receiving more family support.[10]

The separation has had an impact on the other members of the caregiving network as well. Kate Farnsworth, Sarah's best friend, laments the change in landscape of joint family activities: "It was a huge loss for me when that sort of system shifted." She has a hard time deciphering how much of it is because the kids are older and have different friendship circles now, and how much is because Sarah and Alex split up. She has made a concerted effort not to take sides: "I have definitely stayed friends with Alex," as well as Sarah. Lydia Dunn, the mother of Jacob's best friend, also maintains a friendship with both. She tries not to be judgmental about the situation and will continue to vacation with the Aldriches, but separately with each parent and the children.

The logistical needs as well as the relationship dynamics have changed. Alex wonders "if it's not almost easier, because . . . since we're not traveling together, usually one of us is available. . . . I mean, one of us will be around to have the kids as opposed to a more nuclear family, where everyone travels around in pairs or whatever." As if to affirm another dimension of his observation, Sarah said: "I don't seem to need a babysitter as much on the weekends. And I only have [the children] every other weekend, so I tend to be here more when I have them." Ironically, in some ways, the separation has diminished needs for nonparental care.

Sarah Aldrich, Anchor

With the posture of a dancer, Sarah stands at the stove as the kettle starts to boil. Her thick hair is cropped short and shapely around her face. She dons an almost floor-length black skirt and a sweater and has a warm scarf draped around her neck. Her sisters, parents, and friends rely on her for straightforward advice and help. Her unfettered honesty sometimes interferes in relationships because most people are not used to such bold truth telling. In this, Sarah's forthrightness is consistent with that of upper-class women who do not have to "make nice" in the same way middle-class women do.[11] It is part of Sarah's personality, as well as of her class position.

Sarah talks about herself in the same matter-of-fact way she deals with others. In evaluating her strengths and deficits as a parent, she observes that she is not a fun person. She reflects on feeling more comfortable as a mother of older children: "Toddlers were like the perfect group. They just made me feel guilty all the time that I wasn't playing with them, and I don't love playing. This is much better, these ages, where you talk with them and do things together that are more interesting to me." Like a good manager, in assessing the needs of her children, she has employed babysitters to fill the gap. She hired April to be fun.

Sarah's mother Jane talks about Sarah as a child, characterizing her as oriented toward caretaking and leading: "She was the little mother. . . . There was a book called *We Help Mommy*. And that was one of her favorite books. 'We dust, and we sweep, and we make a pie for Daddy.'" Now Jane sees Sarah indulging less in the soft parts of caretaking and more in the sharper aspects of managing: "Sarah's just a super, efficient parent." Further, Jane, feeling guilty as the mother who raised her, adds: "The one thing I think maybe Sarah's lacking in some is some empathy, and I wonder where I missed." Sarah comments on the effects of holding multiple executive responsibilities in her family: "My mother said I was completely the one who had to take care of everything, and that is the role I play in the family to this day. When you ask if I'm asking for advice? No. I'm giving it. I'm still the one who's the family board chair. People rely on me for my strength and can-do ability." Sarah elaborates: "I'm good at trusteeship now. I'm really good at it."

Several years ago, Sarah was a director on eight educational and cultural boards across the state. April, the nanny, observed, "They were both just busy constantly, for a while." Sarah has continued to turn down invitations to join other boards. Through the frenetic haze of high-powered work demands, Sarah discovered that she was in an unhappy marriage: "I was out many nights during the week, at either meetings or functions that came my way that were interesting to me—part of the fabric of my causes. And that may have been . . . part of being in a marriage that wasn't too good for me. I was very, very busy and looking for other places to be fulfilled than being fulfilled in the home." She sees her current situation as a new opportunity to reacquaint herself with her children: "So now that I'm separated, it has been like this world opening up for me. I really love being home more; . . . my kids' relationship has blossomed. I feel like we're so much closer. I find myself much more interested in cooking them a dinner; . . . I imported food much more than I do now.[12] And I never was available. I mean, now I'm picking up." Her many competencies and personal unhappiness drew her into overcommitment with work. Since her separation from Alex, she has cut back on her board commitments, sees her children more, cooks more, and feels immeasurably better about her home life.

The Aldrich Network Members

ALEX BROLIN

I drive to Alex Brolin's office in Marin County and park behind his recently renovated building. With short, salt-and-pepper curly hair, he has a winning smile and an air of sweetness about him. Informally dressed, he prefers the pleasures of his new work flexibility and the casual work environment of his own consulting firm, as opposed to the formality of dressing and commuting to the city to a corporate environment. Jane Aldrich's observation that Alex is a "very likeable person" proves true. Alex attended business school after college, and since then his interests and expertise have concentrated on land development. From the beginning of his marriage to Sarah, he has been supported by the Aldrich family and increasingly drawn into the family businesses. A philanthropist in his own right, he serves on several boards that promote environmental conservation. He has been absorbed into the Aldrich kin system. Jane reports one daughter's expression of loss: "'I've known Alex since I was fifteen. He's like a brother.'"

Not ever the main organizer of child care while the children were younger, Alex nonetheless was a participant in some of the decisions regarding them and paid attention, at least in the big picture, to their child-care history and central concerns. Since he moved his office, he can pop in and out of the children's schedules more easily than when he had to commute into the city. Sarah reports that Alex "does none of the midday pickups unless I call him into it, which I do, particularly when they're at his house." He identifies his own network of care as consisting of the mothers of some of his children's friends, Lydia Dunn being the most important one. April is obviously a centerpiece, although Alex did not explicitly mention her; April works for Sarah, not for him. He also has a new girlfriend who has her own children, and she has become a resource for child-rearing advice.

APRIL MILLER

April Miller could single-handedly act as a public relations firm for the extended family. Effervescent and optimistic, she is an upbeat fan of the children and her employer. Undoubtedly April's job requires that she put on a sunny face and celebrate the strengths of the children. In turn, she is worshipped and adored. Sarah displays genuine affection for her: "She's the most wonderful person you'd ever want to have nanny. I love her—great energy, she's very fun." Jacob concurs: "April is really fun. Yeah, she's cool." Other people in the network feel similarly about April. Sarah's friend, Kate Farnsworth, says, "God, she is unbelievable! . . . she's amazing." April sets a standard against which satellite networks judge their own family helpers.

When I first interviewed Sarah, I mentioned to April that I would be getting in touch with her after the holidays to schedule an interview. She suggested that we get together some time before work, because her starting time is flexible. "Right?" she queried Sarah. They both laughed. April has enormous flexibility in her work hours as long as she gets things done. She also gets paid vacation whenever the Aldriches go away, which amounts to about three months a year. She cannot imagine a better position. Speaking about Sarah and her job, April says: "She does my IRA generously. She pays two-thirds of my health insurance, she pays monthly for my car upkeep and the gas, because I use my own car, . . . gas, and you know, just general upkeep, you know, whatever it is a mile. . . . It works out. . . . I can't even tell you how fair it is." April views employment as a nanny, her preferred job title, as her ideal day job. It supports her evening work as a singer in a rock-and-roll band. After April's four years with the family, everyone speculates about how long she will continue. April jokes that when Jacob starts shaving she will have to look for another job. But she concedes that Sarah will continue to need an assistant. She feels appreciated and knows she is needed. "The money is great," and "it's a fun job, pretty much. [Laughs.] They're great kids, and I love it. It's a good way to be able to be around kids without, you know, being a teacher in that other way."

Her job responsibilities have evolved over time. When she began, she worked twenty-eight hours a week and focused exclusively on the children.

As she put it, "I was just the entertainer." When Sarah's personal assistant quit, April was offered additional hours and she enthusiastically accepted. April speaks of Sarah with deep respect and feels respected in return. "It's a really funny line to walk between working for a family and being part of a family. It's a funny line, but this way, this time, it turned out great. So I scored. [Laughs.] We all scored." Although her multiple competencies lead her to manage many parts of the household, she clearly communicates what she will *not* do on the job: She does not do cleaning, although she does the children's laundry and occasionally helps them straighten their rooms. She does not do the parents' laundry. She works with the pest-control people and touches base with the plumbers but does not supervise them. Also, she is adamant about not getting mixed up in the conflicts of the marriage and separation. While she manages the transitions for the children, she refuses to act as an intermediary.

April grew up in the Midwest, where her father is a lawyer and her mother a schoolteacher who took many years out of the labor market while April and her sister were growing up. April has a large circle of friends and no children of her own. She says she used to want to have ten children, but now she has scaled back her family plans, "unless they're just like Kimberly and Jacob. Then I could probably handle ten." Like other nannies, her aspiration is to rear her own children, not to hire a nanny:[13] "Well, I can't imagine having someone in the house all the time with my kids. . . . I can't imagine—except for me, you know what I mean? I could see if I had another me in the house with the kids, which is a pretty snotty thing to say, but I can't imagine, . . . unless you handpick someone who's exactly how you want them to be with your kids. You know, you don't know what they're gonna say around your kids. You know, I've heard horror stories about nannies preaching religion to kids, you know, all this weird stuff." Given her gifts with children, her plan to raise her children herself bodes well for the next generation. It does prompt one to wonder what she thinks of Sarah's delegating the fun parts of mothering to her.

JACOB AND KIMBERLY BROLIN

When I arrive to interview Jacob, the family is just finishing supper. I bring a plateful of cookies that quickly usurps the healthy bowl of strawberries sitting on the table. At Sarah's suggestion, I tell Jacob and Kimberly about myself and my study. I ask them if they have ever interviewed anybody, and it turns out they have. I get the distinct impression that Sarah has agreed to let them be interviewed because she thinks it would be a good experience for them. Inevitably, their futures hold the prospect of more interviews of various kinds. I perceive my main task as making the children feel comfortable talking to me, and since I have a child about Jacob's age, that seems a reasonable goal.

I chat up baseball and the season's prospects for the Giants. Jacob cares passionately about baseball, especially his Little League team. When I ask Jacob what he might like as his pseudonym in the study, like any other self-respecting, hero-worshipping, baseball-aspiring eleven-year-old boy, he says, "Mo." Who would not want to be named after Mo Vaughn, given the chance? His mother laughingly exclaims, "Jacob!" and he promptly retracts his request. Sarah sits at the table a bit protectively through the interview, interjecting comments a few times.

Slightly shy, Jacob has a mouth full of braces and an easy laugh. April observes that Jacob has an emotional division of labor with his best friend, who acts as his alter ego and spares Jacob getting in trouble. "Jacob's best friend is this wild, crazy, hysterical weirdo guy. And Jacob's like the straight man. He's really popular and funny too, but he lets [his friend] get in all the trouble. And Jacob just laughs. He's just so smart!" Jacob listens to the ensuing conversation more than he speaks. Slightly awkward, he does not yet have the poise of his older sister, Kimberly. Sarah describes Jacob as a sweet, "cling-to-your-side kind of boy." Her friend Kate confirms that. She comments that both Jacob and Kimberly are a little less adaptable than her own children about where they feel comfortable: "They always wanted to be in their house."

At fourteen, Kimberly falls outside the formal purview of my study, but she has insights to offer about the Aldrich network. She has a healthy glow and is very self-possessed and assertive in an adolescent, anything-is-possible, my-life-is-an-oyster kind of way. By the end of the interview, she refers to her own "network of care" in a slightly mocking but nonetheless charming way. She even inquires about *my* network of care and who its members might be. In enumerating her own, Kimberly adds her grandfather to the list Sarah has given me. Jacob agrees. After I completed all of the Aldrich interviews, Sarah confided that were I to begin the research process again, she too would include her father in her network of care.

Everyone in the network describes Kimberly and Jacob as perfect children. No one except April reflects on what kind of pressure that might create for them. Jane Aldrich says: "They're such special, unusually cute, wonderful children. . . . You know, smart, verbal, all that stuff." As a mother, Sarah can hardly be unbiased and concurs: "They are really good kids. They are nice and they have integrity. You can trust them; they're calm; they're lovely, and they're good-looking too. They're great kids." Their father, Alex, says: "Someone said to me, 'Do your kids ever fight?' I said, 'Nope.' I have never seen them have a fight, you know. Not even who gets to sit in the front seat on the way to school. They don't pull, poke, punch, tease, you know. There's none of that stuff. Reprimanding them—have I ever reprimanded them in any way? No. You know. Jacob's bouncing a ball in the kitchen and I'll say, 'Jacob, stop, would you?' You know, it's just not a big deal. We are just so lucky that way."

April brags about the children in a similarly approving but almost disbelieving way: "I've never met kids like this before. . . . You know how brothers and sisters fight and pick on each other . . . ? They're like . . . fake kids. I'll say, 'Don't you guys cheat? When I say go to bed, you're not supposed to go to bed!' You know. They didn't know how to cheat at Monopoly; they didn't know how to do any of the things you do! You know, they just never did them. They get along great. They think that the other one is the greatest." When first employed, April thought they behaved well for company. But she later realized their presentation of family authentically reflected their relationships.

The only time I see the children openly disagree with each other is when I ask how they care for each other. Kimberly babysits Jacob occasionally. Jacob cannot think of anything he does to take care of Kimberly, until we begin discussing events and performances. Jacob takes credit for *always* going to Kimberly's dance performances; in turn, he thinks she *never* comes to his baseball games. Of course, he has about twenty games to a season compared to her single performance, and his grandfather attends virtually every game. Nonetheless, the performance support feels lopsided to Jacob. When I ask if there is anything else I should know about her network of care, Kimberly implies that she feels entitled to the transportation and support she receives for all her activities. At the same time, she recognizes that not all her friends have so much support and so much in the way of resources on the home front: "We rely on it a lot, like so much, that it's just so common for me to be able to call home. Like if . . . I'm at [dance] and find out we have some really mean teacher. And I'll be like, 'Hey, come pick me up!' And somebody will be able to pick me up. And that's totally common for me. But then, I have friends at [dance] who can't get picked up. So, yeah. They're very important, our networks of care. We're very lucky to have a network of care."

I then asked Jacob if he thought the network enhanced his ability to play sports. He said, "Yeah." He later added: "I would have to learn how to use public transportation if we didn't have networks of care. I still don't know how to take the bus." Again, their class privilege alters the world he has to navigate.

April's account of daily life points to how much driving the network has to do, the plight of children in California, especially when they are children of privilege and reach the age of lessons and games when their transportation needs expand: "I should've brought this birthday card [Jacob] gave me in December. It was so cute. I faxed it to my mom. Everyone just cried when they read it. It said something like, 'Thank you for—all these games we used to play,' you know, since I first got there, and then it said, 'I feel like I've spent half my life in your car and I cherish every moment.' Something like that. And I went, 'Oh my god! I'm gonna cry!' And I cried. And I sent it to my mom, and she cried. [Laughs.] But it was cute." As if to affirm the importance of transportation, Kimberly says: "I think I'm very self-sufficient, so I think that helps. I get up by myself, get myself organized, and I just rely on them to drive me places."

JANE ALDRICH

When I first called Jane Aldrich, Sarah's mother, she modestly tried to wriggle out of the interview. She denied that she did much for Jacob and Kimberly. I assured her that because she did some things, particularly provide a great deal of early morning transportation to school, Sarah thought her indispensable to the network. Then she replied that she certainly hoped that I was going to interview other families that did not have as much in the way of resources as the Aldrich family. This concern reflected her politics and her life work as an advocate for poor people. It was also a means of deflecting attention away from herself, an interactional technique at which upper-class people are suavely adept.[14]

Her stately house stands close to a busy road, protected by a high fence. Jane greets me at the door—an unassuming woman with a pageboy haircut, sporting small round glasses. Jane Aldrich seems as humble in her presentation of self as Sarah seems commanding. She invites me into the kitchen to get something to drink. I follow her from the entryway into a formal dining room, proceeding through a swinging door into a roomy kitchen with high ceilings and lots of windows. We settle in a room I take to be her study, on the other side of the dining room. Jane sits at the roll top desk, a ceiling-high wall of books behind her, two walls of windows looking out onto the verdant back yard in front of her. Before we begin the interview, Jane takes me on a tour of the photographs on her shelves, introducing the various people in the family whose names I know but whose faces I do not.

Despite having successfully reared four children, Jane feels incompetent as a mother: "I think some people are natural with children, and I didn't think I was that; . . . my daughters . . . didn't have much of a role model, I think. John was a very strong parent and I was a weak one." As if to confirm her mother's perspective, Sarah characterizes her mother as not very good at domesticity. Astutely reflecting on the 1950s context in which her mother reared children, Sarah adds that for Jane, "living for her husband was difficult." Her husband, John, "was not really involved in the caregiving part of it. He was more someone we could talk to about our homework," according to Sarah. She describes Jane as a bright woman who has gotten more strong and forceful with age, to the benefit of everyone.

Sarah reports that her mother was always concerned about the underprivileged and the homeless, and continues to do rescue kinds of work today. When the children were young, Jane raised money for UNICEF and sent supplies to the Mississippi Box Project, Sarah remembers: "She's always interested in the down-and-out. She'd roll up magazines when I was little—send them to Russia for people who had nothing to read, . . . the irony being that she was raising kids with needs, but her real love was [charity]." Jane talks about her sense of mission while the children were young: "I was writing letters to congresspeople, telling them not to have nuclear testing and all that kind of thing. I was worried about the children, and so I was trying to make the world better." She continues to volunteer virtually full time, collect money for UNICEF every year, and subtly encourage her grandchildren to join her in garnering resources for those less fortunate than themselves.

LYDIA DUNN

Lydia Dunn, the mother of Jacob Brolin's best friend, was the only person in the entire study who refused to be tape recorded. A woman who knows what she wants, she controls situations. Alex says about her, "She's a boy expert and she's great, and she doesn't take any prisoners." She has three sons—two teenagers and an eleven-year-old who is Jacob's best friend. She cultivates their independence, giving them a lot of autonomy and facilitating their school-based and traveling adventures. She claims that some people in her community are horrified by what she lets her children do, for example, take the bus into the city for a day, or go to boarding school in the East. But she does not care because she maintains faith in her children's common sense.

She has worked in her current position as the director of development of a nonprofit for three years. No one else in the office has children, which feels odd to her; nonetheless, she leaves work early to go to her children's sporting events on a regular basis. She works four days a week, and from her perspective, flexibility is a necessary condition of her work. She is fully prepared to quit if her employer objects or sets too many limits.

Lydia takes a hypervigilant approach to managing the lives of her children. She is the original carpool queen. She participates in several carpools, all organized around the schooling of her children and their multiple sporting activities. When I settle into her office, she points to the blue sheet posted on her wall, about eye level in front of her desk. That is the school carpool, for which she is the schedule coordinator and distributor. Two other women participate in the carpool—Lydia drops off in the mornings and they do afternoon pickup. But according to Lydia, they are more lackadaisical about it, which bothers her. She clearly has different standards of efficiency. While the women are dependable, they do not understand her compulsiveness. She has so much to keep track of, she does not feel she can be casual about transportation. Therefore, she takes charge and organizes everything. She assures me that she and Sarah are of a similar mind about this and take an executive approach.

Lydia met Sarah when their sons entered kindergarten, and they have been close ever since. She characterizes Sarah as "one of my best friends in the world." She feels she could ask Sarah to do anything; they infinitely trust one another's judgment. Sarah acts as a sounding board for her, especially in regard to educational issues. They sometimes carpool together and they regularly help each other cover the logistics of daily child care. The two families have vacationed a great deal together—camping in the mountains and rafting down wild rivers. The boys go to camp together. Lydia's son's first swimming lessons were in Sarah's pool. As if to seal their fates well into the future, they own dogs that are sisters. They are a dynamo team. They understand each other and their respective approaches to family management and child rearing. Sarah always lists Lydia on the school emergency-contact forms, because she lives a five-minute drive away and she is involved in their lives, and "because her husband's a doctor, so that's a great person to write down."

Lydia grew up in the East not too far from New York City. She says she is trying to recreate for her children the kind of community environment in which she grew up. She lives in a town adjacent to Sarah's, equally wealthy and conveniently nearby. Lydia observes that in her community people watch out for each other's children. And unlike Sarah, she encourages, indeed solicits, that involvement. Last summer when she was looking for one of her older sons, she called the grocery store where she shops and charges food and asked if they had seen him. If he was hanging around outside, could they have him come to the phone? She did not hesitate to call on people to rise to what she sees as their community responsibility.

Besides trusting her residential community, Lydia constructs more webs than Charlotte the spider. Her husband works all the time, so he seldom enters the caregiving picture, although she says he helps out when he is around. Her current after-school care strategy is to hire mature high school students who can drive. One of the students likes to cook, and since she herself hates to cook, she is thrilled and has him prepare meals whenever he works for her. She tries to hire "April-type" babysitters, which means they are intelligent, high energy, and responsible. She says her standard is to think about how a person would handle the situation if an earthquake struck. If that person could manage it, then she or he has met her standard of care. If not, she does not hire them.

KATE FARNSWORTH

A little brusque in her manner, Kate Farnsworth and her big, aging dog greet me at the front door. A tall striking woman, she gracefully maneuvers the grand spaces of her house. It has taken me three-and-a-half months to schedule the interview. Without the referral from Sarah, I am certain Kate would have turned me away. But I was persistent, and she eventually agreed.

Sarah and Kate speak on the phone virtually every day and try to see each other regularly. Until Sarah and Alex's separation, they brought their families together for dinner once a month and took joint family vacations. Because of the ages of their children—Kate has a sixteen-year-old daughter and a thirteen-year-old son—and because of the traffic-packed miles between their houses, they are no longer involved in the logistics of each other's everyday life the way they used to be. Nonetheless, Sarah confides, Kate helps her immensely because they are so close. Kate is her best friend and their staunch affection for one another is mutual.

In contrast to Sarah and Lydia, Kate does not see herself as having much of a network. Her parenting strategy has been to work part-time so that she can handle the child and family dimensions of life without too much of a struggle. Her husband heads a foundation and "travels like a maniac." Although she has hired a housekeeper for two-and-a-half days a week consistently since the children were born, she takes responsibility for much of the driving necessary for getting the children to school, sports, and dance.

The way Kate tells her story, she has purposely set out to parent differently from the way she was raised. "It's partly because I felt compelled to do it because my mom wasn't around particularly, so you know, I wasn't going to do it the way she was going to do it. And I think, just balancewise, I wanted some help. We could certainly afford someone to help. But I didn't want . . . that person to do it all. That wasn't comfortable." She grew up with lots of brothers and sisters in a wealthy urban neighborhood in an elegant house designed by a famous architect. As a child, she hated her house because she found it big and lonely.[15] Her father died when she was young, and her mother overcame her own sorrows by becoming ever more active in volunteerism and philanthropy; as a result, she was rarely around. Kate says, "We were raised by other people." She reports that she and her siblings were able to survive childhood because they were this "gaggle of kids, because we were all really close and had a good time together." Her mother remarried twice, the second time to a man Kate adored. His daughters from a previous marriage continue to be part of her extended kin circle, although he has since died. And Kate relishes her involvement in the lives of her siblings, although that is limited to holidays and special events.

That her daughter loves the house they currently live in Kate interprets as symbolic of her own success in changing the family pattern. Kate says, "I feel really close to my kids." In retrospect, she thinks she would have had an easier time as a mother if she had hired more help. "You do kind of give something up when you're not around as much, not just of your kids, but for yourself—you know, being in the trenches kind of thing." She also feels that a successful part of her arrangement is her good fortune in finding skilled child-care workers: "We have this unusual karma of having fabulous child-care people, from age six months to sixteen [years], consistently." This means she has exercised good judgment in matching people to her family needs.

Interestingly, Kate waxes nostalgic about communities and networks but does not like to get wrapped up with others in a way that reciprocity and networking requires. She commented on my study and preliminary findings: "Are you interviewing people who feel they have a real network of down the street, bringing a cup of sugar? I mean, this is my fantasy. God, if I could have anything, that's what I would have wished." Yet, her actions belie her words. She does not know many of her neighbors and attributes her isolation to sending her children to private schools. She imagines that public school life would provide more of that local connection, and has found that private school has been "a disappointment socially, because you don't have the fabric the same way." Her son did play some town sports, but that did not lead to local community ties.

AIDAN MACLEOD

Aidan Macleod has worked for the Aldrich family once a week for the past ten years. As a regular, she is a minor, albeit stalwart, part of the caregiving system. She is a tall woman with a friendly round face and brown curly hair that falls softly to her shoulders. Aidan Macleod is as shy as April Miller is outgoing. In her midthirties, she is married and planning to have children. And because she currently does not have any, she sees no need for a parallel network system of her own. Her day job also involves caring for children.

As with April, Aidan's contract with the family is mediated by Sarah, because Sarah is the scheduler and formally her employer. Aidan is unlikely to work for Alex because he goes out less when the children are with him. Unlike April, Aidan is not extensively involved in the rhythm of Aldrich family life. She says, "We simply don't see each other that much," and she had less to say about the children and their development. But she says: "We've gotten quite attached over the years. Of course, because they were so little when I started." She commented, especially after having done a lot of temporary babysitting for an agency: "I like the continuity. I like staying with the same family."

When Aidan talks about Sarah, she uses the language of obligation. She reports that if they skip a regularly scheduled Saturday night, then she will fill in another time, whenever Sarah needs her. Aidan does not feel she has the right to ask anything of Sarah—not advice, nothing that is not work related. From Sarah's perspective, she has the obligation to pay Aidan well and to provide her the promised amount of hours of employment. The reciprocity extends only to working conditions and commitments.

Executive Style and Public Service

The Aldrich network can be uniquely characterized as exercising an executive style that rises above mere household management and an approach to public service that extends beyond helping friends and family to providing resources to the truly needy. The philosophy of public service, a sense of noblesse oblige, and the practice of trusteeship on many boards inform Sarah's child rearing, her sense of herself, and the way she anchors her network.

Sarah has proven successful at running corporate boards and making decisions; in the household she is no different. She understands that complexity demands organization and decisiveness, both of which she can offer. In the Aldrich household, "the book" sits in a sacred space on the kitchen counter. "The book" details the master schedule for the household—who goes where, when, and how; the hours April works; the time Sarah will be home; at which house the children will sleep; and the like. While some leeway exists, between two different school schedules, lessons, games, evening meetings, and shifting back and forth between two households, a slipup in the schedule can spell disaster for someone.

With this executive style, some things can be delegated and some things cannot. Sarah understands that she is interdependent with April and others in her network, on her board of trustees as well as her paid staff. As in other large organizations, those on top depend on those in the middle and on the bottom to get a job done. There is no illusion that an executive director can do everything herself. She needs her board; she needs her workers. Like Patricia Crane, Sarah Aldrich feels comfortable with the knowledge that the success of her child rearing requires that she depend on others. They in turn depend on her to earn a living and responsibly, respectfully govern. Most importantly, the anchor has to have confidence in the sound judgment of caretakers and members of the network. Given this approach, the relationship between April and Sarah seems especially remarkable. April has passed a very high threshold of expectations and has been embraced by Sarah as a partner in rearing the children. Sarah said, "She and I work together to manage their schedules." Like a small percentage of mothers and nannies, they form a child-rearing partnership.[16] Whenever Sarah or April makes an appointment, she records it in "the book." April has come to be empowered, in her middle-management position, to schedule dental appointments, haircuts, cable repairs, and the like. She and Sarah used to hold weekly meetings about the schedule and the week's projects, but the level of trust is very high and the communication constant, and so they find weekly meetings no longer necessary. But April is the exception, not the rule. She has earned her status; Sarah does not award it easily.

Consistent with Sarah's executive approach, Lydia Dunn exercises a managerial style that relies on technology and other expensive services. She has a cell phone and three separate voice-mail machines, all of which have to be checked for possible changes in sporting schedules, and each of her children has a beeper. Lydia recounts an example of how she handled a transportation challenge for one son's weekend swim meet, about an hour-and-a-half drive south. Only one other family in the area had a child on that traveling team, and it had an unlisted phone number. Lydia was outraged—how could a person expect to get by in life without being accessible to other people? In order to arrange a carpool, she sent the mother of this other swimmer an overnight letter and told her to call her so they could coordinate travel. She expected an immediate reply. Through her example, Lydia teaches her children a sense of entitlement, the importance of being organized, the way to exercise authority, and the need to set high standards of community help to which she holds people accountable. This assumption of privilege and self-importance reaches beyond what Lareau describes in middle-class child rearing.[17] It produces expectations that the children will become powerful adults who run organizations and manage armies of workers.

Not all anchors in upper-class families in this study fit the household-executive model. Kate Farnsworth, for one, prefers to do child-related activities herself rather than delegate them.[18] She has employed babysitters and housekeepers over time, but she derives satisfaction from performing the nitty-gritty tasks associated with child rearing. They offer her a means to connect with her children and a method to alter her family's historical practice of child rearing, which she experienced as alienating, for the next generation. Likewise, Jane Aldrich is an example of someone who felt uncomfortable asserting her authority over caretakers while her children were growing up. Nonetheless, Sarah's executive style of mothering must be understood in a context of her family legacy, including its enormous wealth, its ethic of philanthropic giving, and its practice of public service.

In regard to kinship, the Aldriches' story differs from the Cranes': The Aldriches do not observe a "family-first" practice in daily child care. However, although Jane Aldrich and Alex Brolin are the only kin members who help out regularly in the network, Sarah's reliance on nonkin does not mean that family is not important. In fact, Sarah's extended family looms large in how she approaches rearing her children. In this regard, the Cranes and the Aldriches share something important in common. However, the Aldrich family office and shared vacation home structurally link extended kin together for financial investments and leisure activities. The Aldrich legacy, and Sarah's paternal grandmother in particular, cannot be overestimated in their power to influence Sarah's attachment to her kin. The family culture of public service significantly inspires Sarah in the values she imparts to her children, as well as how she has organized her professional life. The family legacy is an important resource insofar as it enables her and her children to think about themselves as part of a large, enduring group.

Through philanthropy and civic engagement, Sarah Aldrich and Alex Brolin convey their unique upper-class status to the children. Jane Aldrich puts the public service philosophy most clearly: "My thing has been trying to get them to think of giving to others, you know. If you're fortunate enough to have money, you should give lots of it away." As people who have money, they have responsibilities that others do not share.

Separation, Privacy, and the Transmission of Privilege

The Aldrich constellation of resources includes insufficient time, plenty of people, and enormous material wealth. The marital separation has prompted a shift in priorities. In fact, both Sarah and Alex report spending more time now with their children than they did when they lived in the same household. When the children are with them, they are less likely to go out and rely on a babysitter. And now, they no longer take vacations together away from the children.

In the upper class, marriage legally clarifies the lines of inheritance in a way that is less important to those without property. Because of their social and financial leadership within the extended family, Sarah and Alex's separation has thus caused a rupture in the kinship system, as well as in the network. But a separation does not inevitably lead to disruption, as the contrast to the Crane network illustrates. Patricia Crane and Robert Holcomb had a child outside legal marriage. Like Sarah Aldrich, Patricia Crane is the undisputed anchor of the child-rearing project. Robert Holcomb, a man without property, nonetheless has material and social resources to offer his son. His commitment to his son goes unquestioned; and, uniquely in his case, marriage was unnecessary to solidify that paternal link. Moreover, the separate residences of Patricia and Robert do not interfere with network functioning. In fact, network members focus on the benefits of Robert's investment in child rearing rather than on the detriments of his physical distance.

Unlike most families in separation and divorce, the split between Sarah and Alex has not diminished the number of people involved in the children's lives or the monetary resources at their disposal.[19] In this upper-class context, the particulars of daily life and child rearing are delegated to those the Aldriches define as "quality people," but values and a sense of identity are deeply tied to family and select friends. The network consists of people who care about Kimberly and Jacob, and also care for them. Some exchanges are structured around a market-based agreement (with April and Aidan) but also on extensive mutuality in a hierarchical context.

Wealth and material resources are assumed in the Aldrich households. Curiously, there is a large silence about money per se. This does not mean that the calculations are absent, or that an awareness of social status and resources is not an ongoing part of negotiating the social world. Economic status is assumed but nonetheless clearly conveyed through philanthropy, family activities, and enrichment for the children. Jane Aldrich ponders what her grandchildren know about their future inheritance: "They probably know they're well off, but they don't know about the amount of wealth they'll have." They do not know the particulars, but their position of privilege is not lost on them. Fourteen-year-old Kimberly now carries her own ATM card to purchase clothes, although she has to stick to a budget. Eleven-year-old Jacob looks forward to working with a baseball trainer in the off-season to improve his batting. While they live largely in a world made up of people similar to themselves, according to their mother, "they have consciousness of people without means. But they have no worries and . . . live a different life because of that." In contrast, the working-class children learn about the limitations of family resources daily through concrete discussions and ongoing calculations of dollars and cents. The upper-class children learn "a sense of broader opportunities," as Alex Brolin puts it, and of responsibilities through the example set by their elders and a loud silence about money. And the wealth that awaits them leverages family connections over the long term that might otherwise be abandoned.

The distance created through privacy—physical and psychological—also figures as a resource and a deficit. Here the class differences also register strongly. As E. Digby Baltzell puts it: "The higher the social class, the more social distance is reinforced by geographical isolation."[20] The Aldriches own their homes and live in well-heeled seclusion. In contrast, the Cranes have no buffer zone—positive or negative—to shield them from their neighbors. Indeed, the walls that separate the Hacienda Apartments are shared, which means that Patricia Crane's bedroom is immediately adjacent to that of her abusive neighbor on one side, and her living room wall provides the slight divide from the bedroom of her friend, Tracy Johnson, on the other. Total privacy is out of the question. Regardless of whether or not it is desirable, it is unattainable. The thin walls mean that Patricia's neighbors' activities are her business, and her ability to screen what Robbie sees and hears is more limited. Sarah Aldrich's property protects her from prying eyes and the annoyances of neighbors. It also means she lacks neighborly support, and her children live with a greater fear about being alone and protecting their property from thieves and intruders.

Chapter 4   The Duvall-Brennans

A Loose Association
of Advisors

MAGGIE DUVALL and Jack Brennan jointly anchor a network, psychically and managerially sharing the work of rearing the children and running the household. They actively coparent, practicing intensive parenting with passionate attention to the children when they are together. An air of resignation to the overwhelming demands of careers and parenthood hangs over Maggie and Jack. They try to schedule time for exercise and friendship, but neither fits easily into an already full schedule. Both feel they are "skating" (Jack's term) on their jobs to accommodate family life. Because they prioritize family, they do not put in standard attorney's hours, sixty to eighty per week.[1] Nonetheless, they work full time in high-powered jobs that place extensive demands and hold high expectations for their performance and commitment. They feel they are barely holding their work and family lives together—inadequate as parents and as workers.

They rely on institutional care for their two children—Danielle, age six, who attends an after-school program when kindergarten ends, and Scott, age three and one-half, who has been in full-time day care at the same center since infancy. Jack explains the equity they have designed in setting up the week's schedule: "The presumption is, I'll take the kids in, she'll take them home. That's the presumption. And that once a week each of us on different days will work late." Maggie leaves early to be in the office by 8:00. Jack drops Danielle at before-school care at 7:30, and Scott gets dropped at his day care by 8:00. From there Jack drives to work, arriving between 9:30 and 10:00 if the traffic is not too bad. When kindergarten finishes at noon, Danielle goes to after-school, which thankfully is at the school, so no transportation is needed.

72

Table 4.1
Duvall-Brennan Network

Co-anchors	Maggie Duvall and Jack Brennan
Children	Danielle, 6 Scott, 3 1/2
Maggie Duvall's occupation	Attorney
Jack Brennan's occupation	Attorney
Class location	Professional middle class
Child-care strategy	Institutional
Network Members	• Tom Brennan, Jack's brother • Teresa Clark, Jack's brother's partner • Byron Russell, former neighbor • Rebecca Hoffman, former neighbor • Ruth Bergman, former neighbor • Lucia Stanley, friend of Maggie • Brenda Emerson, friend of Maggie • Amanda Brennan, Jack's sister

Maggie has to leave by about 4:30 to pick up both kids by 6:00 P.M. Like other formal child-care institutions, profit making and nonprofit, both day-care centers have strict pickup time policies.[2] The children spend approximately ten to eleven hours a day in school and at child care, at institutions that offer stability and reliability.

The downside of institutional stability is inflexibility. Despite this full-time care arrangement, Jack and Maggie still need and want an informal network. A sick child, a traffic accident on a major highway, or the slightest disruption to their carefully crafted schedule precipitates an emergency. The Duvall-Brennan network is well off financially but stretched extremely thin in terms of people and time. The caregiving network they enumerate consists of Jack's brother and his coresident partner, three former neighbors, two friends from Maggie's women's group, and Jack's sister, who lives on the East Coast (see Table 4.1). The network list is substantial in its numbers—eight people in addition to Jack and Maggie—but the ties are thin and brittle. It is well situated to care about the children, but ill prepared to care for them. All of its members have multiple commitments, and none live immediately nearby. As Maggie puts it: "They're all working. . . . I don't know of anybody who'd really help me out with [an emergency] because everybody I know is a working parent." Jack Brennan says, "The network is both split up and not there, if you know what I mean."

Ironically, Jack and Maggie's partnership in parenting leads to labor-intensive self-sufficiency. As one former neighbor put it: "I don't think they used a lot of support. They really did everything themselves." Like that of Robert Holcomb, Robbie Crane's father, their practice does not match their espoused ideology. In a reversal of Robert Holcomb's belief in independence, they articulate a hunger for community involvement and a political commitment to communitarianism, yet they practice parental and familial independence. They yearn for a network of interdependence. While they have friends and kin upon whom they rely, at least for advice and emotional support, they lead isolated lives structured by the demands of their employment. Ultimately, they depend primarily on each other.

Searching for Family-friendly Jobs and Good Schools

Not long ago, Jack and Maggie lived in a bustling urban neighborhood. As Danielle reached school age, Maggie and Jack deliberated about the public school system and its ability to educate their children. Politically committed to public education, they nevertheless found it inadequate. Therefore, they sought a better school system in a nearby suburb rather than sending their children to private school in the city—the choice as they saw it. In their old neighborhood, they were not alone. Their former neighbor, Rebecca Hoffman, describes the deliberations of white middle-class families in the area with children of school age: "We know about ten families in the neighborhood with kids either [our son's] age or a year older, and nine of them were sending their kids to [private] school. We were the only ones who were seriously considering [the local public school], and we looked at it. And we talked to teachers, and we met with some parents. . . . I think it's an okay school, but it has a lot less parent involvement than [the one we have chosen] and some of the, quote, 'better schools' or hill schools, or whatever you wanna call them." Indeed, Thorne's research in the same area of northern California confirms the way white parents clamber to get their children out of this multiethnic, multiclass public school.[3]

Once they moved to a new neighborhood with a better public school system, Maggie and Jack's fragile backup support system unraveled. They left behind their neighborhood, their friends Byron Russell and Rebecca Hoffman, and their downstairs neighbor, Ruth Bergman, a single woman who loves children and had voluntarily filled in some of the gaps in child care. Maggie and Jack do not see their old friends as much, because the two miles that separate them from their old neighborhood makes popping in to play or visit no longer convenient. Maggie seemed baffled: "It's not like we moved to a whole different state or something. But those networks are not as easily [accessible], they're not next door." The distance means they are not involved in each other's child-rearing projects in the same way. As Maggie acknowledges about her former downstairs neighbor, "Since we moved, I'm not sure if I can call on Ruth the way I used to."

The move from an urban neighborhood to a suburban enclave took the Duvall-Brennans to another universe. In their new neighborhood, which is decidedly more upscale, single-family homes with three bedrooms and two baths averaged over half a million dollars in 1998. In describing the neighborhood, Jack contrasts his warm expectations with cold reality: "Maybe it's because we were both raised on *Ozzie and Harriet* and, you know, *Leave It to Beaver* and all that. You know, there's [an expectation of] a seamless web of warmth and intimacy in your neighborhood. You know, it is astonishing to me; . . . it seems much more difficult to make contact with casual friends, neighbors, what have you, than it seemed to be when you lived in a scuzzy little flat and you were just out of college two years. It seems very different." Absent are activities on the street and the bustling hum of human interaction that makes a neighborhood vibrant and engaged. Maggie and Jack rarely even see their new neighbors. When they do, the neighbors appear to be in transition and anxious to maintain their privacy. They have thus far foiled Jack's efforts to make eye contact on the street.

Maggie affirms his perception: "There's one neighbor that we've met. We've kind of said hello to a few others. But there hasn't been as much warmth as we might like. There's one neighbor down the block that I know. We belong to the Unitarian Church here, and I know her. She's a single mom, actually, who just adopted a child. . . . She actually called me on Saturday night because her baby had a high fever and she had apparently been running a fever for about five days and just wanted me to walk down to see how things go. So . . . that's developing." Although the neighborhood feeds into the local kindergarten that Danielle attends, few children play in their front yards. Jack has resolved to change the situation: "I've decided the next time . . . they, like, have their feet on the street long enough, I'm just gonna walk over and say hi. It's been difficult; it's been unusual."

Ironically, in detailing her own childhood experiences, Maggie reiterates her determination never to end up in the isolation of a suburbia. Until she was twelve, she lived in an urban neighborhood, where she was part of "literally roving gangs of little kids." Then her parents moved to another city, into an expensive community with huge lot sizes that created a secluded privacy not conducive to neighborhood play. She expresses the sense of loss she felt without her gang and the child-friendly neighborhood and says, "I never wanted to go live like that again." One wonders how her choices may have led in that very direction.

As with many parents, Maggie and Jack's child-care strategy has changed as their children have grown and developed. They adopted Danielle as an infant, and Jack stayed home with her as the primary parent. When he prepared to return to work, they answered an ad posted several blocks from their apartment announcing that a family in the neighborhood was looking for a "share-care" arrangement and already employed a babysitter. Maggie and Jack, philosophically predisposed to sharing, answered the ad and passed ideological muster with Byron Russell and Rebecca Hoffman. In essence, the share-care approach worked well for them as they developed a friendship with Byron and Rebecca, and for Danielle, as she bonded with their little boy and their highly touted babysitter. Like all child-care staffing, the situation was subject to change. After three successful months of share care, the babysitter received a call from her family in Central America and left their employ with only one day's notice. Maggie described the feeling that, suddenly, "we were quite in the lurch."

The couples jointly hired another shared babysitter, who stayed for a year and a half. However, her behavior prompted concerns about truthfulness and trustworthiness that proved unsettling for all four parents. In retrospect, Byron regrets not checking her references more carefully but notes that their decision was made in the context of the babysitting crunch and their own desperation about work. The situation ended when the children went off to nursery school. It left Maggie and Jack with a sense of unease about employing someone they could not directly supervise and a distrust of in-home babysitters.

Given the demands of their jobs, like other families with mothers who work full time, they decided instead upon institutional care.[4] Because of this "mixed experience," Maggie said, "we decided we wanted a place that we knew exactly where everybody was at all [laughs] times. And it has a really good ratio of infants to caregivers." So they shifted strategies when they adopted their second child, Scott. Although they liked the share-care philosophy, individual in-home babysitters had proved untrustworthy and unreliable. In light of their needs as full-time attorneys with little workplace flexibility, and in the absence of help from their families or friends, it was the only form of dependable care that could ensure their ability to work and guarantee the safety and well-being of Scott. The upside to the share-care, in-home babysitting arrangement had been greater flexibility, given the structure of the workday.

Their work schedules now have to meet the structure of the day-care center and adapt to its inflexibility. Jack talks about the pressure of the rigid schedules: "I think our default schedule is stressful but not complicated, is how I'd put it. The level of stress is fairly predictable unless I get caught in traffic and, you know, I don't have a cell phone or anything, so I can't call them and they do shut down at six. At 6:30, they have some arrangement to call Protective

Services or something—I don't know what they do." For example, the day of the interview, Jack reports: "Literally, they were both outside the front door waiting for me so that they could leave. I got there at six o'clock. At six o'clock." Scott's child-care center is about five miles from their house. "It's not a long distance. It's not a neighborhood place." Jack's older brother, Tom, and his partner, Teresa, live about fifteen miles away, although Teresa's workplace is fairly close to Scott's child-care center. She has picked Scott up several times when neither Maggie nor Jack could make the six o'clock pickup time.

Both Maggie and Jack commute to work, one south to Santa Clara County and the other across the Bay Bridge. Both can make the drive in about an hour each way, if there are no accidents or traffic jams, but there are never guarantees. As Jack puts it, it is "high-demand driving," with a lot of accidents and stop-and-go traffic. The commute, long days, and unbending work structure prevent Maggie and Jack, like other parents, from easily checking in with staff at the child-care center.[5] Maggie finds this frustrating, because she does not drop off kids in the morning, and "the late afternoon caregivers frequently don't speak very good English. And the director who kind of sees Scott and might have some assessment is just there kind of like in the middle of the day, so I don't get a chance to interact with her." The same problem exists with their daughter, Danielle, who goes to a before-school program as well as an after-school program. Maggie would like to be able to speak to her kindergarten teacher. However, unless they schedule a special meeting, she finds it virtually impossible to see the teacher in person.

Tom and Teresa take care of Danielle and Scott for events planned well in advance. Maggie reports on one such time when she and Jack went to a Bruce Springsteen concert· "Jack is from New Jersey and he loves Bruce. I was, 'Okay, Jack, I'll go. For you.' And it was fabulous. But anyway, [Tom and Teresa] babysat the kids then. But we really probably for that type of thing are more inclined to pay for a babysitter if we can." Given that the concert is precisely the kind of care Tom and Teresa can do, planned well in advance, one may wonder why Maggie and Jack prefer paying someone over accepting a favor. (The trade-offs between paying cash and paying in obligation are discussed at length in Chapter 7.)

Occasionally, they hire a woman from their church to cover evening dates, at the rate of eleven dollars per hour. But more often than not, at the end of the day, they simply stay home. Other members of the network provide invaluable support and advice, but not practical care. Byron and Rebecca remain friends, but they are not close enough geographically and no longer fill in for emergency child care. As a result, Maggie and Jack are at risk when emergencies arise.

Maggie Duvall and Jack Brennan, Co-anchors

MAGGIE DUVALL

Maggie is tall, with short dark brown hair cut fashionably asymmetrical. She has a long chiseled face and sad eyes. She grew up in northern California, where her two brothers and divorced parents still live. Her sister has moved to the Pacific Northwest. Maggie and her siblings were raised in the Catholic church and claim a primarily Irish heritage. As children they did not have extended kin in the neighborhood, although they visited their grandparents in the city for holidays. Maggie's mother was a "stay-at-home mom. Very clear division of roles." Her father ran a small business and later went to law school and became a practicing attorney. Her mother returned to graduate school even later in life and now teaches in the field of early childhood education. Maggie comments: "In early childhood development with these beautiful grandchildren that she never visits! The irony of it all." Teaching suits her in a way that grandparenting apparently does not.

I am struck by how few people Maggie has to turn to for child-rearing advice. I ask her what she does when she encounters a "parenting challenge"; she responds that she reads books. Her mother, a trained child-development professional, is "not a grandmother," according to Maggie, and is not sympathetic to the children's circumstances. Maggie explains that Scott has issues of "anger management. He's fundamentally sound and healthy and smart. But he's . . . got a very intense anger. And he doesn't know how to control it." Maggie does not trust her mother to reserve judgment: "I told her we were going to a class on 'spirited children.' . . . I have not really shared with her how difficult it is, though. . . . We don't have that kind of a relationship. Part of it is that she's not close enough to him to share it. . . . How do I put that? If she was more emotionally involved it would be easier. But I don't want to have her prejudge him. 'Cause he's hard . . . I mean, we haven't told her for example that we are going to possibly get some counseling on his anger management and how to deal with it. And I'm not sure we will tell her."

In contrast, Maggie does find great solace and advice from her mothers' group. The group meets one evening a month; they send out for pizza, hand their children off to their husbands, and then talk, muse, and commiserate. Maggie finds them a "great resource"—sympathetic, supportive, and not judgmental. Maggie includes both the other two women (the group has diminished in size over time) in her list of network members. Neither lives nearby. They are devoted to her, however, and provide what they can during meetings and by phone.

Being a high-powered professional makes it difficult for Maggie to be a hands-on mother. She chronicles the tensions she faced in trying to be a responsible worker with two small children:

> I had real conflict at my last job about child-care issues and my hours. It was part of why I left, actually. Because I—interestingly enough, I worked for a woman. Also a woman who had two kids; . . . she has a nanny. Very, very hard-driving ambitious woman. And I got scheduled on a couple of cases that were going to take me to trial outside of the Bay Area. And I just couldn't imagine leaving my kids for six weeks. . . . I went and actually asked to be transferred off of the case because I have small children, you know. The effect of traveling like this is not something I can do. I was told, "Sorry." [Other workers] . . . would perceive them as favoring me because I had children. And that everybody then would be seeking to [have] their caseloads be rearranged for personal reasons and stuff like that. So they would not switch me off. That was a really big thing for me. It really, really pissed me off.

Her hostility toward the ambition of her supervisor and her ability to hire a live-in nanny (which Maggie feels she cannot afford) to finesse her job-family conflicts appears to have fed Maggie's resolve to quit. The deck at that law firm seemed stacked against her.[6] And the woman from whom she might have expected most compassion, her supervisor, who was also a mother of young children, exercised the least. However, Maggie says that the organization of the legal profession in general makes her angry; she wishes she had known earlier "how unrelenting it would be in its demands."

Maggie is plagued at home just as she is at work, afraid she is insufficiently sensitive to the children's needs, aware that she cannot accomplish everything that needs to be done, and convinced that at some time in the future her actions will come back to haunt her.

JACK BRENNAN

I did not see Jack until the end of my interview with Maggie, but I could hear him cleaning up the kitchen. He had put the children to bed. The baby monitor was on; Scott stirred once or twice and Jack helped him settle back down to sleep. When Jack came in, he had on an apron and was carrying the family address book, a Personal Digital Assistant (PDA) that included even Maggie's friends from her mothers' group. Jack looked up the list of network members' phone numbers and gave them to me.

The evening I arrived to interview him, he had picked up the children from day care so Maggie could work late. About five feet, ten inches, with steely gray hair and a kind face, he carried a grim air of dogged resignation about him, which was punctuated by a dry wit. As I enter the house at nine o'clock in the evening, the children are asleep and Maggie is eating her dinner in the dining room.

Jack reflects thoughtfully on his life, the network, and their parenting. Pathos dominates his talk: "I wish the network was bigger. We really do. I mean, every parent must feel this way, but we feel like we did the other night after you were here, just like we're totally on our own." He and Maggie are in the midst of the intense years of parenting young children. In probing their sociability, I ask if he and Maggie socialize with the families of the women in Maggie's mothers' group. He answers: "We generally don't socialize. I don't socialize with the men separately, and we don't socialize as couples together, really. [Pause.] Unfortunately not. Got any phone numbers?" Ironically, both Jack and Maggie express a desire for more community. They say they want more involvement, more help, but they are not getting it. They seem at a loss to find a solution in the context of their overextended lives.

Jack recounts his own painful childhood in contemplating the childhoods of his children. His father died when Jack was seven, leaving his mother in charge of the four children. His mother moved the family back to a community not far from her extended kin. Jack described her cousins as "world-class drinkers" who were part of a "dysfunctional support network. There were people we spent time with that had a safe place to be, while my mother tried to destroy her liver." Jack described his grandparents' involvement as "benign presences." They lived three hours away. "They were nice people. We had good relationships with them, but [they] weren't really providing a lot of parental support to—because they didn't live there." Jack's brother, Tom Brennan, talks more about their mother's alcoholism. "We essentially raised ourselves. Amanda, [my older sister,] and I ran the house. Yeah. At age nine, I was fixing toilets. And I had no assistance from anybody." I ask whether nearby relatives provided any help. Tom resentfully replies:

> They would come when she was so drunk she couldn't stand up; and they would try to sober her up. And they would just leave. . . . At nine years old, I just couldn't figure it out. Is something wrong with my mother? I didn't know what "drunk" meant. I knew she drank a lot of beer. She drank a lot of beer. And I said, "Make her better. This is your job." And they would just come, and they would rub her shoulders and they'd put her to bed, and they'd leave. The next morning, she drank another case of beer. So, essentially, you know, Amanda cooked and cleaned. And I did the dishes, and I washed the

car, and I cut the grass. And Jack got so involved in school he was
never home. And [our younger sister] did drugs.

He saw himself and his older sister as taking responsibility, while the two younger siblings escaped. "Jack went to college and disappeared. I got married young. Amanda got married young. [Our other sister] disappeared into the drug culture, but she got married young. And Jack finally got married." Tom's resentment of Jack seeps into much of his account of family life. As he sees it, Jack built his success on Tom's and Amanda's backs. From his perspective, Jack simply bailed, as had the rest of the extended family. From Jack's perspective, education had been a promising path out of a bad situation.

Jack's move to the West Coast ten years ago took him another step farther from his kin but closer to Tom, who had also moved there. His reliance on his older brother continued, despite the emotional gulf between them. And now, married with children, Jack struggles with a parallel set of tensions about work and family commitments, although the family side is more compelling: "You have to continue to make those choices, those trade-offs." His choice has been to make his children's life as different from his own as possible.

The Duvall-Brennan Network Members

DANIELLE DUVALL-BRENNAN

Danielle, age six, snuggles up to her mother on the couch in their family room as I interview her one sunny afternoon. Cheerfully and with no small amount of giggling, she answers my questions about who takes care of her. Danielle mentions her babysitter, Grace, who comes occasionally in the evenings, and her aunt Teresa and uncle Tom. When I ask whom she would call in an emergency if her parents were not home, she names the parents of her friend from kindergarten who live in the neighborhood. Danielle reasoned, in a real emergency they could get there faster. At six, she does not see herself as taking care of anyone, except perhaps her brother, with whom she sometimes generously shares a cookie or performs other such acts of magnanimity.

Maggie is worried about Danielle now, not because anything is wrong per se, but because Danielle's behavior is changing and Maggie feels out of touch, not sure with whom to talk about it, not sure how to interpret it:

She's decided that she doesn't like pink and that she doesn't want to
wear dresses. And it's all related to the fact that she has established
this friend. And . . . that's fine. I'm not a pink person either, but it's
this clear reaction to being a girl, and she's got this, like, friend that
she likes who's a boy. . . . But it is something that I'd like to bounce off
someone and I don't quite know where, you know? . . . I was talking to

> her today about trying not to let other people decide whether you like this color or not. But it kind of got lost on her, I could tell. She's convinced she doesn't like pink. Last year it was her favorite color.

Thus this moment in her child's development becomes another opportunity for Maggie to feel anxious and uncertain.

Before I leave, Danielle pulls out a photo album to show me some treasured photographs of herself as a baby. And importantly, she proudly points to photographs of her birth mother, with whom the family has been in touch. Her history is a part of her she feels I must understand and charmingly offers.

TOM BRENNAN AND TERESA CARTER

Jack's older brother and only relative who lives close by, Tom Brennan, lives with his partner, Teresa Carter, about twenty-five minutes south. Tom and Teresa live in a corner stucco house in a quiet suburban neighborhood. When I enter, I am greeted by a rotund golden tabby and a roaring fire. The front door opens into a spacious L-shaped room. Just to the right as you enter, gracing a high arched window, is a tall ficus tree tastefully decorated with Christmas lights and ornaments.

Despite the Christmas cheer, an edginess in the air keeps me uncomfortable. The subject matter of my interview generates tension. Tom's feelings about Jack are built on a bedrock of commitment, layered with acrimony and long-held resentment. Tom and Jack's mother, at eighty, still effectively manipulates her children, getting them to vie for her favor; and she plays favorites with her grandchildren.

Tom and Teresa have been together five years. They come to the relationship with different backgrounds—Tom, in his midfifties, has grown children whom he raised as a single divorced father. Teresa, a decade younger and comfortably assertive, has never had children but always liked children in general, and is fond of Danielle and Scott in particular. Tom reports: "I raised my own children myself. I'm very children oriented." He also admits that he relied extensively on his sister, who lived near him, and his mother. "They were always there for me, babysitting, or advice, or whatever. Jack . . . was a single young man having a good time. He was about two hours away from me." Again his resentment of Jack seeps into his narrative. From Tom's perspective, Jack took no family responsibility, he refused to participate, and he distanced himself from the family to have a good time and to improve himself.

As a systems programmer, Tom is on call all the time and yet also has a lot of flexibility in where he works. He presents himself as willing and able to be backup caregiver to Jack and Maggie: "I have a laptop computer. I can take my job with me anywhere I go. So I'm really mobile. So if [Scott] was sick, or

Danielle was sick, I could just take my computer with me and if they paged me, I could work from Jack's house very easily." Teresa clarifies that in regard to babysitting, of whatever kind, "usually, we do it together." And she herself has flexible work as a social policy researcher, with a few constraints posed by scheduled meetings.

Indeed, at a strategic point in Jack and Maggie's family formation, Tom and Teresa took care of Danielle for two weeks. It was a story each member of the network hashed over with me, the torments of the period still not completely resolved. Jack and Maggie were in the process of adopting Scott and had to travel to the Midwest to retrieve him. The experience continues to raise questions for all of them about how nonparents in the network effectively care for children. Danielle, who was almost three years old, attended day care during the day, while both Tom and Teresa worked. They found their evening time, which was devoted to her, extremely difficult.

TOM: She had her good days and her bad days. She was terrible at nighttime, because Jack would always tell her a story or sing to her. And she would just cry. After—what?—three or four days, she just kind of settled into a routine.

TERESA: No, that's not my perception of it at all. [Laughs.] Because I think . . . she had a lot of anger towards her folks for leaving her. And I understood what was going on—and I think, especially probably at her mom, so I probably represented her mom. And so she expressed her anger towards me. And so she really rejected me during that time. And so it was really difficult because. . . , Actually, Tom had to do most of the—

TOM: Bath time and everything, yeah. She was very close to me.

TERESA: Because of the way she was reacting to me. And it was hard. Even though I understood, you know, psychologically, what was going on with her, because she had thought I was so great. And then she didn't, nothing at all. So I just had to remind myself, you know, what was happening to her.

Jack and Maggie, also traumatized by the separation and the difficult experience had by all, have not left the children overnight since then (except individually on business trips). Admittedly, two consecutive weeks is a long time for parents to be separated from a young child. They both felt guilty about the level of distress Danielle experienced and the grief her emotional reaction caused Tom and Teresa. Tom says, "We've offered, but they don't take us up on it." Maggie and Jack worry that it would be damaging to Danielle and Scott, in part because they lack confidence in Tom and Teresa's ability to handle the children well. To add another layer to their considerations, they recognize that weekend caretaking requires more time and energy than an occasional evening, and they may be reluctant to be so deeply indebted to Tom and Teresa for doing such a huge favor.

Tom resents the differences in Jack and Maggie's approach to child rearing. He thinks there is nothing like experience, and parents should rely on those with experience—like him and his older sister, who raised five children. He feels angry that Jack and Maggie do not call on him and that his experience is not valued more. "They don't generally listen to my advice, nor anybody else's, I don't think," about child rearing. When I probed about why that might be the case, he said: "I'm not sure. Too smart? They think they know too much. I don't know. . . . They're two yuppies raising babies! And they're old and . . . he reads a lot of books, which are great, but hands-on experience is more useful, I think. But that's just what I think." Again, the tension of upward mobility and the changing perceptions and values about child rearing that accompany it play a role. Jack's emphasis on learning via books offends Tom. Tom interprets Jack's lack of reliance on him as a rejection of those comforts he attempted to give Jack over the course of his life, the skills he has tried to teach him, and in essence, everything for which he stands.

Nonetheless, in the last instance, Tom says, "we're family." And "we'll take care of each other," although they may not enjoy it along the way. Not only is Tom identified as the emergency contact in case of an earthquake, he will be guardian of the children if anything should happen to Jack and Maggie.

REBECCA HOFFMAN

Rebecca Hoffman, who stands about five feet, three inches, with short dark curly hair and tortoise-shell eyeglass frames, answers the door and invites me to sit on the L-shaped couch in her small living room, crowded by an oversized Christmas tree. Rebecca immediately reveals that she and her husband, Byron Russell, have been discussing how they could possibly fit me into their tight schedule around the holidays. As journalists who interview people for a living, they felt they owe it to the karma of their profession to do so, although it feels enormously inconvenient. As freelance writers, both have some institutional ties and some flexibility. Both work at home a lot.

Rebecca and Byron have two children—one son in kindergarten, a good friend of Danielle, and another son who, at two, does not get along with Scott, who is three and a half. Life has gotten more complicated since they had their second child, and so they do not get together as much with Jack and Maggie as a family. They still arrange play dates for Danielle and their older son about once a month.

One theme of the interview emerges as consistent with the other network interviews—Rebecca is not that close to Maggie or Jack. This created some discomfort for me and for her. Maggie had told me, "We became extremely close to this couple and continue to maintain a close relationship." But Rebecca's way of characterizing Maggie is much more distant and formal than the way Maggie talks about her. From Rebecca's perspective, their relationship began as business and evolved into friendship; her confusion about it and her ambivalence conspicuously spill into her language. At one point in the interview she referred to Jack and Maggie as "contacts" that she might (or might not) incorporate into her own caretaking system.

Their share-care arrangement when their children were toddlers worked because of convenience and shared child-rearing values. As Rebecca puts it: "We were very intricately involved in each other's lives. One of the things that made sharing child care work so well was shared values in regard to child rearing. They agreed on limiting television exposure and monitoring junk-food intake" (see an in-depth discussion of shared child-rearing values in Chapter 6). Feminism and flexible gender roles also figure importantly into their calculations about compatibility. Rebecca notes that when Jack and Maggie come home they are completely involved with the kids. She likes and admires that.

She would not call Maggie or Jack in a pinch for help with the children because they live an inconvenient distance away and are too overwhelmed with their own lives. Besides, Rebecca has her own network, which includes her mother-in-law and sister-in-law, who live nearby. They do a lot of babysitting, she adds, "depending on what the emergency is or what the need is." Byron's father and stepmother live up north and take the children occasionally on weekends. "And then, we're pretty friendly with the family across the street." Rebecca says she really likes Maggie and Jack, but she loves Danielle. Scott goes without comment. Rebecca still counts Maggie as her friend, just not a close friend. Rebecca would not call Maggie for advice; for advice she has another friend with a son one year older than hers, who helps her with "boy issues," which she sees as developmentally different from girl issues. She has also organized, along with a friend of hers, a group for second-time mothers. In other words, for needs large and small, Rebecca and Byron have their own well-functioning system of support independent of Maggie and Jack.

BYRON RUSSELL

I return to the Duvall-Brennan's old neighborhood to interview Rebecca's husband, Byron Russell. He greets me with his two-year-old son in his arms at ten o'clock on a Saturday morning. Aware of the ways that this project invades family time, I am determined to be succinct. As I set up my recording equipment, the little boy decides I am sufficiently interesting that he might hang around. He watches, fascinated, but keeps a respectful distance.

Byron assures me that he and Rebecca share parenting: "We pretty much split everything fifty-fifty." Rebecca concurred: "I think we're pretty unusual in that way. We both worked full time and so . . . there really isn't a division." Both of them boast that "we also have never hired somebody to take care of the kids." That said, during the week, their children spend about forty hours with paid babysitters. Byron comments: "That's already way too much. It's more than we'd like, and to add on evenings or weekends seems like way too much, and so that's why we've avoided it. Now that they're starting to get older, I think maybe we'll begin to do that." Someone who takes his parenting seriously, he is also part of a men's group.

Byron makes it clear that he and Rebecca moved back to northern California, his childhood stomping grounds, to be near his family while they reared children. He elaborates on the role of his own parents, divorced and living in different towns, who take the children on weekends so that he and Rebecca can have some adult restorative time. "It's very important for us. We really need to do it at least a couple times a year."

Byron is no more likely than Rebecca to approach Jack and Maggie for help, although he continues to honor the friendship between their children. Byron's only modification to Rebecca's portrait of their own network adds a group of families who organize a monthly Shabbat gathering. Like Byron and Rebecca, many of the families observe different religions, but all actively celebrate Jewish holidays and rituals. Byron says he would never rely on these other families for child care, but he relies on them extensively for child-rearing suggestions and advice. The person noticeably missing from their own network, from Byron's perspective, is his brother who lives on the other side of the bay. As a recently divorced man, his brother is absorbed in his work and nighttime leisure activities. Byron wishes his brother wanted to be more involved.

RUTH BERGMAN

I wait in a neighborhood café to interview Ruth Bergman, another former neighbor of Jack and Maggie's, whom Maggie had described as a "delightful woman" who had "bonded" with her children. I had set my tape recorder conspicuously out on the table because I realized I had not given her any clues about what I look like or how to find me. When a woman walked slowly through the door, a little hunched over, I wondered if that might be her. I knew Ruth had been ill recently. She had short black hair and dark eyes. Slender, she wore black pants, a turtleneck, a fleecy gray vest, and a Star of David necklace. She walked directly to my table.

Ruth has lived alone in her apartment for about six years and in the community as a whole for about eleven. She has set up a network for herself, made up exclusively of friends, mostly lesbians, not blood kin.[7] As I predicted, Ruth informs me that if asked to construct a list of people in her own network, she would not include Maggie or Jack. She likes them but, for example, if her dog needs to be cared for, she would not ask them to do it. "My dog has people in line waiting to take care of her, so it's not an issue." And now that she is having health problems, she turns to others: "I have a pretty wide support group." In thinking about the best metaphor for her own network, Ruth suggests a web: "Once you tend to meet someone new, in an extended way that you see how they're connected to some of the people in your inner circles. And inner circles seem to change and shift over time, for no real fallout, breakdown reasons. Just, you know, your life changes a little bit; and so they change, and another one develops for a while. Those people don't go away, it's just . . . you talk to them less frequently. . . . You change jobs, or they get a new partner. You know, however it happens, it just shifts a little bit." But it remains intact and pliable.

When Maggie and Jack lived upstairs from Ruth, she became involved in their network of interdependence as a neighbor and an occasional babysitter. Ruth says, "I don't have kids of my own, so it was easy for me to fit Danielle into the schedule." And she has a flexible work schedule as a health-care administrator. In talking about Ruth, Maggie emphasizes her attachment to the children: "She loves my kids." Jack has a more skeptical perspective: Ruth "was very involved with the kids and the kids were very involved with her dog, I think was the right way to describe the relationship." Ruth herself is less cynical in talking about the Duvall-Brennans: "They were very, very, very busy, so . . . I had more of a relationship with the kids in a lot of ways. The kids weren't quite as busy." In fact, Ruth sees her primary relationship as with Danielle, not Jack or Maggie. When they were neighbors, Scott was a baby and did not figure into the picture much. It was Danielle who would come and hang out with her and her dog, while Maggie was cooking dinner or the family was preparing to leave in the morning. The visiting was of the drop-in, hangout, spontaneous variety, although Ruth did babysit on occasion.

When Maggie and Jack moved out of the neighborhood, they moved Danielle out of proximity and easy engagement with Ruth's web, with some regrets on Ruth's part: "I feel like I haven't kept up on that relationship. And it feels bad to Danielle, not to Maggie. I mean, I feel bad for Maggie because Maggie is Danielle's mother and she's probably more aware than Danielle. . . . But I also . . . appreciate that, because then I wouldn't have had so much time with their kids if they weren't that stretched." She stumbled in her attempts to articulate the limitations imposed on her relationship with Danielle because of the busyness of Maggie and Jack. Their overwork created an opportunity for her to get to know Danielle in the first place, although ultimately, the parents' imperatives displaced the relationship.

LUCIA STANLEY

After several failed attempts at scheduling, I was able to interview Lucia Stanley, a member of Maggie's mothers' group, in the middle of the week while she was home with two sick children. I rang the bell to her house, not entirely confident she would answer. Lucia, looking a bit haggard and askew, answered the door. With the help of a *Sleeping Beauty* video and with only a few interruptions, we discussed her involvement in the Duvall-Brennan network and got to the heart of the work-family issues that plague her.

Lucia works as a technical writer in the computer industry and has a great deal of flexibility in her current job, where she has been working for the past year and a half. Although she works full time, she spends two days working at home, as does her husband, an academic. The other three days she commutes about an hour and a half each way; she and the man with whom she carpools take turns driving and working on a laptop in the back seat. She has to work nights to make up for time lost on sick children and other family emergencies, and the dark circles under her eyes suggest that work flexibility does not undo the stress and fatigue of overwork.

Lucia expresses an empathic attachment to Maggie that has been absent in the interviews with other network members. Although she and Maggie met as neighbors, they have sustained and deepened their relationship through being in a mothers' group together. Common values—such as "spirituality, our attitudes toward raising children, . . . trying to raise them to be good and as nonviolent as much as possible"—establish a base of rapport and have led them to support each other in their parenting and in their lives. Lucia characterizes her husband and herself as "very left-wing Catholics. And we've just been involved in a lot of social justice and human rights kinds of things. And the peace movement. And the refugee sanctuary movement when things were really bad in El Salvador and Guatemala." They are actively involved with their church community and send their eldest daughter to parochial school in their parish.

For Lucia, the mothers' group provides "support and sympathy and empathy and fun." Lucia emphasizes how important the group had been at certain moments in her life. After having two children, reaching her ideal family size, she recounts: "I had unexpectedly gotten pregnant with my son, and . . . it was really hard. I went into a deep depression. I didn't want to have another child. It was very difficult for my husband and I. And the group—I remember just crying with them. And they were just so supportive, and not pushing me one way or the other about what should I do, but just being there. . . . They really helped support me through a dark time that, you know, now I'm on the other side of it." Now with three children and a full-time job, Lucia continues to rely on the mothers' group. And yet, for her child-care needs, she has her own elaborate network of care.

Like Maggie and Jack's, Lucia's child-care arrangements have changed over time as her children have grown through different developmental stages and her work situation has shifted. When she and her husband had the first of their three children, Lucia worked at freelance technical writing, like so many involved in the dot-com economy, which means dramatic fluctuations in work time. Her husband was a freelance, part-time academic. As Lucia puts it: "The day care really has to match your work needs; . . . especially if you're a contractor, it's so hard. Because you don't know. Suddenly you're working full time for a couple of months." She could not afford to pay for child care while she was not working, so she had to find a situation that would flexibly adapt to the ebb and flow of her work. They tried share care, but "we just couldn't make it work out. We realized that my work situation just wasn't reliable enough." And at that time her husband did not have a full-time job. She found a small family day-care center not too far from her house, which worked extremely well for a while. At a certain point her work became more regular, and then the day care seemed too "chaotic."

When her youngest child was born, Lucia's husband cared for him during the mornings and they hired a woman to come to their home in the afternoons. Like all situations, this was subject to change.

> [The babysitter] left to have a baby, and one woman almost started and at the last minute she wanted more money; . . . it was becoming so hard to make it work that we just said, "All right, having a person in the home was great when [our son] was a baby. He's now almost one. He loves going to his toddler center; he loves it. What can we do differently?" So now, [my husband] is basically starting work very early and gets home by the time [my daughter] gets home from school at three o'clock. We have that set up with the neighbor, where we take her daughter in the morning to school, to the elementary school, and she brings them home in the afternoon. [My husband] is here by the time they get home, and then he picks up [the other two children]. And so basically . . . from three o'clock on, he's home; and usually, by four everyone's home. So they have a couple hours with him, which is really nice.

Lucia also has emergency backup relations with two families on her block. Both she and her husband maintain flexibility in their schedules. Lucia says:

"We're so lucky that we don't have to punch a clock. Because otherwise, we'd be calling in sick." Although one could hardly describe this elaborate plan as streamlined, it works for the family. Lucia adds: "I do the morning. And basically, we're gone by, like, seven, which is, like, real early. But in order for me to get to work at a reasonable time, that's the way it works. Now, on two days a week, . . . Monday and Friday when I'm home, we don't have to leave that early. . . . So that's what we have now. So now there's nobody coming to our home, and it's really working great." After this narrative, she shows me the elaborate chart her husband has designed to keep track of their schedule. She says, "You've gotta almost have something written to keep it all straight." A woman from their church continues to babysit on Wednesday evenings. "In the middle of the week, it's like this oasis" for Lucia and her husband, who go out for some alone, adult time.

The division of labor between her and her husband is a source of conflict. They embrace an egalitarian ideology but have different perspectives on how fair their arrangement is. They evenly split the pickup and drop-off of children, time in the afternoons with the children, meal preparation, bedtime, and school-lunch packing. However, details of everyday needs—such as when one child is supposed to wear red to school, or another has a dental appointment—do not register on her husband's radar screen. Like other women in this study, Lucia feels the weight of the psychic responsibility for running the household (see Chapter 8 for a discussion of the gendered dimensions of child rearing and networking).

Lucia's family of origin lives on the East Coast, where she grew up, so is not an active part of her network of care. She said: "This mobility is tough on a family, you know? My family is just spread to the four winds." She speaks fondly of her sister who comes to stay with her when her husband goes to a conference once a year, and helps her take care of her kids. Should anything ever happen to her husband, Lucia thinks she would move to be close to her sister, because she cannot imagine raising children by herself. Her husband's family is scattered around the area, but no one lives sufficiently nearby to help with regular child-care needs: "They're too far away; they're too old; they have jobs; whatever." His sister who lives about an hour's drive north exchanges child care with them occasionally, so they can take adult retreats.

BRENDA EMERSON

The power of the mothers' group also operates for Brenda Emerson. Like Maggie and Lucia, for her the group provides advice and support, but not babysitting. That, however, does not diminish its importance. As one of the founders of the group, Maggie is closer individually to Brenda and Lucia than they are to each other. The intimacy and respect Maggie and Brenda share is immediately apparent in the way Brenda talks about Maggie and their relationship.

In many ways, Brenda is similar to Maggie. Like Maggie, she is an attorney who began her career in corporate law and switched to the public sector in an effort to find a more family-friendly work situation. She is married to a professional man who has job flexibility and is deeply involved in child rearing. Both Brenda and Maggie have two children, the same ages and genders. Both live away from their parents and do not have easily accessible or engaged in-laws. And they both moved from "walking neighborhoods" to houses in the suburbs as their eldest child reached school age. The two of them even look alike, except that Brenda seems happier.

But despite the similarities, some profoundly different decisions have led to a more manageable family-work situation for Brenda, who touts a better balance in her life. Importantly, she works four days a week instead of full time. She comments that both she and Maggie have made conscious choices, scaling back their professional ambitions to accommodate family life. Since they are so similar, Brenda chafes at some of the decisions that Maggie has made differently. Brenda's child-care arrangements give her more of a cushion when crises arise, as they inevitably do.

Her own network centers on a paid babysitter but includes neighbors, former neighbors, her brother-in-law and sister-in-law, and the women in the mothers' group. Brenda discusses her reasoning for organizing care around an in-home care provider: "I didn't want to put my kids in day care. I wanted somebody at our house. I wanted another family so that the kids, you know, would have social interaction. And it was at times difficult, but for me it was well worth it." She had employed one babysitter consistently for four years who was the linchpin of the arrangements. When that babysitter left, she referred friends and family to work for Brenda and has continued to do occasional backup babysitting.

The in-home babysitter arrangement is expensive, as Brenda points out; her total child-care expenditures amount to approximately two thousand dollars a month. The cost includes salary for the babysitter, before- and after-school fees for her daughter, and nursery school for her son. She drops her daughter early at kindergarten and then commutes to work. Her husband takes their three-year-old to a later-starting nursery school and then he commutes to work. The babysitter picks up the boy around 1:30; then she picks up the girl, who stays in the extended-day program at school until 2:00; and then the babysitter takes them home and stays until Brenda gets home around 6:00. Her husband arrives closer to 8:00 or 8:30. The current babysitter does not have a car, however, and so Brenda and her husband are contemplating the purchase of a third car to make the system work more smoothly. Even with the large repertory of personnel and the ability to pay the high costs, Brenda admits that "the logistics . . . are a constant battle."

AMANDA BRENNAN

Jack Brennan's sister, Amanda, still lives on the East Coast and describes the Brennans as a "very close family." She has raised five children, helps care for her elderly mother, and, according to Jack, continues to be a fountain of wisdom. Five years his senior, Amanda helped raise Jack in the wake of their father's death and their mother's alcoholism. Jack continues to appreciate her; he describes her as a "very strong, powerful person—wouldn't leap tall buildings, she would lift tall buildings."

They visit each other about once a year, which means she barely knows Danielle and Scott. But she and Jack talk on the phone, and in a crisis related to child rearing, Jack does not hesitate to ask her advice about anything. Maggie does not call her, although they do occasionally talk. Amanda explains this from her own perspective: "I wouldn't call my sister-in-law. I would call my family first." Apparently her sister-in-law does not rank as family.

Demanding Careers and an Inadequate Network

Maggie Duvall and Jack Brennan are parents wedged and squeezed by the conflict between their demanding careers, a deep, abiding belief in intensive parenting, and an inadequate network to help them rear their children.

Maggie's and Jack's jobs make unyielding demands, although both parents have sought jobs that better accommodate their family situation. Maggie left her last corporate job because her employers demanded that she travel for six weeks. She switched to public sector law, which pays less but demands fewer hours.[8] Being new on her current job, she feels she must establish herself and her credibility. As of yet, she has not accrued much sick leave or vacation time. Maggie talks about her job:

> It's not onerous. It's just kind of oblivious to the fact you have a family. And most people I work with are not dealing with small children; . . . it's kind of a mixed bag. Sure, I don't want to . . . be perceived as this *mom*. But on the other hand, I am one. And my son is sick and I have no flexibility. Basically what I'll tell my boss is that my gig is up—Jack can't cover. [Laughs.] And it's up to me. . . . It could reflect badly on me and maybe it does. And maybe people, my boss in particular, perceives me as someone who isn't gonna have the kind of fire power that he needs because I can't be there in every

predictable situation where I'm needed. But it is what it is. But I have to kind of swallow it.

Like other professional women, she has to hide her family life or at least pretend it is not there.[9] She has had to work late some nights, but not weekends. She has to rely on her partner in parenting to make the situation work:

> So far I've been able to negotiate with Jack. It may come that I need to work weekends. And you know Jack and I have talked about this. With my job the concern, the problem is that there is just so much to do and there is just not enough time to do it in the hours that I work. So something is going to fall through the cracks. Something's got to get not done. I'm in a situation where I don't have someone breathing over my shoulder and looking at this and telling me I have to be there. And that may have an effect at some point. And what will I do? I'll just take that. But the problem is that it fills me with anxiety.

Anxiety is her operational mode: fearful, pressed, anxious, feeling like she never does enough. And yet, embedded in her story is news of success as well: "They're quite thrilled with me so far. But you know, who knows a year from now when all these things I would like to get done are not getting done may catch up with me. So it may. I may be paying the price at some point down the line, in my more honest moments, I think I have to face that." While she gets rave reviews of her work, she fears being unmasked. What if her employers find her out? What if she cannot deliver? Even at the height of the 1990s economic boom, Maggie understands that her success as a lawyer requires the appearance of professional commitment as well as high-quality productivity. More than many other middle-class careers, commitment to lawyering is measured in hours clocked and degree of availability for the demands of work.[10] People who are not considered serious in their commitment to their jobs and to the profession are marginalized, denied upward mobility, and are in danger of losing their jobs. This reality shrouds the relative privilege Maggie enjoys in a high-status career and threatens her security. Jack recognizes the feeling and knows the danger: "I think she's definitely skating, and she knows it. She's skating bigtime. They could pull the plug on her any minute, because she basically says, 'I'm not gonna do it,' and they keep telling her to do more. She keeps walking out the door at 4:30, so . . . " Maggie also ponders how and when she could work more, if forced to.

> I come home at six and I, you know, make dinner. I eat dinner; the kids eat dinner. We give them baths; we put them to bed. And they usually get to bed about eight thirty, quarter to nine, and then Jack and I usually like doing the dishes, making lunches. I'll pay a few bills.

I don't know when people work [at home]. And then I'll go to bed. [Laughs.] I mean, I have no idea when I would work. . . . As a matter of policy we don't watch TV in our family. It's not like we are sitting around watching TV. . . . I couldn't take work home if I wanted to. And the weekends are the same. They're the only time I'm able to spend time really with the kids.

Maggie imagines her solution as working four days a week, like Brenda Emerson. Her current office does not have a policy that would enable her to work a shorter week, but she holds out the possibility as a beacon of the future: "If I could snow them for a year and then maybe ask." One has to ask, in a larger sense, how much difference one day would make. If Brenda's experience is any indicator, a four-day workweek holds the promise of making the work-family system operate more smoothly with less anxiety and exhaustion. However, it also comes with the stigma of "time deviant," which goes along with part-time status.[11] And, as sociologist Mary Blair-Loy observes about the high-powered executives she studies: "By requesting reduced hours, senior managers revealed their infidelity to work devotion and risked being banished from their organizations."[12] Maggie hopes that four days of employment would scale back not just time, but also expectations of what has to be accomplished. However, a slightly shorter workweek and its associated lower status still fail to resolve the fundamental structural problem: Children need time and attention that cannot be squeezed easily into the corners of a crowded, long workweek. More give-and-take on the job would help. "I think we manage, one, because Jack's got some flexibility in his job. A job where, one, he's the boss and, two, it's fairly family friendly."

However, when Jack talks about his work life from his perspective, he does not sound free of a similar anxiety. Even with its greater autonomy, his job does not feel much more forgiving than Maggie's: "I'm seen walking in at 9:30, if I'm lucky, in the morning." And then "they see me walk out at 4:30. You know, they're there when I get there and they're there when I leave . . . and there are just things that don't get done." Jack discusses the consequences of those structural imperatives: "I found myself today in a meeting with my boss, where I was picking up the slack on something I had delegated to someone, but not like really closely supervised. And that person had not shown up, and I just realized, I'm skating. It could all fall apart at any time; but you just make a judgment. Your family's more important; . . . you rely on your instincts a lot."

Both Maggie and Jack work as hard as they can and see their children only a few hours a day. Despite their hard work, both feel like shirkers on the job. Their sense of inadequacy comes from their own internal expectations, not others' criticisms of them. Because they cannot possibly accomplish the amount of work at the high standard they expect of themselves, they feel anguish and insecurity. Both set limits; neither takes work home, although Jack has to work one Saturday a month. When he does, he feels guilty, in part because of his awareness of the onerous work of being a single parent for even one day: "Maggie knows that she's gonna be sand-bagged with the kids." Maggie and Jack set boundaries around work that result from a very clear commitment to themselves as parents, to their children, and to the kind of life they want their children to have. But the consequences of their choices are not yet something to which they feel reconciled.

This couple experiences acute anxiety about keeping their jobs and they have a minimal crew upon whom to call for practical help. The demands of their work, including a two-hour round-trip daily commute, place severe limits on their ability to stage a network of people who could help them care for their children. Jack Brennan says: "I think, for us, it's been a challenge. I think, to some extent, we were resigned for better or worse that there was only so much in the way of a network we really have. I mean, from time to time, we'll say, 'Well, you know, we've gotta get more involved with the church, and if we do that, we'll develop deeper personal, social relationships with the folks there,' and blah blah blah blah blah. But you know, there's only so much we end up really doing."

Maggie and Jack have joined a church in their search for community and a network of support. And it has served some purposes well. Jack describes it as "a big tent, and it's very good for us as a source of community." However, it does not and cannot change their structural dilemma in regard to ongoing child care. Maggie described the kind of support it provided when they were moving: "We e-mailed folks and we got a lot of response from folks who took the kids during the weekend and stuff while we packed." That kind of help can make a difference. However, their work-family dilemma remains intact.

Neither the Duvall nor the Brennan kin are easily engaged. Maggie and Jack's socially recognized local kin are not sufficiently like-minded to join them in child rearing. On the list of members of their network of care, Maggie and Jack did not include a single Duvall. The exclusion of the Duvalls from the network results from reasons other than proximity, however. Many of them live about an hour's drive away, sufficiently close to be helpful in some situations. But not so, says Maggie. She elaborates: "Both my parents are rather distant grandparents, unfortunately for my children. They are not into children and they are not into really being a part of their lives. So I don't think living in the area would have helped." She then contrasts them to her siblings, whom she thinks would exchange care and favors if they lived closer. I ask if she relies on them for advice about child rearing. "Not really. No." Her alienation from her mother is philosophical as well as practical: "We don't share some of the same values" in regard to child rearing. Conditionality similarly shapes the engagement and availability of the Brennan relatives, including Tom and Teresa, who are part of the network. Nonetheless, overall Tom says: "Considering our differences it works pretty well. You know, I adore those kids and I love my brother and Maggie. We're family."

In the absence of family, some people turn to friends who share their values, who live nearby, and who help each other rear children. Maggie and Jack have constructed a network, but they have reached the limits of what they can ask of their friends. Some of those they count as friends do not similarly count Jack and Maggie as close friends or part of their networks. This leads to an uncomfortable imbalance in their relationships. And they do not yet have neighbors upon whom they can call.[13] Because of their limited capacity to reciprocate, however, they cannot construct networks that can care for the children (see Chapter 7 for an elaboration of this argument).

The combination of professional work demands, high-intensity parenting, and a network inadequate to helping care for their children combine to leave Jack and Maggie feeling out on a limb.

Tensions between Ideology and Practice

A major theme that runs through the Duvall-Brennan interviews is the tension between the contradictory impulses Jack and Maggie feel and the choices they make—between ideology and practice, between what they want and what they have, between how they would like things to be in contrast to how things are. Consciously or not, they sometimes make choices that lead to the opposite of what they claim to care about. It is not just their old neighborhood they have left behind, but also, earlier in life, their extended kin. In part, their distance—emotional and geographic—from kin results from relocation for jobs and education. In effect, the distance is partly the consequence of upward mobility, or the promise of it. More profoundly, their outlook on life divides them from their families of origin.

The "family-first" principle does not apply to the Duvall-Brennans. Even so, family acts as an ultimate safety net for them; they rely on family "in the last instance." They feel that they have only Jack's brother, Tom, and his partner, Teresa, as kin upon whom they can rely for their immediate child-care needs. And Jack feels strongly attached to his sister, Amanda, on the East Coast, who gives sage counsel. While Jack and Maggie use a minimum of family ties and feel ambivalent about family help, in the terrible event that something should happen to them, Tom will take the mantle of guardian of their children.

The choice of institutional care, which is a rational outcome of the step-by-step process they went through with Danielle and her various babysitters, means that the primary caregivers for the children are not part of Jack and Maggie's network. Jack and Maggie must negotiate child care within the institutional setting, but their relationship is different than it might be in family day care or with a babysitter or nanny at home. This reliance on an institution means they have less wiggle room, as they must now abide by the rules and regulations of a business. Another consequence is that Jack and Maggie do not have specific people on whom they can call. To compare, even though she relies on a market model for primary care, Sarah Aldrich can implore April Miller to cover an unusual event (and of course she has the rest of her network as well). In contrast, Jack's and Maggie's relationships with the primary caretakers of their children lack mutuality. Their dilemma is not simply that they depend on a market-based model for the lion's share of their children's care, but also that the institutional structure inhibits outside relationships with care workers that might otherwise be helpful.

By national standards, the Duvall-Brennans have plenty of money. They hold prestigious jobs and have recently purchased a large house in an affluent neighborhood. However, they do not have sufficient resources to cover easily the costs of child care that would offer them more flexibility and still guarantee reliability. Their destiny is not their own: Their careers dictate a great deal of their weekly schedule. The structure of their work impinges not only on their time with their children, but also on their ability to construct a supple network and reciprocate with its members.

Shared parenting and shared anchoring has resulted in an unanticipated trade-off. Instead of relying on others, Maggie and Jack depend on each other for almost everything. Their self-sufficient child rearing means they ask less of others and more of themselves. Like other employed married couples, they rely more on each other for care than on other relatives.[14] They articulate an ideology of engagement and interdependence but practice self-reliance, against their better judgment. They have a long list of people they call their network, but no one who can help in a child-care crisis. The network consists of people who care *about* them and the children, but who have limited capacity to care *for* them. Because their network is a "loose association," its members are not densely knit together. Their network members are not interchangeable parts of the association; one person cannot be easily substituted for another because of disagreements in child-rearing philosophy, different degrees of intimacy and connection with the children, and varying degrees of availability. And they lack a group identity with a shared culture that makes a sustainable difference for the Cranes, the Aldriches, and, as we will see, the Beckers.

Chapter 5 The Beckers

A Warm Web of People

THE BECKER NETWORK, wealthy in people and moderate in income, is based in a solidly middle-class neighborhood in a diverse urban area. At its center is Dina Becker, a freelance photographer, mother, and wife. She and her husband, Mark Walde, a middle school teacher, have two children—Donalyn, age eight, and Aaron, age six. Dina and Mark struggle to maintain their place on the economic ladder; rather than experiencing middle-class comfort, they experience middle-class insecurity.[1] Dina loves being a photographer—but it is her occupation, not merely a creative outlet. Like most middle-class women of her generation, she has to work so the household can maintain its economic position. Her contribution to the family income helps make the expense of their home mortgage and the tuition at the children's private schools manageable.

Dina and Mark try to meet their parenting and work responsibilities by relying on a split-shift strategy—they take turns working different shifts and alternately taking care of the children. Dina leads the charge in the morning, getting the children up, dressed, fed, and delivered to their respective schools. She works at home during the day and hands over the children to Mark when he walks in the door between four and five o'clock. He presides over dinner, does the dishes, and supervises the children's evening bath and bedtime rituals. Dina retreats to her office, which is in the basement of their home. There, she meets with clients and deals with the complicated details of her work. Weddings are a big part of her business. So, in addition to the evening shift, Dina works most weekends, leaving responsibility for the children to Mark.

In theory, the split-shift child-rearing strategy sidesteps the care-gap crisis families face when both parents are employed. Approximately 20 percent of couples with children in the United States use shift work to solve their child-care needs.[2] In practice, though, this approach is vulnerable and difficult to sustain without outside help. Mismatched work schedules and school schedules (e.g., school holidays, early dismissals), illness (a sick child cannot go to school; a sick parent may not be able to transport or feed a child), fatigue, transportation glitches, and simple happenstance can undermine shared child-rearing responsibilities. For Dina, the solution lies almost literally around the corner: She turns to her sizable family of origin for help. Dina lives in the city where she grew up, less than two miles from her childhood home. Most of her seven siblings have homes within a five-mile radius of the old neighborhood. Her mother, her father, her two brothers, and three of her five sisters are ready and willing to help Dina out. The extended Becker clan has a strong sense of family solidarity. "Helping" defines their family culture. Dina's brother Ryan notes, "I don't know any other family that really spends as much time doing other things for members of the family as my family [does]." Dina Becker puts it metaphorically: "Family is like sort of our warm web of people."

The combination of her family's proximity and its willingness to help frees Dina from the expense of hiring babysitters. "If you have to pay for child care," she explains, "that would just push us right over the [edge]—we would not be able to try for this new house." But even with the financial savings the Becker network provides, Dina and Mark's split-shift strategy is costly. They have traded time with each other for time with the children and time to work. The multiple demands of employment and parenting mean that they see little of each other as a couple, and they have no time to devote to nurturing their relationship and their marriage.

The Beckers' vibrant network embraces a large group of people, all of whom are related via kinship. In their strong culture of kin, family comes first. And more than in any other network, men are active in the Becker network. In addition to the long hours logged by Mark Walde, Dina's father and two brothers help her out weekly. Nonetheless, the split-shift strategy and the army of people do not alleviate the issues of gender equity in the marriage nor adjudicate the question of who holds ultimate responsibility for the children on a daily basis.

The Making of a Tradition of Family Solidarity

Dina, Mark, Donalyn, and Aaron live in a two-bedroom house with small neat flower and rock gardens on each side of the garage. Many of the pastel-colored stucco houses on their street boast arches faintly reminiscent of Mexican

Table 5.1
Becker Network

Anchor	Dina Becker
Children	Donalyn, 8 Aaron, 6
Anchor's Occupation	Freelance photographer
Class Location	Middle class
Family Culture	Helping and learning
Childcare Strategy	Split shift
Network Members	• Mark Walde, Dina's husband • Peter Becker, Dina's father • Susan Becker, Dina's mother • Kent Becker, Dina's brother • Ryan Becker, Dina's brother • Shannon Becker, Dina's sister • Michaela Becker, Dina's sister, • Caitlin Becker James, Dina's sister

architecture. Home prices in this middle-class neighborhood are higher than the average for the city as a whole.[3]

Less than five minutes away is the house where Dina and her brothers and sisters grew up. Peter and Susan Becker, Dina's parents, still live there. The senior Beckers' house seems to exert a gravitational pull. Like Dina, most of the siblings live within what Susan calls a "useful radius." Dina's two brothers, Kent and Ryan, share a house that is located, like their sister's, only about five minutes from their parents' home. Dina's sister Shannon lives just outside the city limits, about a fifteen-minute drive south; and another sister, Michaela, lives east, over the hill, about fifteen minutes away. Caitlin and her husband and children live farther south, about a thirty-five-minute drive. Two of Dina's sisters are not on the list: Barbara, who lives about twenty miles east, and Lila Becker McKendrick, another married sister, who lives with her family in the Pacific Northwest. (Table 5.1 details the members of the Becker network.)

The local presence of so many family members, coupled with a firmly established tradition of "family first," means that Dina's children and her siblings' children have easy, frequent access to their extended kin. This had been much less true for their parents, though. In general, extended kin did not play a significant role in the life of Dina's family of origin. Dina's mother's family, who lived about an hour's drive south, visited in the summer and on holidays. Dina's father's mother lived in the same city and saw the family frequently, but even she remained a peripheral figure. Describing her grandmother, Dina says:

"My grandmother lived a couple miles away, but . . . she didn't get along with my mom, so she—she was over a lot for holidays and things; . . . she wasn't babysitting for us or anything . . . and my mom was home, so she really didn't need much support that way." Similarly, the Becker siblings' contact with their neighborhood peers was limited. "When there's eight of you," Dina explains, "there's always somebody to play with, anyway, even though our block was full of kids."

Large and unwavering, Dina's family of origin was able to successfully establish its own ecosystem, complete with symbiotic relationships and rules of nature. Susan and Peter, whom Shannon describes as "natural-born teachers," deliberately instilled a strong family ethos. They made learning fun and interesting. And, as verification of the fruits of their labors, all the Becker children attended college, and more than half went on to do postgraduate work in education, mathematics, medicine, or art. Several of Dina's siblings have formal positions as teachers. Others simply adopt a "learning-as-play" approach to life.

The Beckers created their own sense of identity in other ways that were less consciously planned but no less effective. Peter Becker recalls: "It's funny how things become a tradition. You do something with a couple of them and then suddenly, 'Well, this is what we do.' And I mean all kinds of things at Christmastime and so on, having been done once or twice, assumed this tradition status. And they want to do this every year because that's what we do. This is what our family does." Lila Becker McKendrick provides an example of the strength of the family's sense of identity. In telling a story about her son's first words ("Timothy's first two words that he put together were 'read books'"), she delivers the punch line: "[It was] such a perfect Becker sentence!" The family has sufficiently defined itself that something called a "Becker sentence" could be identified. Dina's sister Michaela Becker calls this process of inculcating values in the next generation "very conscious parenting. . . . [My siblings are] educating their kids on what it means to be in the Becker family."

The family cohesiveness and capacities make the members almost interchangeable parts. For example, when the children were all living at home, a neighbor might call and request a babysitter, and invariably, somebody could do it. Michaela reported to me an example of how this played out in adulthood. Recently she had sought help with the managerial aspects of her job: "So, like, the other day I called Caitlin and Shannon and Lila, you know. And Caitlin and Lila were not available, but Shannon was. And so, like, you know, I called them up and said, 'This is something I need to figure out how to handle.' And so she called me back." In this situation, one sister was as good as another. They shared the capacity to help, and in a moment of angst, one could step in for another. This holds true regarding babysitting as well, contributing to that "just-in-time" availability made possible by the family's large size and proximity to one another. And, finally, it is common for Becker family members to refer casually to what "everybody" thinks, or what "everybody's" values are. Caitlin is perhaps the group's most enthusiastic pollster, routinely determining what "everyone" thinks about one topic or another. These opinion polls serve to affirm among family members a sense of the Becker group, and also to differentiate minority viewpoints when they emerge.

Talking and doing represent a continuum of help within the Becker family— both implying a lot of activity. From Caitlin's perspective, "everyone's a talker," although she adds the caveat that communication is sometimes indirect:

> So if . . . someone is going some direction that no one likes, then you can just keep talking and talking. And if everyone talks about it enough, . . . I mean, we can't change each other exactly, but at least then whoever's going this direction is doing it with their eyes open. And they know they're making everyone else really worried. . . . They won't necessarily bring it up in a group, which is probably better. . . . Everyone has a couple of people they confide in much more, and everyone else knows who those people are, and so if you need to access someone that isn't the one that you confide in the most, you can talk to someone else who does confide in them the most. . . . There are siblings that I couldn't just say, "Oh, what a terrible choice, I can't believe you're seeing that person. What a horrible influence they are on you." There are some siblings I could say that to, but some I couldn't. And the ones I couldn't, I could say it to someone else who could say it to them for me, in a different way.

Her brother Ryan, however, in emphasizing the "doer" aspect of the family ethos, clarifies that talking a lot does not mean talking about feelings. He observes: "At the same time, my family is probably not the family that, like, spends as much time talking about things that are bothering them; . . . we are all super available for each other to do errands because we're less available for each other in an emotional way. But in a sense, it is available emotionally. It's just not a verbal emotional way." This difference in perspective between Caitlin and Ryan may reflect their respective gender or sibling order in the family.

As the youngest, Ryan is keenly aware of cultural divisions between the "older kids" and the "younger kids":

> There are sort of two generations of children in my family. I think the four oldest girls were raised in a different way even than the four youngest children a little bit, because when the four oldest girls were

raised, it was really a time in my parents' life when they were more conscious about money. They were . . . younger, less experienced. I think parents change as they get older and more relaxed. By the time I was, you know, in school, my parents were still exceedingly thrifty, but not to the same degree they had been when my older siblings were around.

Ryan's next-oldest sister, Michaela, offers a similar view, although in much more vivid terms: "The older siblings think the younger siblings are all spoiled or something, that we didn't have harsh enough, you know—sleep on needles type-of-thing." And, later: "There's a tendency for, like, the younger siblings to know more about what's going on with each other, and the older siblings to know more about what's going on with each other. Except for someone like Kent. Kent helps everybody." Michaela thinks the generational differences also mark a political divide; she characterizes Dina and her older siblings as more conservative socially and politically. Shannon, from the older side of the divide, sees the younger Beckers as "less traditional" and "funkier." Still, as Ryan says, overall, Becker family members are "incredibly close." They share a deep commitment to one another that is readily converted to action when the need arises. For Dina, this great wealth of people resources makes a crucial difference. With the child-care help her parents and siblings provide, she and her husband Mark are able to cling to their middle-class position, rearing their children in a safe neighborhood and a loving family.

Dina Becker, Anchor

When Dina opens her front door in response to the doorbell I have just rung, she says, good naturedly confirming the obvious, "You found me." I have, indeed. Dina is about five feet, six inches tall. She wears her dark hair pulled back in a ponytail. Her deep-set brown eyes are big and intense, but the dark circles below suggest fatigue. She has an easy smile that reveals even white teeth. Stepping back from the doorway, she ushers me into the house. With two children and a home business, their two-bedroom house feels crowded to Dina. Her work requires more surface space than her basement office provides, so she stacks photos and papers in little piles all around the living room and dining room, covering table tops and sections of the floor. This contributes to the house's rumpled, lived-in feeling. Dina acknowledges the clutter, saying that if she has a choice between cleaning house and spending time with her children, the children win.

We head for the living room, where a pure-black cat lies asleep on a stool in front of the picture window. I sit on the couch; Dina chooses the wooden rocker, which she then draws closer to me as I inform her about the study and solicit her consent. When Dina begins to tell me about herself, it is immediately clear that she is a take-charge respondent. The eldest of the eight Becker children, she characterizes herself as "bossy" and confidently asserts that her siblings would agree. She is correct in her prediction. Her sister Shannon casts Dina as a straightforward woman of authority: "Dina is very honest. . . . She'll happily say what you don't want to hear. [Laughs.] And I think that's good. You know, she tells it like it is. . . . She's the oldest, so she's lived a life of telling us what she thought. Do you know what I mean? That's from childhood, like, 'You know, Shannon? That's stupid!' . . . And so now, it's like, she might say it like, 'You need to re-think that!' . . . There's nothing I wouldn't ask her about." Although Dina typically does not ask advice of others, she accepts unsolicited counseling amiably. Her mother, Susan, says, "I'd rather give Dina child-rearing advice than tell my other married daughters, because Dina either will agree with me or not agree with me [laughs], but she doesn't mind that I tell her what I think." Dina's husband, Mark, characterizes her as "a little more reluctant to kind of joke around" than he is, a tendency he attributes to Dina's having "played the big mother role, the big sister role," all through her childhood. As an adult, though, she is less likely to mother her siblings, in part because her own life leaves her little time to do so. Dina's sister Lila marvels at Dina's ability to simultaneously sustain her career and raise two seemingly happy, smart, and well-adjusted children: "I don't know how she can do everything she does as well as she does." Lila, too, is married, has children, but is employed part-time. But both Lila's and Caitlin's (the only other married Becker sister) spouses are highly paid professionals. Thus, unlike Dina, these sisters are economically secure and do not have to pursue paid employment as avidly as Dina does.

In answer to my question about the shape of a typical day, Dina explains how she juggles her parental responsibilities with her occupational ones. In addition to getting the children to school (one single-sex secular, one co-ed religious—in opposite directions from the house), she organizes carpools and after-school lessons. "I do the afternoon activities and drive around wildly, you know, picking them up, getting them to dance or . . . whatever it is." The evening activities are different but no more relaxed: "Then [I] come home and make dinner, and then at dinnertime we do a switch. And my husband comes home from work, and I say, 'OK, here's dinner on the table. I'm downstairs.' And then I see my clients." Dina is also the primary organizer of her family-based child-care network.

Dina views her life as "a lot more frantic" than her mother's was. Susan Becker raised eight children, compared to Dina's two, but she did not work for pay outside the home, and her husband, Peter's, income (augmented by his diligent frugalness) was sufficient to cover the expense of a weekly housekeeper, as well. Dina does not consider her own hectic pace a good thing, but it seems to be a necessary one: "If I'm running around all the time, you know, getting groceries and doing da da da, and all my photo stuff, then when I come home, I'm frazzled and I haven't started the dinner yet. And so I'm trying to cram way too many things into my day, and I know that." Her mother, on the other hand, perceives the stresses of the "speedup" as self-imposed.[4] That is, there is more work to do in the same amount of time, and Dina is employed full time. From her mother's point of view, Dina is making choices that make her life more difficult for her. Dina reports that her mother will say something like: "You need to look at the things that you're doing. Your life would be better if it were less frantic and you weren't driving your kids around and doing all these things." Dina laments that her mother lived in an era when children did not have to be driven to school, and schools started at the same time. And, while she was rearing children, her mother did not work. Her perspective leaves Dina, like many other middle-class working women, feeling misunderstood—although in her case, supported—by her mother.

Turning to the topic of photography, Dina explains that although weddings are the core of her business, she also shoots family portraits. She says she strives to represent the families she photographs "as they would like to be," meaning outdoors and "pretending they have loads of quality time." She also occasionally teaches workshops about the fundamentals of photography. The dramatic growth in her client base took Dina by surprise. She was unprepared for some of the conflicts that arose, and that continue to surface, as a result of her efforts to weave work and family: "When I first opened my business, it took me about six years to really get it rolling, so I assumed, since I had closed it for four years, that it would take me some time to get the ball rolling again. It didn't. It grew much faster than I thought; . . . my husband would go off to work in the morning, I would have the children all day, both of them, all day. He'd come home. I'd feed them dinner. Occasionally I'd have a client, and then on the weekends, I would have some weddings. Not that many."

She then moves to discuss a conflict of perception at the heart of the division of child-rearing labor, and hence of her marriage: "But I'd have them all day, every day. And I didn't think I was babysitting them. I thought I was parenting them. And so then as I got more and more [jobs on] weekends, and I would hand them to him for the weekend, he would say, 'I'm babysitting *again?*' I'd say, 'No, you're parenting.' Because for him, it's really hard. He works very hard Monday through Friday, and he really thinks he ought to have some weekends. Well, actually, some time every weekend."

I asked if she meant free time.

Free time that's his time. And in the beginning, when I just had a Saturday wedding randomly, . . . I think the first year I did eleven. That's not that many weddings. It wasn't such a big deal. But when you go from eleven to forty-eight, it's a big [laughs]—it happened pretty fast, too. I was kinda surprised. And now I'm turning down a lot of people because I can't possibly handle as much as I could book now. So he gets pretty annoyed [laughs] when weekend after weekend after weekend—he comes home Friday. He's really tired. I don't usually want to go out on Fridays because (a) he's really wiped from the week, and [(b)] I don't want to get too tired for my wedding on Saturday. So I'm gone Saturday night . . . because I'm mentally gone. If I'm about to go to a wedding at one o'clock, by nine o'clock I'm useless; . . . they're very stressful.

I suggested this was because she had to capture the moment. "Right. Right, you have one chance," she said. "So, do I have the film? . . . I'm sort of in 'wedding mode.' And then I leave, and then I come back in the middle of the night. He's had the kids all day. Then we get up and go to church on Sundays, and often this year, I've had Sunday weddings as well."

Like others who use a split-shift strategy to care for their children, Dina and Mark find that they have little if any time together to nurture their relationship and their marriage.[5] Dina's unorthodox work schedule made parenting possible when Donalyn and Aaron were younger. Now, with the dramatic increase in her business, the same sort of flexible schedule creates strained relations with Mark and makes it increasingly difficult for Dina to organize her family life effectively. Dina has chosen to develop her business and is willing to make the trade-offs necessary for her own success. Although she places some limits on its growth, she sacrifices some aspects of family life to the imperatives of her profession. Without her many network helpers and an available husband (albeit reluctant), she would not be able to do this.

The Becker Network Members

MARK WALDE

Mark Walde, with piercing blue eyes and thinning, curly brown hair, puzzles through his thoughts about the ups and downs of his marriage and his status as a father. A man of medium height, his ample musculature conveys the seriousness of his commitment to athleticism. He trains as a tri-athlete, biking to and from work each day and running long distances, as much as his family schedule permits. Like Dina, Mark is struggling to adjust to many of the consequences and complications that have accompanied her burgeoning business. He feels driven by a compulsory family schedule over which he has virtually no control: "The weekends are mine, basically, with the kids. And if it's not weddings, it's sessions, either photo sessions at the studio here or off somewhere outside, so that is a schedule I have to accommodate myself to. So, I am still adjusting [laughs] to this because her photography is increasing, and so I have to accommodate my schedule. And the calendar—which finally is kind of up on the wall, that we can kind of look at—is something I have to accommodate to."

As Mark sees it, he does 50 percent of the child care, and maybe more. He voices doubts about nearly every aspect of his and Dina's split-shift strategy. Although he is not responsible for morning activities (because he bikes to work, he leaves early and alone), in his assessment, the routines do not work smoothly. "It's a tight schedule," is how he puts it. During the week, Mark teaches school all day, comes home, and then is "on" with Aaron and Donalyn. "It seems like I'm cooking dinner most of the time," he tells me. "She's either busy getting ready for finals or off to photography meetings, which happens once in a while. And I do dishes." He notes, as well, that he is the one who "will put [Aaron and Donalyn] to bed, usually," at the end of the evening. (A comparative discussion about these issues in all the networks, particularly as they pertain to fatherhood, appears in Chapter 8.)

Although he acknowledges that Dina takes responsibility for a lot of the organizational and managerial aspects of the children's lives, from Mark's perspective, she does not do as much hands-on care as he does, especially now that both children go to school full days. Time equity is an especially sensitive issue for Mark. He feels shorted, deprived of free time to pursue his own interests, whether those involve work or leisure. "I never have enough time for school. . . . I mean, I would like to do a lot more preparation and get into projects that would be interesting for me and my students," but that does not happen. Weekends fly by, and "then Sunday evening, it's time for perhaps lesson plans for the week, which never seem to get completed thoroughly the way I would like them to." Mark feels anxious, worried that he is underperforming at his job and walking a tightrope in his family life.

An important source of the tension between Mark and Dina stems less from the growth of Dina's business than from its increasing importance to her. Dina's photography is a creative form of self-expression, as well as an economic endeavor. In Mark's view, she—unlike him—has downtime while Donalyn and Aaron are at school. Freed of responsibility for the children, she has large chunks of time to devote to her photography. He acknowledges that, in effect, Dina works all the time, but because she derives enormous satisfaction from her work, Mark finds it hard to count her efforts in the balance of marital sacrifices.[6] And, like other men who minimize the paid employment of their wives,[7] he does not mention the critically important income Dina's photography generates for the family.

Overall, Mark is weary from the press of work and the loss of leisure time. He feels that his basic life needs are going unmet. He wants more fun in his life and in his marriage. Both he and Dina feel overextended; on the relatively rare occasions when they have an evening available to spend together, they are too exhausted to go out. They do not take vacations. "We don't even have time to sit down and decide how to do that," Mark complains. Contemplating his current situation, he muses, "I don't think I have completely . . . accepted . . . okay, is this fair or what? [Laughs.] "

Like Dina, Mark looks to the Becker network for support as he struggles through the undulations of his marriage and his changing status as a father; and the clan comes through, enfolding him, as well as Dina and the children, in its warm embrace. He describes Becker family gatherings as "very animated and sort of hard to get a word in edgewise," but he makes it clear that he finds this appealing. His own family of origin is relatively small and is nowhere near as verbal or fun loving as the Beckers. Unlike the other Becker brothers-in-law, Mark does not deliberate about where to spend holidays or which family to turn to in times of need. He prefers Dina's family to his own, and he fits right in.

KENT BECKER

Kent Becker lives with his brother, Ryan, in the house that used to belong to their paternal grandmother; it is now owned by their parents. The neighborhood is well maintained, with lots of stucco-fronted homes with red-tiled roofs. When I arrive for the interview, a housecleaning crew is at work inside the house. Kent, tall, fair, and brawny, greets me with a somewhat high-pitched voice that seems ill matched to his size and appearance. After he greets me, he suggests we go to a café so that we will not be bothered by the noise of the vacuum cleaner. We head for the local Starbucks in his new SUV.

Kent has a reputation in his family as a child-oriented man. According to his mother Susan, he has always liked children. He started babysitting when he was twelve years old. As an adult, his goal is to spend as much time with his nieces and nephews as possible. Kent's commitment to helping members of his family, Dina included, seems to be a mainstay of his existence. Although he is currently romantically involved with a woman, several members of the kin network expressed their severe dislike of her and their bafflement at how he could even consider letting his love interests conflict with his deep commitment to family involvement. According to a few of his siblings, this created tension in the network. Kent himself spoke of his lack of privacy but jokingly laughed it off in the interview. Clearly his intense involvement with the family hinders his ability to cultivate his romantic life and to choose with whom he wants to have a relationship, even at the age of thirty-two.

As an emergency medical technician, he works a block schedule that provides him with large chunks of free time. Virtually everyone I speak with in the Becker network mentions Kent's flexible schedule, and all enter it into their calculations of favors and responsibilities. He seems completely agreeable to this: "I can arrange to pick [the children] up. And because . . . they don't have huge schedules where, you know, 'Kent, can you pick them up? And then can you take them to piano lessons? And then can you take them to soccer?' . . . which . . . would be more difficult. But if it's one activity or just, you know, 'Can you kind of fit them into whatever you were doing?' You know, have them around the house, play with them, entertain them, take them with you on errands, then there's no reason not to." Today, for example, in addition to setting aside time to be interviewed, when school lets out he is planning to pick up two girls in the neighborhood for whom he used to babysit full time, take them to soccer practice, and then drive them to a pizza party. Sometimes, at the end of a nonworking day, Kent will ask himself, as so many other care providers do, "But what did I do? I have all this free time, and it just disappears." [8] In general, though, he seems content to use his time off to help others, especially family members.

In the Becker family spectrum, Kent is, by all accounts, more a doer than a talker. Ryan discloses that if someone needs support in an emotional crisis, Kent typically would not be the first choice. However, if a child needs tending, Kent rises to the top of the list.

PETER BECKER

Dina's father, Peter Becker, is a not-so-recently retired physician, slender, and of medium height, although slightly stooped. His sprightly step contrasts with his shock of white hair. When I spoke with him on the telephone, he seemed like a man in the know, curious and not shy. My impressions are confirmed when I meet him on the street as I approach the house for my interview with his wife. He is direct ("You must be Karen Hansen."), well prepared (speaking to me in Norwegian, briefly), and, later, generous (offering to buy some bread for me at the thrift store, his next destination).

Peter keeps popping into the kitchen when I first interview his wife, Susan. He is going about business of his own, but he is also monitoring me, listening to my questions, noting how long I stay. When I tease that he will be the next candidate for an interview, he assures me that he has nothing to add to whatever his wife might say. They have the same perspective on things, he says, and they share a common history. Nonetheless, when I call the following week to request an interview, he accedes and I am pleased.

Peter Becker is a good storyteller, summoning evocative details from his clear memory. A man of his generation, his accounts focus less on personal relationships and more on actions, places, and events. He grew up with one sibling, a brother, in a family that was poor, clean, and hardworking. His father ran his own moving business; his mother, who had emigrated from Ireland as a young woman, was a housewife. His mother raised Peter and his brother as Catholics, a faith his German Lutheran father did not share. Peter became a surgeon; his brother, a butcher. Over the years, Peter's strong sense of civic responsibility has motivated him to work as a volunteer doctor in South America and Europe, and on an American Indian reservation in the Midwest.

According to his son Ryan, Peter is the archetypical doer of the family: "My father is not like a chit-chatter about something troubling you. The way he interacts and lets people in his family, particularly, know that he loves them is by spending all this time doing everything for everybody else in the family and never having a selfish bone in his body." Mark, too, notes that his father-in-law is not a talker. Although he frequently drives Aaron and Donalyn to and from sports events and after-school lessons, he typically says very little to the children during these trips. Peter seems to be the kind of person who is happiest when he has something to do. In addition to chauffeuring his grand-children, he provides transportation for Susan, because she does not drive. He has set up a free clinic to clip the toenails of elderly people in the area. He also administers the affairs of some of his elderly widowed former patients, including managing an apartment building for one of them. And, he shops for any-one who is interested. Peter is a serious bargain hunter. Each week, he peruses the farmers' market as well as the discount bakery.

Shannon and Caitlin rave about their father's distinctive characteristics. Shannon calls her father "Mr. Grammar" and relies on Peter's language exper-tise over and above what she learns from computer programs, web sites, and hotlines. Praising Peter as a fount of knowledge, Caitlin says: "Out in the world, Dad knows all the things about how to handle that. He knows all the . . . re-sources that exist in the world for how to take care of anyone." Child-care advice, however, she seeks from her mother, because her "father just thinks we were just all perfect all the time. I mean, he can't remember it."

SUSAN BECKER

My arrival at the senior Beckers' home is announced by their dog, a shepherd mix, who has spotted me through the front picture window. Susan opens the door, dressed in pants and a sweatshirt and wearing her hair drawn back in a no-nonsense bun. Moving with agility and energy, she walks straight ahead into the kitchen. We walk past the dining room with a commanding, long oak table at its center. When we reach the kitchen, I look around while Susan finishes refilling the humming bird feeder. There is an eating alcove at one end of the room; the nook's small space is dominated by a table and benches. The tight fit is offset by a sunny bay window that provides a view of a beautiful tree and the house next door. Susan tells me that Peter built the table and benches to accommodate the horde of small Becker children. I eagerly accept the cup of tea she brings to me at the table and then sit back to listen to her reflections.

Susan marvels at the difficulties contemporary women, including her daughters, face as they try to rear children. She does not seem judgmental as she remarks on the profound cultural changes that have occurred since 1959, when she and Peter married. At that time, there was no question that she would have children and then stay home and rear them. Trained as a scientist, Susan set aside her research and professional ambitions until the youngest of her children reached school age. For the past twenty-five years, she has been a volunteer research scientist at a local research institution. The senior Beckers have reversed the conventional gendered division of labor in retirement.[9] While she pursues her scientific calling, Peter volunteers in various helping capacities.

Susan has a teacher's spirit; she respects and admires the enormous capacity children have to learn. She enjoyed the process of posing questions and discovering knowledge with her children and continues to do so with her grandchildren. Mark Walde describes her as "a very wise person, and although she doesn't think her answer is the last possible answer—I mean, she's not arrogant at all; . . . she's the exact opposite." He considers Susan an expert at child rearing. From his perspective, the proof of her skill lies in the remarkable children she reared. Therefore, when Mark has questions about his children, he turns to Susan, rather than to his own mother, for help.

SHANNON BECKER

Shannon Becker is a high school teacher. Although unmarried and with plans not to have children of her own, she is Ms. Family Values, or as Caitlin describes her, "the world's [most] perfect aunt." When she first walks into the café where I meet her, I recognize her as an unmistakable Becker. More than any of her sisters, she looks like her mother—of medium height, with brown hair, a bright white smile, and incandescent energy. Even in a family of highly committed, can-do people, she stands out as someone who acts on her philosophy of "family first." Other aunts and uncles are child friendly, but for Shannon, maintaining deep relations with her nieces and nephews amounts to a kind of life mission. Because she treasures her relationships with them, Shannon says, "I try to make time with me very special and memorable." She takes them to movies about mountain-climbing adventures or concocts special birthday presents. The children respond with a matching ferocity. Dina reports that her children "love [Shannon] wildly." Donalyn calls her aunt a "baseball freak," a description that delights Aaron. Caitlin's four-year-old son, who refers to Shannon as "my tia Shannon," grieved when he found out that she was his cousins' tia Shannon as well. He cherishes his relationship with Shannon and longs to have her to himself.

Shannon makes an effort to see Donalyn and Aaron regularly. Most frequently, this happens at her parents' house rather than at the children's home. "I would see them more," she tells me, "but they're just too busy." She makes up for not being able to see her nieces and nephews who live farther away, especially Lila's children, by talking to them on the telephone. She tries to get to know each one as an independent individual. According to Caitlin, Shannon is thoughtful, considerate, deliberate, practical, and successful with the children. Dina provides an example of a typical adventure with Aunt Shannon: "She had a cowboy theme sleepover for the boys, you know, and arranged all this cowboy food; . . . they drank sarsaparilla and, you know, they rang a bell, a triangle, to come to dinner, and her roommate—who cooks—was called Cookie, and . . . they ate victuals at the chuck wagon. I mean she really goes all out, and so she's having as much fun as the kids." According to Caitlin, Shannon need never fear becoming a lonely old person, because she is laying the groundwork for lifelong relationships with her nieces and nephews.

CAITLIN BECKER JAMES

Caitlin, her husband, Mike, and their two children live in a solidly middle-class suburb, about thirty-five minutes south from the senior Beckers' house. Their neighborhood consists of tract houses with few exterior architectural embellishments; the homes are comfortable and the area is staunchly crime free. The community has a reputation for having a high-quality education system—one of the best in the state—but Caitlin notes dryly that this is hardly worth bragging about, given that California now ranks forty-eighth in the nation in its spending on education.

The Monday evening of our interview, Caitlin looks a bit harried. Her long, dirty-blonde hair is pinned up in a messy bun that unravels bit by bit over the course of the evening. Surprisingly, she does not seem tired, even though she had been away all weekend teaching a workshop. Mike is just about to put their seventeen-month-old daughter, in her pajamas and rubbing her eyes, to bed when I arrive. Their older son is already sound asleep. Caitlin offers me tea and we chat while waiting for the water to boil. When Mike returns, the couple's emotional division of labor quickly becomes evident. Caitlin is a gregarious people person; Mike is reserved. Without being unfriendly, he makes it clear that he is interested in neither me nor my research project.

Caitlin and Mike had lived in the East for many years before deciding to move back to California. For Caitlin, that choice meant not only leaving their friends but also giving up a well-developed professional network. She decided that being close to her family was worth the sacrifice. "I knew I was throwing away my professional life by moving," Caitlin admits. "I mean not totally, but to a great extent." Now she pieces together employment by reviewing books and teaching workshops. Her expertise registers high on the Becker family index. Dina, awe evident in her voice, had told me earlier, "If anybody's written a book, [Caitlin has] read it, if it's for children." Caitlin acknowledges her own role as the family's "idea person"; everyone including her father calls her for suggestions about how to deal with people creatively.

Caitlin and Mike's calculations about where to live weighed commute time, affordability, and proximity to the Becker family. Living very close to the senior Beckers would have made Mike's commute unreasonably long. On the other hand, they reasoned, living next to his workplace would erase some of the advantages of moving to the West Coast, since visiting family would require an hour's drive across the bay. Their compromise location meant paying a higher price for their home, however. A family emergency that occurred shortly after they had moved reinforced the wisdom of their choice. Their daughter, then an infant, contracted meningitis. Caitlin had to accompany her to the hospital because she was still nursing. When she telephoned her mother in a panic, Susan dropped everything and arrived at her doorstep twenty-five minutes later, ready to take care of Caitlin's older son while she went to the hospital. Mike could stay at work and Caitlin could focus fully on the baby, knowing that her other child was in good hands. As she puts it, "That kind of stuff, . . . you just can't pay for it." Nor, in Caitlin's opinion, can that kind of unconditional availability and support be supplied by anyone other than a family member.

RYAN BECKER

At age twenty-seven, Ryan is the youngest in the Becker family and still in school. With his dark hair, brown, sad eyes and thoughtful manner, he seems more serious than his brother and housemate, Kent. As a medical school student he has very little free time, so he is now less central to Dina's network than he has been in the past, but he remains a willing participant. Ryan reports that his relationship with Aaron and Donalyn is one that brings him a great deal of pleasure. He notes, though, that he is not as active an uncle as Kent.

On the other hand, unlike others in the Becker network, Ryan consciously makes himself available to talk about emotional issues with his siblings. From his perspective, he puts effort into the larger network, and then he gets things back, although not necessarily directly from the individual he helped. So, while he sometimes helps Dina, he gets most help in return from his father and his brother.

Ryan describes himself as very close to his father and similar to him in temperament: "I'm, for better or worse, a lot like my father, in that I interact with the world in a very practical kind of way. And so when I talk about relying on my father, it's because I'm talking about relying on him to go to, like, help me put in a new garage door. Because that's the way I interact with the world. . . . So, yes, my mother is super emotionally available for me. My mother isn't gonna go out and find the right part for my car when I need to fix my car." But his father will do that, and more, which is one reason Ryan values his relationship with him so highly.

DONALYN AND AARON BECKER-WALDE

Primed by Susan's and Shannon Becker's descriptions of Donalyn and Aaron as fun, beautiful, and bright, I bring high expectations to my interview with the children. They do not disappoint me. The free-floating energy is palpable as Donalyn, Aaron, and one of their school chums sit twirling in the swivel chairs of Dina's home office. Their lively physical selves seem to punctuate their verbal proficiency. When I begin asking questions, third-grader Donalyn quickly establishes a clear advantage as the older sister, but Aaron nevertheless manages to make his views known.

In answer to my asking who cares for them before and after school, Donalyn replies, "Well, not really Dad so much, because he's a teacher." Aaron chimes in, "So he's at school." They are right, of course, but this is not the direction I had intended the question to take us. My goal is to gather information about the time periods immediately before and after school, which I know their mother covers. The children's ability to interpret my questions literally and precisely lays waste some of my carefully constructed child-interviewing strategies and leaves me scrambling to rephrase without being overly directive. When I prompt them about the care-provider roles their aunts and uncles play, Donalyn is again the first to answer: "Kent and Ryan don't actually do it. They used to do it a bit, but they don't really do it anymore. Because now—"

Aaron, interrupting, adds: "Yeah, because they took me over once, and I played this game on the computer."

Donalyn, taking charge once again, corrects him: "Aaron, we're not talking about computer games right now. We're talking about—"

Aaron shouts: "I know!"

Donalyn continues: "Because, now one of them works. They all work, they both work full time. One's [an emergency medical technician]; one's a doctor."

Unwilling to concede completely on the topic of relations with his uncles, Aaron brings up Ryan's role as his personal barber: "When I asked Ryan to have a haircut—when I called him, and I called him on his pager, so he—and he didn't really come. And when I called him on the pager, he said he would come the night that I called him." In addition to communicating his technical adroitness, Aaron makes clear the access he has to his uncle, and hence affirms his own importance. He knows that his uncle feels a sense of responsibility toward him, and that Ryan would understand the importance of getting a haircut when one was needed.

On the subject of household chores, Donalyn tells me she helps take care of the cat, and, "if Mom isn't up, I feed the fish. And if I am asked to take care of Aaron just for a little bit, I do. It's not often." Aaron's contributions are weightier: "I usually make the dinner with my mom," he says, adding that he likes doing dishes. "That's one of my favorites."

Ever vigilant, his older sister notes, "You don't actually do it much."

In asking the children whom they might call in an emergency, if their parents were not home, I precipitate a series of misunderstandings that verges on the comical. "Nine-one-one," is Aaron's immediate reply. I realize, belatedly, how illogical the question is for children who are never left home alone. Trying to recover the intent of my question—namely, to find out which member of the network the children would seek help from first—I parry, "After nine-one-one, if you had to call another adult—say it wasn't like a fire or somebody who got sick . . . " That sloppy rephrasing prompts Aaron to pose a question of his own: "Well, how could somebody get sick if we were the only ones here?" Indeed. I improvise, "Well, it would be an unusual situation, right? Because you guys don't stay home by yourself. Maybe even a babysitter was here who you didn't know. Who would you want to call in an emergency?"

Obligingly, Donalyn considers this farfetched scenario and then comes to my rescue, saying without hesitation, "My grandparents." When I restate in confirmation, "You'd call your grandparents?" Donalyn agrees, expanding, "Yeah, we might call Oma and Opa. We'd probably call them first."

Aaron explains why: "Yeah, 'cause they're the closest." Now fully into the spirit of my inquiry (they are from a family of helpers, after all), the children begin to speculate. Perhaps, if their parents were not home, they would first try to reach their parents. Maybe, Donalyn hazards, they might call the neighbors across the street (she admits that she does not know their telephone number, however). The conversation turns to the topic of the neighbors, about whom I begin to learn more than is strictly necessary. As the interview draws to a close, I realize that Donalyn and Aaron have answered my questions in spite of, rather than because of, my efforts.

MICHAELA BECKER

As the director of an after-school center for young girls, Michaela has an enormous amount of responsibility and works long hours. Dina warns me that this youngest Becker sister, as a thirty-year-old single woman, is seldom home and, because of her professional commitments, spends little time with her nieces and nephews. Nonetheless, Dina counts her as a network member. According to Dina, Michaela is so frequently unavailable that even a telephone interview could be hard to schedule. In fact, though, when I call, she is home and with no cajoling agrees to a face-to-face interview. When we meet, I am struck by her appearance—Michaela looks like a petite female version of her older brother, Kent. She promptly explains, although I don't mention Dina's warning about how difficult it can be to reach her: "I don't own a car, and they don't really know what my schedule is [laughs]—don't really know what's going on with me. You know, like, 'Where is she exactly?' Then I get called upon last. Because I think that everybody perceives me as having my hands full already with other things." Michaela sees Aaron and Donalyn about every three to four weeks, usually at her parents' house. She is glad to see them there, plays happily with both, and thoroughly enjoys herself. Unlike Kent and Shannon, however, she does not purposely involve herself in their lives.

Michaela lives geographically close to her family, but she inhabits a psychologically and culturally distant neighborhood. Still, like the rest of the Becker clan, Michaela is willing to contribute effort to help others, when called upon; and her zone of privacy notwithstanding, she relies on her family for support and help of various kinds. Her apartment, for example, is in a Victorian building her father manages. Maintenance is a family affair, much to her friends' amusement: "My friends tease me. . . . My bathroom right now needs to be painted really desperately. So my brother's supposed to do it. And he's been being supposed to do it for months, but he's very busy. You know, so—'Why doesn't your family ever pay anybody to do anything?' And I'm like, 'Well, why pay somebody to do it when you know you have a relative who's perfectly capable of doing it?' You know. Just as well—better than—somebody you're gonna pay. So, you know, eventually I'm sure my bathroom will be painted." Her mother, Susan, mentions a time when Ryan and Kent helped Michaela take some of her girls from the center to a professional women's basketball event. Examples abound. Despite her careful distancing techniques, Michaela is deeply embedded in the Becker way of life.

LILA BECKER MCKENDRICK

Lila Becker McKendrick is the second eldest, immediately following Dina. She too has an older-sister attitude and sense of empowered authority with regard to her kin system and her children. She is not formally a part of Dina's network; she lives too far away. Lila's husband's career took them to the Pacific Northwest, and although they have considered returning to California such an option does not seem professionally or financially viable. Dina speculated that her two brothers-in-law had a harder time being absorbed into the Becker kin network than her own husband, Mark, did. They struggled a bit more to maintain their independence as family units. And in fact, her two married sisters and their respective husbands and children live outside the fifteen-minute radius that the other siblings purposely maintain.

Because her husband is an employed physician, Lila feels she has the luxury of working parttime while she anchors the project of rearing her three school-age daughters and one toddler son. She rationalizes, "He's overpaid for what he does, and I'm underpaid for what I do." In the big picture, this division of labor and level of compensation works out. In the Becker educational tradition, Lila teaches advanced math at her daughter's middle school and tutors other children who need help with math. "I love teaching," she confides, and she concedes that she is good at it. The education ethos infuses her mothering as she structures daily reading time, sets weekly letter-writing goals, and limits after-school activity for her children, in effect creating an enriched learning environment at home.

Lila has constructed a vibrant network of her own that trades child minding, caring for the infirm, and a variety of other activities. She says, "There's always somebody to call when you need something or there's an emergency." Her network is rooted in the neighborhood, her daughters' parochial school, and the church community. No kin live nearby. Lila and her husband considered moving to be closer to the Beckers and to his mother in California, but realized they would "be giving up a daily support system for a weekend support system," because of where they would have to live. In the end, the move did not seem worth it. The ties to the California Beckers are sustained through regular visits, phone calls, and letters. Lila's involvement in Dina's network is thus limited primarily to the six weeks she spends near the senior Beckers every summer.

As one of the three sisters with children, Lila is a philosophical resource for Dina, and vice versa. Lila affirms that they help each other maintain their child-rearing approach when it differs from that of the outside world. Lila's distance from the Becker epicenter does not explain the entirety of her distance from Dina, however. Lila observes that she greatly respects Dina as a person and likes the way her children are turning out. Explanations for their social distance did not surface in the interview.

Familism, Children, and a Culture of Helping

Three dominant themes run through the accounts of the Becker network of care: familism, the centrality of children, and a helping ethos. Each is the result, at least in part, of deliberate decisions and careful teaching. "For both of my parents," Ryan explains, "their priority has always been family—like number one through ten." He says: "I think my father basically had a million kids because he likes family more than anything. Honestly, there's nothing more important to my father than his children and family." According to his mother, Susan, family relationships best all others because "a family person is always going to be there" to provide help and support. Susan and Peter purposely instituted an ethic of "family first" when they had children. Susan had grown up in a small family, without any extended kin nearby. "We were pretty self-sufficient," she says. The Becker children did have aunts and uncles and cousins who lived relatively near, but extended family members did not interact frequently.

Michaela characterizes the Becker family as a core unit that all others interested in participating must join. Caitlin is equally clear, informing me that the "expectation is that you spend time with your family." And Kent, though joking, also emphasizes the Beckers' commitment to familism: "What's that quote that Ryan always says? Oh, it's from Wyatt Earp. 'After blood there's nothing.' [Laughs.] Wyatt Earp was talking about his brothers." Pondering his family's collective commitment to one another, Kent sums up the network this way: "I think the only thing that makes it work is, I think that everybody wants it, you know, kind of feels the same way, and so is willing to give and take." Those who feel differently do not participate in the network. (See Chapter 6 for a longer discussion of the issues of inclusion and exclusion.)

Susan, in talking about other things she and Peter did to knit their children together, recalls that they taught them to buddy up when they were small and went out as a group. Even as the children reached adulthood, she continued to devise ways to keep the family together: "I wanted it to be close, so that—for example, when we had various kids away at college, they were always free to use our telephone credit card to call each other, so that we would pick up that, or to call home, so we encouraged everyone to keep in touch that way." Similarly, the senior Beckers encourage the presence of their grandchildren. As Susan puts it, "The house is very child friendly." They have toys available and bunk beds to accommodate multitudes.

Another element in the Beckers' sense of themselves as a unit stems from their ethnic and religious identification. When I first interviewed Dina, she presented the Becker family as "Irish Catholic," seemingly unconcerned about the devil in the details. In fact, her father was raised Catholic by his Irish mother, although his father was German and Lutheran. Dina's mother was Irish on one side, but Scandinavian on the other. The Irish side was bigger, however, and exerted a stronger influence. It is not unusual for American families to engage in "ethnic choosing," identifying with one group despite the options revealed in family lineage.[10] In the case of the Becker family, however, identifying as Irish Catholics includes an atypical element of conscious intention. Michaela recalls: "My parents have always told us about our ancestors and their struggles. And there is that sense of lineage." Susan, answering a question I posed about the role of the Church in supporting their family culture and practice, feels that Catholicism per se had less of an impact than did participating in a shared activity, like going to church or synagogue. "It's a shared part of your family culture," she concludes.

One widely shared perspective in the Becker clan regards the importance of children. "Children are a major focus for all of us," Shannon asserts. "Everybody's good with kids; everybody loves kids." She and many of her siblings attribute the values and perspectives they hold today to the senior Beckers' efforts: "My parents did so many things right that we imitate; . . . we were raised with a very strong philosophy about children." Children are not only valued, they are actively engaged.

A focus on children is central to the network operation and to what Michaela dubs "very conscious parenting," notably parallel to Hays's concept of intensive mothering and entirely in keeping with Lareau's notion of the concerted cultivation of middle-class children.[11] In the Becker context, the children can be showered with attention, essentially parented by aunts, uncles, and grandparents, and, unlike the scholarly descriptions of intensive parenting, the Beckers describe it as fun. Michaela, who characterizes herself as not involved in the weekly lives of her nieces and nephews, nonetheless intensely focuses when she's with them. The children get full attention.

> So, if they want to . . . play a game and, you know, it's Bookstore, . . . then you know, we play Bookstore. And we do the whole nine [yards]. . . . We find books, we make books, we write books. . . . I participate in the game with them, you know? . . . If you're babysitting them or if they're there to play. . . . Then that's the focal point; . . . it's sort of that conscious parenting thing again. It's not like I do anything particularly spectacular with them. But I think they have a really good time when they hang out with their aunts and

uncles because we're not just like: "Okay, guys! I'm gonna be in here, reading, and you're gonna go upstairs and play." Or whatever it is. It's like: "Okay, we're here! What do you wanna do? What are we gonna do today?" . . . I think that's why they think of their aunts and uncles as so much fun. It's because we participate, you know, with them; . . . that makes them feel safe and have boundaries and all that stuff, because they know their aunts and uncles are not gonna let them get away with stuff that's gonna make them get hurt. . . . And they talk a lot, and they like to be talked to. So that's mostly what I do, is hang out with them and find out what's going on in their life, and talk about the things that are important to them in a way they know they're important to me.

The third and final important characteristic of the Becker network is the ethos of helping others. Michaela says: "We are helpers, . . . that's what we do; . . . it's cultivated from within, and I think it's definitely perceived from the outside that if you call on somebody in the Becker family, they will help out." Reflecting on the family culture, Kent notes that it "was kind of instilled, I mean from Dad and Mom, that you just—whenever you can help, you do." Dina's husband, Mark, maintains that "they would sacrifice anything for any-body, especially family members." While the Beckers put family first, they are generous toward friends and neighbors as well. For example, Michaela's sisters helped her photograph the girls at her center and then stayed up virtually all night developing and printing the photos so the children could take them home as holiday gifts. Network members drive people to the airport, help them shop for groceries, babysit their children, and the like. Michaela remarks: "When-ever anybody needs anything, it goes out on, you know, the family tree. [Laughs.] And whoever fits the bill best can do it." Kent explains the system in more detail:

> What goes around comes around, you know, that it all works out. I mean, I do favors for Dina, Shannon does a favor for me, you know, Dina does a favor for Shannon. It's all kind of circular [laughs], you know, in the family kind of thing. But, yeah. So Dina—I've had Dina take pictures of friends, you know, do portraits of friends for much-reduced rates and stuff, where I'm just covering, I guess, just like the cost of film or whatever, not her time or anything, as gifts for them. . . . And, of course, as I said, when I had the girls [the children he babysat for], there were times when . . . I'd ask Dina, and she'd pick them up from something or whatever, or [keep] them for a while.

Michaela points out that the helping is not necessarily seamless: "Sometimes there's negotiation between siblings. Like, I can do it, but it's gonna kill me, so could you do it instead? Whatever it is, and so people try to accommodate each other with their demands. But somebody's gonna fill it." The highly skilled and highly functioning Becker network was built upon the senior Beckers' firm intentions and cultivated through an ethic of help and the sharing of considerable resources to insure members' success in their chosen endeavor. Dina Becker and Mark Walde, even as they move in a separate galaxy with its own sun, benefit from the dynamics of the Becker universe. The Becker network bolsters their marriage, enriches the lives of their children, and helps them remain, however precariously, in the middle class.

An Abundant Labor Force Shaped by Middle-Class Anxiety

Among the panoply of resources, the Beckers have their greatest wealth in people. Not only do they have a long list of network members, but those on the list are fun, committed, and have many skills to offer, especially an interest in and ability with children. The network consists of people who both care about and care for the children. In addition, the Beckers have a sense of family solidarity. This collective commitment helps everyone do a lot more than would be the case if they saw themselves as independent individuals.

At the same time, it constricts the choices they can make with regard to their individual lives and the autonomy they can exercise separate from the family. In the Becker commitment to kin, the tension between independence and interdependence becomes most apparent. The Beckers forcefully articulate their belief in a "family-first" ideology and in the ethos of helping. They contribute practically to each other's lives almost daily. And yet, the cohesiveness takes a toll on individual privacy (as clearly vocalized by Michaela and Kent) and autonomy—so much so that two of the three married sisters have moved a strategic distance away from the Becker epicenter to create a modicum of independence. The gravitational pull is still great and they show no need for or interest in breaking away entirely. To the contrary. Nevertheless, Michaela's ambivalence speaks to the conflicts that arise when one is interdependently embedded in a network while living in a mass culture that celebrates and promotes independence.

Dina and Mark do not have an excess of time, particularly with each other. Dina and others around her describe her life as frantic. In the marriage, the trade-offs for using a split-shift strategy to rear children become evident. With two middle-class jobs, working a swing-shift schedule, they see each other little. Dina Becker and Mark Walde, like many other working parents, find that coordinating care for their two school-age children is by no means simple, even with a platoon of helpers to buttress their child-rearing efforts. Dina feels fortunate to have her family so close and so helpful, but the network does not completely resolve her child-rearing tensions. Even with the amount of care the network supplies, Mark resents how much he has to do at home. The network helps, but it cannot completely assuage the tensions of their strained marriage.

Using the lives of others—her friends, families at her children's schools, her sisters, her mother—as a yardstick against which to measure herself and her circumstances, Dina concludes that she is lucky: "We're actually in a much better position than a lot of people I know." She means this in regard to material resources, as well as in regard to her warm web of people. Ryan aptly observes: "Dina and Mark don't have lots of money. Still, the people they hang out with are certainly sort of the middle and upper-middle class." They feel a deficit of monetary resources, although it is not just their lack of money per se, but their sense of a deficit of resources relative to those around them.[12] It is in this context that Dina's professional employment and income need to be considered. Unlike her two married sisters, Dina married someone who does not earn a family wage, at least not a wage sufficient to own their own home and live near their parents. So Dina works full time and anchors the network. To others, her life seems unnecessarily frenetic.

A comparison of the Beckers to the other middle-class network, the Duvall-Brennans, is useful. In terms of support, Maggie Duvall is on stronger ground in some ways than Dina Becker. Maggie has a mother's group to advise and emotionally sustain her. While she lacks the deep, reliable, practical support of the Becker network, she has in her egalitarian partnership with her husband a good source of support and comfort for many of the tensions and frustrations for which Dina Becker has no outlet. In fact, one way of thinking about the Becker network is that, while it supports Dina and Mark's marriage, it has its costs, permitting a lot of unresolved tensions to exist.

Both of these middle-class networks have large constellations of resources in comparison to the situations of the vast majority of U.S. parents, yet both sets of parents can be characterized as anxious about their economic status. All four adults have meaningful work. The Duvall-Brennans are driven more by professional career demands, the Beckers by the effort to maintain a foothold in the middle class. Work drives them all, compels them, motivates them. The contrast to women in the working-class and upper-class networks illuminates this dynamic. Several working women in these networks—Sarah Aldrich, Lydia Dunn, Patricia Crane, and Tracy Johnson—consider their jobs contingent, an attitude fundamentally different from that of Dina Becker and Maggie Duvall, the middle-class women. These women express clear priorities: They are willing to make do without employment and the money and dignity that come with it. Admittedly, Sarah Aldrich and Lydia Dunn do not need the wages because they have wealth. Nonetheless, their prioritizing of family commitments and their willingness to forgo employment renders them fundamentally different from Dina Becker or Maggie Duvall, or from either of their husbands, for that matter.

Work demands feel overwhelming to these middle-class parents. However, it is the combination of work and their expectations of themselves as parents that generates a great deal of anxiety. All four parents are committed to parenting intensively. The contradictory demands of full-time work and the need to care for children remain the challenge for the twenty-first century. It is a structural conflict that these parents experience as a personal problem. Economic insecurity and the primacy of work that it fosters exacerbate tensions that already exist and generate others.

Networks create an environment where those problems do not feel so individual and where, in fact, the work of parenting can be shared. Here the contrast between the Duvall-Brennans' deficit of people and the Beckers' wealth of people is instructive. Flourishing networks can alleviate not only the family labor shortage but also the sense that one is alone in this struggle. At the same time, the drawbacks of heavy familial involvement—such as the lack of privacy, the need to conform to the dominant culture of the network, the control exerted over one's time due to the obligations—can be perceived as not worth the trade-offs. For the Duvall-Brennans, they are not. For most members (although not all) of the Becker family, they are.

Part II

Constructing and Maintaining Networks

Chapter 6 — Staging Networks

Inclusion and Exclusion

NETWORKS OF interdependence are not naturally occurring social formations; they are actively and purposely constructed. Employed parents face sometimes worrisome and often time-consuming decisions about where and with whom to leave their children during nonschool hours. Should they rely on institutional care, family day care, individual care, or familial care? Parents must decide not only which of these situations is sufficiently affordable and convenient but also which best matches their child-rearing philosophy.[1] Even then, their child-care dilemmas are not resolved. Most working parents also need to construct their own networks to bolster the child-care system they select.

Parents go through a *process* of staging networks of care. Staging involves three phases. This chapter examines the first—identifying and screening potential network members. (Chapter 7 examines the remaining two phases—the dynamics of engaging people via reciprocity and of mobilizing their sense of responsibility.) To select members of their network of care, anchors actively sift through candidates from their own socially recognized kin, in-laws, friends, neighbors, and parents of their children's friends. Inevitably, some people are included in the network and others excluded.

Identifying and screening members from a given universe of potential caregivers is a continual process. Sorting occurs at many levels. For example, anchors' decisions about where to live, with whom to associate, how to organize their work lives, and where to send their children to school shape the size and composition of their pool of network candidates. Anchors assess who is appropriate and conveniently available for each of the various aspects of child care they need help with (e.g., furnishing transportation, watching over children, providing advice). They also try to determine whether the potential candidate's values and principles are similar to their own, paying special attention to the person's child-rearing philosophy. Kinship is neither a necessary nor a sufficient condition of network participation. Neither is friendship or neighborliness. Anchors eliminate from consideration any potential member they judge incompatible, and any they view as incompetent with children, unreliable, or inaccessible. Even a very large potential group can shrink to a handful of candidates.

Sometimes, however, the pool expands, thanks to network members' efforts to recruit others on the anchors' behalf. Children, especially, may be active agents in the process of staging networks. Middle-class children often link parents to neighbors and kin.[2] Their desire to pursue friendships with schoolmates; their involvement in after-school activities, sports, and lessons; and their connections to other children in the neighborhood require parents to make phone calls, arrange carpools, and extend invitations for play dates, sleepovers, and trips. Over time, these kinds of contacts between adults with sufficient resources to afford these childhood amenities may deepen into friendships or overlapping networks of care. Similarly, a child's friendship with or special fondness for a relative can spur a family connection, perhaps recruiting that person into the network. Mark Walde, Dina Becker's husband, notes that his children like to spend time with his niece. His daughter "obviously loves and looks up to this older cousin," he explained, "so that is part of the reason perhaps that we see my brother probably more" than other relatives on his side of the family.

Some people never make it onto the list of potential caregivers. Intentionally or unintentionally, they exclude themselves. These individuals opt out of the burdens of involvement in a network by not expressing interest in the anchor's children, moving away, staying busy at work, not answering their phones, or not living up to their "role" as kin.

The Social Construction of Network Candidacy

Consistent with the findings in much of the literature, social class affects the composition of networks: the affluent middle- and upper-class networks include more friends than kin.[3] However, in all four networks, kin are present as key figures. Logically, networks that center on caring for and caring about children would be more family linked than other kinds of networks. Family members are likely to be more invested in child rearing, given that its success means perpetuation of the clan, the family culture, and, in some cases, the family property and historical legacy.

Across the economic spectrum, the involvement of extended kin is shaped by beliefs about families and about the role(s) families and other adults should play in the life of a child. Some people express a belief in the value of having multiple adults involved with their children because it teaches them to be flexible. Children learn that there is not just one way to do things and that adults can approach a particular problem in many ways—and those adults bring different kinds of personalities, skills, and strengths to a network. Sarah Aldrich states clearly, "I think kids can have different relationships with lots of different people; it doesn't have to be their parents." Kerry Becker concurs: "It's so good that kids are exposed to all different adults, all the different ways of doing things." Her mother points to the ways her daughters act as counsel to their nieces and nephews. Speaking to the emotional and confidential nature of relationships, as well as physical babysitting backup, she says about her grandchildren: "They are willing to ask [my daughter] all kinds of things that they either haven't asked their parents or aren't comfortable about; . . . that kind of a relationship is invaluable." Presumably those who think that only a parent can and should care for a child would opt out of networks altogether.

Once a parent expresses the value of multiple caregivers, the question arises as to which adults fit the bill. The networks vary in relation to the way they view nonkin as opposed to their extended kin. The middle-class Beckers and the working-class Cranes adopt a "family-first" approach; the upper-class Aldriches privilege family history and family ties, although they delegate large portions of child rearing to hired help; and the professional, middle-class Duvall-Brennans operate on a principle of "family in the last instance." Nearly all parents face an overwhelming number of challenges and need to be able to ask for help. The Cranes and Beckers expect family members to provide that help. As Kent Becker puts it, "You always got to be able to just call the family." The Aldriches, in contrast, expect to pay for the help they need rearing their children. Their reliance on paid help in no way diminishes the importance of family, however. It simply reflects an emphasis on the managerial dimension of child rearing and expresses a confidence in the anchor's ability to influence the children via the babysitter, however much time she spends with them herself.

Giving family members and family matters priority is not something that happens naturally or inevitably. The Beckers clearly honor family, but this is an ethic the senior Beckers, Peter and Susan, purposely developed with their children. The Becker siblings, in turn, have taught their own children to recognize and act upon the importance of family. Michaela Becker explains the approach: "People will say, like, at certain times, 'After family, there's nothing.' Or, you know, like, 'Family is gonna be with you when you're at your deathbed,' . . . or, like, Lila will say to her kids, you know, 'That's your sister. You need to look after your sister. You are her ally. You guys need to be good to each other.'" The Beckers' strong family culture extends beyond helping in a crisis to encompass routine aspects of daily life. In addition to providing the sort of overt instruction Lila gives her daughter, the Becker clan reinforces the family ethic in frequent, fun-filled family gatherings.

In all four networks, some biological kin are included as network members and others are not; some kin are trusted, some are not; some kin, but not others, are considered reliable—sure to be there when times get tough. Even in networks that embrace the "family-first" ethic, genealogical kinship status does not automatically grant kinship privileges and responsibilities. This constructed quality of kin relationships became apparent periodically in the form of large silences about certain relatives during the interviews I conducted with network members.[4] When I noticed these glaring absences in the list of network members, I asked additional questions. Patricia Crane, for instance, talked freely about her brother Ben but offered no information about any of her other three brothers until I inquired directly. She told me that one brother calls her occasionally; she has no contact with the other two. And among her still-living maternal aunts and uncles, Patricia remains in touch with two aunts. One uncle who lives nearby she described as "bad news." She has no interest in hearing from him. None of these relatives is part of the landscape of Patricia's everyday life, nor do any participate in her network of care. Tracy Johnson, who has eight biological brothers and eight biological sisters, is similarly selective in calling on kin for help. She counts only two sisters and one brother as part of her network. Musing over what makes these three siblings special, Tracy said: "Maybe because we have the same mom, probably. I don't know. I don't think so." She went on to say that the two sisters in her network are her best friends. One of her brothers, in contrast, she dismisses as too self-centered to be trusted with her children's care. Tracy also depends on people she considers family, including her "play mom" (a woman in her church who is her "mother in the Lord") and a friend she describes as "like a sister." In the Becker network, several members mentioned a feud between Peter Becker and his brother, which ended only after their mother died. And Susan Becker admitted that she found Peter's mother difficult in many respects, so much so that she limited the amount of time her mother-in-law spent with her children.

This process of sorting through with whom one stays connected and from whom one parts is a fundamental aspect of constructing active kinship and a network of care. The reasons for omitting biological kin are not necessarily related to tensions or hostilities. Most families experience conflict; some hold together in spite of it, or because of it; and others separate into branches or splinters. Which kin end up participating in networks can be shaped as much by the haphazard exigencies of life as by deliberate acts of inclusion or exclusion. Well-liked kin may live at a distance or have too many other responsibilities to participate in networks of care for children or have physical or emotional limitations that would make caring for children burdensome.

As with kin, not all friends are tapped to participate in networks of interdependence that focus on children, in part because of class differences in the expectations of friends. Karen Walker's research on friendship reveals that middle-class men and women tend to expect friends to be emotionally supportive and share leisure activities, whereas working-class men and women expect material interdependence as part of their friendship.[5] As with kin, a sifting process and different levels of active engagement sort out which friends or neighbors might help with children. As Byron Russell, friend and one-time neighbor of the Duvall-Brennans, observed: "There are people who are really good at taking kids in, who really enjoy doing. And not all parents fall into that category." For caretaking to succeed, both child and caretaker need to feel a certain level of "comfort" and familiarity.

In U.S. culture as a whole, friendship is seen as voluntary, in contrast to the obligatory nature of kinship.[6] And yet the actions and comments of the network members I interviewed reveal the contingent nature of kinship and the steadfastness of some friendships. In three of the networks, the anchors recruited friends because they provide support, advice, emotional stability, and, when possible, hands-on care. Many of the women in the networks spoke passionately about their commitment to, reliance upon, and admiration for their friends.

Witness the relationship between Tracy Johnson and Patricia Crane. Tracy comments: "If I need Patricia, hey, I call Patricia real quick. And she's on it every time. So, you know, we're there for each other, and that's friends, you know. And you can't get no closer than that." Patricia and Tracy recognize their interdependence. As Tracy puts it, she and Patricia have a "buddy-buddy system"—"I need my buddy!" Each views the other as prepared to "do anything" to help. "I like to share things," Tracy explains, "and if I have it, hey, it's yours—just like Patricia. Go right ahead." She claims she developed this generosity with selected people as a defense against her family of origin, which was decidedly *not* generous. She characterizes her father as "a stingy person, and he's out to get whatever he can get. And with my mom, she always took away from me." Even her grandmother, who raised Tracy and her brother for a while, seemed to withhold affection, favoring her brother over her. As a result, Tracy has set her sights on creating a different kind of environment for her own children by selectively choosing the people with whom she rears her children—some kin, some friends.

The exchanges between Tracy and Patricia, as part of the important role each plays in the other's care network, contribute to their overall sense of well-being. Tracy says, for instance, that she is now a more confident and effective parent. Her own voice has more authority with her children because Patricia reinforces it. She reports, "I've had no problems out of my kids since I met Patricia and [my boyfriend]." Patricia understands that through their friendship and the contributions she makes to Tracy's network, she makes parenting easier for Tracy.

Parallel to Patricia and Tracy, Sarah Aldrich has two completely devoted friends in her network. They think the world of her and would do anything for her. The feelings are mutual. Her best friend, Kate Farnsworth, said, "The thing that is so great about Sarah is that I can always count on her to tell me the truth." She later elaborated on the depth of her trust and reliance: "For some reason we're at a place right now where a lot of people are getting sick and it's been really bad, . . . so I thought, 'Well, who would I want?' Sarah's one of those people. I just would want her to be here. I just want her to be around. Because I know, I feel that kind of comfort with her. It would just be like, we'll do it together, you know what I mean?" While not friends with the same level of intimacy, Lydia Dunn and Sarah Aldrich share a major part of the logistics of rearing their eleven-year-old sons and trust one another implicitly. Lydia pays Sarah Aldrich a high compliment: "She makes me able to work."[7] Sarah is bedrock for her, in part because of her unwavering dependability.

Interestingly, women in the working-class and upper-class networks spoke more passionately about friendship than women in the middle-class networks. Even though the women in the mother's group with Maggie Duvall clearly articulated appreciation and commitment to one another, their contact largely evolved in the context of the group. Their accounts are consistent with the middle-class women in Walker's research who lacked the time to devote to developing friendships, and expressed expectations of advice and support but not of material help. The working-class women and the upper-class women in this research seem more comfortable with the interdependence of hands-on help and babysitting exchange. None of the men in the networks articulated an emotional reliance on friends, male or female, to support them in their child rearing, although some male members were involved in fathers' or men's groups of various kinds.[8]

Inclusion Principles

Anchors use certain principles of inclusion to sort potential members: proximity of time and place, and individuals' expertise and specialization (the latter two include adults' level of skill and comfort with children). None of these criteria, either alone or in combination, is sufficient, however, unless the potential member also shares the anchor's child-rearing values.

INTENTIONAL PROXIMITY IN PLACE AND TIME

Research consistently confirms the importance of proximity in constructing networks and activating extended kinship systems.[9] Potential network members' physical distance or lack of time can create social and emotional remoteness and establish a general lack of availability.[10] In identifying individuals who are eligible and desirable as child-rearing helpers, anchors consider two dimensions of availability. The first involves geographic closeness. Physical proximity affects the convenience of a potential member's participation and his or her accessibility to the anchor's home and to the location(s) of the children's activities. The second dimension addresses the person's availability in terms of time.[11] Free time is shaped both by employment and by the individual's interpretation of his or her nonwork time as available for network participation.

These network members emphasize the importance of being nearby; however, they also make clear that more than geography is involved. Proximity in a network of interdependence includes an element of purposefulness, something I call "*intentional* proximity." Unquestionably some network association results from convenience, but studies underestimate the intention behind proximity. While some kin live conveniently close, their location alone is insufficient to recruit them into a network.[12] In other cases, not living nearby does not preclude kin from participating in the network. Some kin systems exert sufficient "family gravity" to pull others toward them, not as a natural process, but as a socially constructed set of relationships that result from intention and action as well as coincidence.[13]

CONSTRUCTING PLACE. Some kinds of activities are facilitated by the convenience of geographic proximity: neighborhood play dates, impromptu visits, borrowing household items, caring for someone on a moment's notice.[14] As Kent Becker put it, "I think being close geography-wise makes everything else easier." Anchors in three of the four networks purposely determined where to live in order to be near some extended family member. The Duvall-Brennans are the only couple whose decision to relocate on the basis of jobs, quality of life, and school systems superceded considerations of proximity to kin. That decision left them without a kin cushion and diminished their pool of available neighbors, and thus they must clamber to put together a system of care for their children.

The importance of intentional proximity is especially clear in the case of the Beckers. Because a critical mass of the network lives within five miles of one another, members are able to provide many different types of assistance and they require little advance notice to do so. Family members' proximity is not coincidental. When Dina and Mark returned to the United States after having lived abroad for a while, they carefully considered where to live: "We thought that it was important for our children to be part of this large group of people that all cares about each other," Dina told me, "and so we moved back" to California. With two children and an expanding home-based business, they are finding their two-bedroom house cramped. In an effort to locate a larger home, Dina has looked at 170 houses over the past year. In addition to the consideration of price, she is bound by a desire to live within a small radius of her parents and siblings. Making clear that her proximity is intentional, not an accident of fate, Dina said: "It's so expensive living in the city. . . . We sorta kinda thought about moving. But with my family here we didn't want to. . . . If I move to Illinois, if I had to do a wedding on the weekend and something happened to Mark, . . . there wouldn't be that network. I couldn't say, 'Kent!' or 'Mom'; . . . I'm really lucky that way." A similar intentionality is true of most of Dina's siblings. Her brother Kent waited three years to get an EMT placement in the Becker's home city rather than move one thousand miles away to take a job that was available immediately. In the interim, he worked as a babysitter so he could live near his family and be involved in the network. For him, the trade-off was worth it. Ryan, Kent's younger brother, chose a medical school in the same area instead of attending a prestigious East Coast school, because he counts on his family for essential help: "I felt like at the end of the day they would keep me sane and keep me having some perspective—being around my family." Several Becker sisters tell of comparable choices. Caitlin, for example, moved back to the West Coast after she and her husband had their first child, in part because she wanted to reap the advantages of kinship involvement in child rearing.

The Cranes, too, operate with great intentionality. Ben Crane follows his mother and sister whenever they relocate. Although Patricia moves frequently, she does so within fairly constrained geographic limits. Ben commented: "We all try to stick around the same area because we all help each other that way, you know? . . . We don't have a lot of money, so there's some things that we need help with. And if we didn't have each other, we'd really be hurting."

The help Crane network members share is economic as well as practical and emotional.

After Sarah Aldrich and Alex Brolin got married, the magnetic pull of the Aldrich family drew them to California. After their first child was born, they bought a house less than a five-minute drive from Sarah's parents' home. Alex speaks regretfully about how far he lives from his brother, whom he likes very much and wishes could be more involved with his children. But dispersion of residence is the norm in Alex's family, not the exception. Relocating to live in "Aldrich country" enabled him to be employed in the family enterprises for a while, and it made it possible to involve Sarah's parents in the ongoing lives of the children.

Modern technology—cars, airplanes, telephones, and the Internet—facilitates social connections across long distances.[15] The quality of these interchanges may be less emotionally satisfying, however, and the kinds of involvements limited. While Jack Brennan's sister can provide child-rearing advice from the East Coast, the three thousand miles that separate the two households prevent her from being directly involved in the daily routines of the Duvall-Brennan children. She can care about the children; she cannot care for them. Connecting becomes "a hassle," according to Dina Becker, if a relative or a friend lives far away. Distance can prevent relationships from developing, particularly with children.

Still, for some people, including Lila Becker, the challenges presented by distance do not seem insurmountable: "Somehow, I don't mind the phone. But . . . you can't share the phone. And it also cuts you off . . . from the rest of the family. . . . And I don't like that. So we just sort of have this tradition of letter writing." Lila makes a concerted effort to stay connected to her siblings, parents, and nieces and nephews, in part *because* they are so far away. Every summer, she brings her children to spend six weeks in her northern California hometown to reintegrate her children into the Becker clan. Continuity requires conscious effort, and it sometimes results in lopsided relationships: "My children are very much involved in their lives, at least. I don't know if they think about my children as much as my children think about [Dina's children]. . . . My children are perfectly happy with that, because they know they fit right in as soon as they're there."

More than any other network member, Robert Crane demonstrates how to overcome geographic distance, which in his case is compounded by physical challenges. His level of psychological involvement with his son transcends time and space. With the help of phones and cars, he can be at Robbie's side within two hours. Moreover, Robert's emotional involvement, supported and affirmed by Robbie's mother and grandmother, makes his presence immediate and powerful in his son's everyday life.

INTERPRETING TIME AND EMPLOYMENT. Proximity can be established through time as well as place. I argue that how individuals organize their time and interpret the demands of their employment profoundly shapes their involvement in networks of interdependence. Some people interpret the time they spend away from the workplace as being accessible to friends, family, and young people; others see their lives as impossibly busy and themselves as unavailable, except in emergencies. Many workers face significant demands in the workplace, including long hours.[16] But the key difference between those who are available and those who are not is not occupation per se.[17] Someone who has unstructured time during the week may still see himself or herself as being very busy with work or overwhelmed by the demands of daily life and unable to assist others or be a part of a network of care.

Kent Becker is a good example of a person who views himself as ready and willing to help people in the network, even though he has a full-time job. As an emergency medical technician, he has a work schedule that consists of long blocks of time on the job alternating with periods of several days in a row of nonwork time. Importantly, when Kent is off work, he sees himself as on call for the network. He is ready to help out with neighbors who need to be taken to the airport or nephews who need to be babysat after school or a brother who does not have enough time to do his own banking. Equally important, Kent's siblings and parents see his free time as a family resource and allocate it to those in need.

Even with more traditionally structured hours, some workplaces are more family friendly and responsive to needs that pull employees homeward. Describing his situation as an employee of a small landscaping business, Ben Crane said: "Yeah, my boss is pretty cool about things. I have quite a bit of flexibility. If I need to get something done, he'll let me go ahead and do it." In the Aldrich network, Lydia, director of development at a local college, has a profoundly different relationship to the labor market than Ben, and yet the two share a similar approach, placing firm limits on the demands of their work. Lydia's perception of her accessibility makes her a valuable network resource, as Alex Brolin explained: "She's the mother of three boys—three very active, involved, scheduled boys. And so she's used to massive amounts of orchestration and logistics, and she's also very flexible. . . . 'Let me know. I'll just pick them up.' Or, 'I'll drop Spencer off and make them play together.' Or 'drop Jacob off at our house.' It's easy to make arrangements. You know, she's not protective of her own [time]—she's a wonderful facilitator of complicated schedules." Time, in absolute terms and in the way it is constructed and interpreted by members of networks, impacts participation in a network of interdependence. In these cases, class status, insofar as it reflects a particular relationship to the labor market, importantly shapes perceptions of work and time.

Virtually all network participants, whether in the core or on the periphery, say they want to be available to the anchor (and often to others in the network as well). However, these declarations are sometimes followed by a conditional escape clause: "*if* I can do it." Referring to Dina, Kent declared, "I can't imagine what she would ask me to do that I would say no, other than not being able to do it for time reasons." Sarah Aldrich's friend Kate proclaimed, "I would do anything for her in a second, if I could do it." Sarah's weekend babysitter (who has taken care of the children for ten years) maintained she would do whatever she could to help Sarah: "If I were available, definitely." The critical issue is how "available" gets defined. Under what conditions does a network participant define helping out as "impossible"? Availability is a social construction. Even as they articulate their attachment and commitment to an anchor, network members acknowledge participation limitations, both hypothetical and real.

People are constrained by the structures of their jobs.[18] Person after person in this study has identified job flexibility as a key factor in the ability to participate in a network. Network members struggle to stretch and shape their work situations to make them amenable to their family and network needs. For some, the goal may be finding a decent job that generates an adequate income. For others, a good job may be one with hours compatible with children's school schedules, or one with some flexibility and fewer demands on time otherwise spent on the second shift.[19] The network members I interviewed define their relationships to work differently, depending on their economic resources and class contingencies. And yet, greater economic need did not translate into increased desperation and acquiescence to employment. Work-related demands seem to dominate the psychic lives of middle-class network members. Newman describes middle-class life in the 1990s as a culture where people feel "a peculiar combination of consumer confidence and employment anxiety," and hence "oscillate between optimism and worry."[20] This description aptly captures many of the middle-class network members in this study. They are anxiously trying to accommodate—their employers and clients, their partners, and their families.

Many of those in the middle-class networks discussed their job choices as ones made to accommodate the needs of children; some went so far as to prioritize job flexibility and work location. Both Jack Brennan and Maggie

Duvall, for example, changed jobs to be in more family-friendly environments. Nonetheless, as attorneys and as commuters, both continue to have enormous and seemingly unyielding work demands thrust upon them. As a result, their days are long, their burdens heavy, and their anxiety levels high. Here, the distinction between jobs and careers is useful. Rosanna Hertz notes that careers offer a "realistic expectation of upward occupational and financial mobility" along with "advancement from lower to higher levels of responsibility, authority, and reward." She makes the point that a vast majority of women are employed in jobs, not careers. "Jobs offer limited opportunities for advancement, responsibility, and authority, are paid by the hour, and promise little significant increase in financial reward for achievement or for longevity of employment."[21] The Duvall-Brennans are both in high-powered careers. Mark Walde and Dina Becker are also pursuing careers, but their work entails less intense external demands than those the Duvall-Brennans face. Dina set herself up as a freelance photographer so she could care for the children and fit her work around Mark's schedule as a teacher. Now that the children are in school, Dina can devote more time to photography and still have some day-to-day flexibility. As an independent contractor, she makes choices and faces constraints as well. She gets paid by her clients for the photographs she produces. Like other freelance contractors, the quality of her work has to be maintained or else she cannot generate word-of-mouth business.[22] The pressures of quality control, however, do not match the time constraints imposed on professionals such as attorneys, whose jobs demand face time and late nights at the office to prove commitment. And Dina Becker has more options than she recognizes. She could cater to a different client base or shift away from weddings as the mainstay of her business to create more time at home with her husband and children. But she does not do that.

The message I heard from middle-class women is quite different from that articulated by working-class and upper-class women. Members of the working-class and upper-class networks are more adamant that work arrangements must accommodate family concerns and needs. They prioritize family commitments. Neither their identities nor their sense of purpose depend upon a particular job. Sarah and Lydia from the Aldrich network, and Patricia and Tracy from the Crane network, each told me that if she found herself in a job that did not suit her needs as a mother and family member, she would quit. Arguably, Sarah and Lydia do not need the wages and in that sense were free to leave their jobs. But both women's resolve to not let the demands of work overwhelm family life is more than a matter of convenience or superficial homage to family values. Lydia Dunn defined her parental responsibilities as requiring more job flexibility and stricter limits on her work time than her current position was providing. She threatened to leave if her employer would not accommodate those needs. Sarah stepped down from *half* her board positions when her marriage foundered and she felt she needed to be home more with her children. On the working-class side, Patricia Crane quit both her jobs when her mother came home from the hospital and needed her attention and care full time. Patricia's safety net does not include a trust fund, but state monies (a small stipend from social services for performing "home health care" and the Social Security payments Robbie receives because his father has a disability) supply just enough of a cushion to allow her to get by for short periods without paid employment. Work is contingent in a way that would be impossible for any of the middle-class network members to imagine. For the working-class and upper-class women, work hinges on care needs. For the middle-class women, care needs are contingent on work. The idea that work is contingent is not a philosophy the middle-class men articulated either (see Chapter 8 for further discussion). Their commitment to breadwinning as a source of identity as well as income superceded their ability to think about their lives very differently. Through negotiating various constraints, perceptions, and practices, the subjects of this study create, or do not create, proximity of time and place.

SPECIALIZATION AND EXPERTISE

Within a network, members specialize in types of care and appear to be drawn into the network because of some special skill they offer.[23] Consistent with the literature, subjects across networks made distinctions between providing services and giving advice. Sarah Aldrich's estranged husband, Alex, talked about several mothers of his children's friends who provide sage advice. At the top of his list is Lydia Dunn, whom Alex described as "a boy expert." Lydia, who specializes in information related to boys' athletic teams and camps, confirmed this designation. She joked that she ought to have a Web site called "asklydia.com." Jane Aldrich, Sarah's mother, remembered how, as an inexperienced and nervous new mother, she greatly appreciated and depended on her mother-in-law for child-rearing advice: "John's mother was a fountain of advice. And she was a very fine mother-in-law. She never, ever criticized anything at all that I said or did. It was amazing, because I was just a totally inept— I had never babysat a child, even, before I had Sarah." Her mother-in-law's on-call, nonjudgmental wisdom calmed Jane. "It was good to call her, because she was so reassuring. And she wasn't intrusive and didn't like to know anything bad about anybody."

The Beckers were the most explicit about the importance of their specialized division of labor. Michaela offered a description of it: "Everyone has their niche or their role or something like that. Or their area of expertise." They recognize and appreciate what each network member has to offer. In the Becker clan, areas of expertise cover a broad spectrum—from children's literature, to photography, to natural history, to medical care. Each individual's special skills and knowledge give her or him a proprietary claim on that area. Caitlin, for example, confidently discusses her capacities as an expert in children's literature: "No one would dare even ask anyone else, and they wouldn't even dare to possibly purchase or borrow a book from the library without asking me. I mean, everyone's too embarrassed, because I might say that was a really bad book. I mean, Dina borrows books from the libraries, but my mother would never buy books for any kids, not without asking me if that's a good choice." Others in the family respect and honor her expertise. Shannon confirmed the unchallenged excellence of her sister's judgment in the children's book category: "Would I *not* call Caitlin before I would buy a children's book? I would never, like, in my life." In the Becker network everyone also offers highly developed child skills. For example, Kent has a magical way with children and chunks of free time; Shannon imaginatively creates special events; and Ryan cuts hair and checks the children's ears for possible infections.

Adults who are skillful with children are great assets to a network of interdependence. The chemistry between adults and children thus becomes a critical factor. Parents in this study used the language of "comfort" in identifying these specially talented network members. Child care is a two-way street, as anyone who has spent time with children knows. The Duvall-Brennans' friend Rebecca, who has two children, reflected on what arrangements worked best between her family and theirs: "Danielle's completely comfortable with us. But Scott's not, and so—so it's a little bit tricky to take care of the four kids." All members of the network of care have some facility with children, although some have a special knack and capably establish mutual feelings of comfort.

The upper-class Aldrich network prizes managerial and executive skills. A preference for these kinds of expertise is rooted in their class position and in the way they organize their lives, which involves coordinating and supervising hired help and carpoolers, as well as monitoring and nurturing their children. Because Sarah's children are a bit older and she has a teenager in her household, she faces more logistical challenges related to lessons and sporting events than the other network anchors do. She says she rarely seeks advice, but if a need arises, Sarah turns to experts rather than to family members. For example, she consults financial managers to oversee the resources for her children, and therapists to help heal old wounds and work through emotional turmoil. Because she has assembled a highly competent board and staff to work with her, she can confidently delegate some tasks as well. Sarah, Lydia Dunn, and the Aldrich children's nanny, April Miller, all have confidence in one another's tastes. Thus, Lydia can supervise the eleven-year-old boys as they choose their Halloween costumes, and April can take them to buy navy-blue blazers for their dance class. One of the great services Lydia Dunn provides to Sarah Aldrich, Alex Brolin, and other friends is coordinating carpools. She participates in several carpools and has discovered that other mothers, with the exception of Sarah, do not take their responsibility seriously enough. To increase accountability, Lydia has taken it upon herself to draw up color-coded schedules for all drivers. She posts the schedules above her desk at work, ready for consultation.

The class contrast could not be greater between the kind of expertise prized by the Beckers and the Aldriches and that valued by the Cranes. Crane network members' skills and knowledge come not from college educations or managerial positions, but from hands-on experience rearing children and providing home health care. Patricia's mother, Fran Crane, has spent decades nursing the sick, beginning with her own children: "The two oldest boys of mine was sick all the time. In and out of the hospital. . . . My oldest one, when he was six months old, had polio. And then by the time he was three, he had had eight major surgeries. So he was just sick all the time. And then my second one, he was born with an opening in his heart, and he was always sick." Fran came to be anointed as the primary home-health-care provider: "I've taken care of people that's been sick, you know? And I've always been the one that, when anybody's sick, they always call on me to come stay with them." She anticipated that her cantankerous mother would thus kin-script her when the time came. Affection did not motivate Fran to provide the care her mother needs. Rather, it is her position within her family as designated caretaker with special skills and her sense of nonnegotiable familial obligation. Patricia too, has provided in-home care for family members. When her grandmother's husband was ill, Patricia left her job and, bringing Robbie with her, went to live at her grandmother's house so her step-grandfather did not have to stay in a nursing home.

Regardless of class, in all these networks of interdependence, members' specializations and the range of skills available across a network mean that people who are *not* qualified for a particular task are not likely to be asked to do it. This is especially evident in the area of advice. For example, Patricia Crane said she would not think of asking her brother for parenting advice. Ben is good at child care, at playing with Robbie, and at being the "man figure" in his life, but giving advice is not his forte. Patricia relies, instead, on her aunt Sherry, who otherwise was not involved in Robbie's care. "Because she works at a school," Aunt Sherry has a perspective Patricia finds helpful. Michaela Becker is certain that her sister Dina would not turn to her for child-rearing tips. Michaela does not have children of her own, and although she runs a child-care center, most of the children are from poor immigrant families. The issues and challenges they face are quite different from those that confront Dina's children. "She's not going to ask me, 'How do you handle this situation?' or whatever, because I'm gonna see it differently." Since the Becker network is rich with members who are experienced parents, Dina can turn to one of these individuals, instead. Lastly, since advice givers, unlike care providers, do not necessarily interact directly with the children or live nearby, they do not need to specialize in child care.

Not all expertise traded across the networks is related to child rearing. And one service can easily get exchanged for another; anything can get swapped for babysitting. Shannon speaks a foreign language and translates documents for family and friends. For bargain hunting, it is Dina's father, Peter, the designated price shopper of the family, who is consulted. Ryan maintains that if anyone needs something done, Kent is the person they should call first. Kent is equally comfortable and competent whether he is babysitting for Dina's children or tutoring Michaela in math in preparation for her GRE exams. However, he is not the right choice if the situation calls for a person who is skilled in listening to and counseling a person in the midst of a crisis—for that, the family expert is Barbara, a Becker family member not named by Dina as part of her network.

The Duvall-Brennans rarely have the time to provide hands-on care for the children of others in their network. They do, however, have other capacities that amount to major assets to the network. Legal advice, in particular, is something both Maggie and Jack dispense generously. They are also free with advice about how to deal with institutions, and they are willing to intervene authoritatively, if necessary. For example, Jack's brother, Tom, enthusiastically recounts Jack's skills in managing relations with the staff at their mother's nursing home: "Jack's great when it comes time to talk to my mother's caregivers. I say, 'Jack, sic 'em!' He knows all the words. He doesn't get flustered. He just . . . gets results. He's really good." Maggie is unstinting in the emotional support she provides to her mothers' group friends.

SHARED VALUES: CHILD-REARING PHILOSOPHIES

The structure of kinship systems and the degree of proximity play crucial roles in shaping networks, but child-rearing values can trump both. Simply being related, being a good friend, or living nearby is insufficient to qualify a person to become a member of a network of care for children. A shared philosophy of child rearing is indispensable, especially in the context of a church or synagogue, a school, a workplace, or a neighborhood, where parents must establish a firm basis for trusting the care of their children to adults they know only superficially, if at all.[24] Anchors seek to build on a baseline level of trust and to establish consistency among caregivers in the treatment of children. "We don't want people taking care of our kids who would do it very differently from the way we do it," was Byron Russell's summation as a member of the Duvall-Brennan network. I asked Crane associate Lee Ramsey, an astute observer of life around the apartment building she manages, whether she noticed any major differences between mothers and grandmothers in their child-rearing practices. She replied, "That part I haven't seen, because everybody's always yelling the same stuff, so it can't be that different."

Anchors' efforts to determine the trustworthiness of potential network members entail a conscious, deliberate process. When I asked Patricia Crane if she felt comfortable with the way Tracy treats Robbie, she responded, "Oh, yes," and then continued: "That's why only my family and her watches him. Because I've seen how she takes care of her children . . . and that's right in the line of mine. She comes home, they do their homework first, they do their chores, and that's exactly what I have Robbie on—doing his homework, doing his chores, like sweeping." Knowing that she and Tracy and shared similar beliefs and values, such as personal responsibility and the importance of children helping out at home, convinced Patricia that Robbie would be in good hands while in Tracy's care. Commonality of perspective on other topics, such as junk food, also may create a basis for trust. Among the middle-class network members, attitudes toward food registered as a sorting device. With her siblings, Caitlin Becker took for granted shared values about the inappropriateness of giving children junk food: "I don't have to worry when Kent has them—I don't have to tell him what to give them for lunch. He just gives them a reasonable lunch. It doesn't occur to him not to, and we don't have to talk about it."

Which values are shared and emphasized varies by network. Consistent with the social science research on child rearing, values appear to vary by class.[25] The Cranes teach themes of respect for adults, honesty, and hard work, consistent with what Lareau terms "the accomplishment of natural growth."[26] Within this approach to child rearing, children are allowed to play and structure their free time within limits established by their parents; children are encouraged to be rather than to perform. At the upper end, the Aldriches and their friends model behaviors that teach the importance of independent decision making and public service. As Ostrander puts it: "Upper-class children are taught early that they are different from children of other socioeconomic classes. They learn that they have special talents and special responsibilities. Their association with children from other classes is limited, their individual abilities are nurtured, and their social responsibilities are disciplined."[27] Members of both middle-class networks emphasize education and limit children's television viewing. These values are not mutually exclusive, nor are they limited to a single class. Nonetheless, the passion of some members as they talked about certain values indicates their importance and suggests that future research should explore these themes further.

In a network composed of working-class members, one important consequence of the ongoing effort to generate sufficient income while also caring for those less fortunate is that children do not direct family life, as they tend to do in middle-class families. Children like Robbie and Paulie Crane are embedded in the network; they are valued, indeed treasured, but they do not define the family schedule or set the group's priorities. Children in working-class homes tend to grow up in a multigenerational environment where they are encouraged to think up and pursue their own forms of entertainment (such as drawing "when it is quiet" or playing "Ring around the Rosies" with younger and older relatives).

Both middle-class networks stress what Lareau calls "concerted cultivation," an approach to child rearing that emphasizes providing children with scheduled activities and lessons that develop their individual skills and capacities. It creates a frenetic schedule that prioritizes individual children's activities above the needs of the family as a whole. And the desire to cultivate their children intensively creates a structural conflict that these employed parents experience as a personal problem. The Beckers practice a collective version of concerted cultivation. Their family culture stresses the importance of children exploring the world, stretching themselves, and enjoying learning, in the context of the extended family. Michaela, who disagreed with Dina on some issues, nonetheless shares with her a notion that you "should nurture a child and you should talk to them." The Duvall-Brennans concur. Jack and Maggie privilege intensive one-on-one verbal interactions with their youngsters. Describing the Duvall-Brennans, their friend Rebecca noted: "When they're home with their kids, they really want to be with their kids. But we share values about that too."

In the middle-class networks, television, more than anything else, acted as a lightning rod, drawing out differences between people and serving as the basis for including or excluding potential network members. Unsolicited, members of both the Becker and Duvall-Brennan networks identified attitudes about television as a defining child-rearing issue. In contrast, television did not surface as a top-of-mind issue among the Cranes or the Aldriches. Lareau observes that watching TV is often something that working-class families do together, often in a multigenerational environment.[28] Members of both middle-class networks in this study consciously tried to counter the influence of the dominant culture of consumption, deliberately stressing instead healthfulness and a strong educational environment.

As proponents of anticommercialism, the Becker sisters who have children each felt part of a cultural minority in her neighborhood and in her children's schools. The extended family provides important psychological reinforcement for the mothers and children in deflecting the influences of mass culture. Lila Becker reflected on the support her kin bestow: "Dina and Caitlin do raise their children, in many ways, the same way [as I do]. And I feel in some ways we're not like many of the people we know here. Just—our children watch less television, eat less junk food. They're just much less media oriented. We don't do quite as many sports. I mean, they do play some. . . . I think my children are a lot more like their cousins than [they are like] many of their classmates." In Dina's network of care, her siblings and parents reinforce the correctness of her approach and trust each other to make similar decisions in similar situations. Caitlin commented that, as a mother, she had sometimes felt out of step in her own neighborhood: "I definitely felt for a very long time that there was no one you could admit that we didn't watch TV, that our kids didn't watch any TV. Everyone just looks at you and rolls their eyes." The Beckers' familywide commitment to certain values creates a sense of solidarity. At the same time, along with establishing consistency with children, it exerts control over network members who might stray from the family culture.

The shared value of minimal television viewing provides opportunities for bonding between some people and for conflict between others. The Duvall-Brennans feel strongly that children are at risk for health and behavioral problems as a result of their saturation in materialist popular culture. These stalwart values were grounds for their initial bonding with Byron Russell and Rebecca Hoffman, with whom they shared child care when their daughter was little. Rebecca reflected on this connection: "We were about the only ones that I knew at that time who weren't having their kids watch TV. . . . We let [our son] watch videos occasionally, but it's a special treat. It's not part of his daily life." On principle, Maggie Duvall and Jack Brennan do not own a television.

These same values, however, contribute to conflict with kin in Jack and Maggie's case. The Brennan extended family sees Maggie's opposition to television as a form of provocative extremism. Even Jack's brother Tom Brennan, the family member closest to them and a participant in their network, expressed disdain for the "no television" policy. He thinks banning TV at home puts children at a great disadvantage within the dominant culture. Tom also recognizes that Maggie and Jack's policy has evolved in the context of a parenting style very different from his own: "The very glaring, obvious thing is they don't believe in television. And I said, 'Jack, okay, that's fine. There's a lot of crap on TV. But what's wrong with *Sesame Street*?' And he believes in *Sesame Street*, but Maggie doesn't. [The kids have] never seen *Sesame Street*. [*Sesame Street* characters] taught my kids to read! [Laughs.] They taught them their language skills and their math. Things like that. Different ways of raising children, I don't believe in doing." Thus, in the Duvall-Brennan network, values similar to the ones Dina Becker and Mark Walde cherish lead to an opposite outcome with extended kin.

Whether individuals condone or condemn a particular child-rearing value or belief, the conflict usually is about parenting in general. Tom Brennan comments on what he sees as the flaws in Maggie and Jack's parenting philosophy:

> I guess part of my theory is that you can't hide children from something forever. Eventually, they're gonna see television. You know, you can't hide them from the world. This is the world. Maybe TV has violence and junk, but . . . they have friends, and they'll say, "Gee, let's watch *Sesame Street*. It's gonna happen, and I think if they grew up with it, they would maybe deal with it better. This is a beast they've never seen before. They see videos, but not TV. You can't shelter your children from the big bad world forever. Someday it's gonna be there.

Many of the feelings Tom expressed about Maggie and Jack included similarly prickly edges. His tone frequently implied that he believes he will be vindicated in the long run. In the meantime, though, he finds it extremely irritating that his brother and sister-in-law do not share more of his opinions or, more importantly, listen to his advice. As a result, while he remains at the top of the backup list, Maggie and Jack do not call upon him on a more routine basis. Their clash of child-rearing values creates too much conflict.

In the Becker extended clan, conflicts over television do not occur within the network. Instead, they take place across generations, specifically, between mothers-in-law and daughters-in-law. Lila and her mother-in-law, for example, disagree over the best approach to television: "At some point I said something about too much television, and she said, 'Yes, but too little television is bad too.' It was hard for me to seriously think about something that's too little television, which isn't that my children never watch because one of the reasons is that I don't want them to feel there's something wonderful out there that they've missed. And, but part of it is that we don't have time for it." When her children go to stay at their paternal grandmother's home, "they get plenty of television during that week to make up for all the television I don't show them the rest of the year. [Laughs.]"

Lila's fate was foreshadowed by her own mother's experiences. Susan Becker felt undermined by her mother-in-law, who lived nearby but who was *not* part of her network. Susan recalled, "We disagreed on most child-care issues." Worse, her mother-in-law deliberately subverted the family rules: "My mother-in-law would wait till I was out of the house" and then "do what she pleased," using television as a tool to provoke Susan. Kent remembered his grandmother trying to tempt him and his brother to watch television on the occasions when she was the care provider. "She'd actually encourage us. 'Don't you want to? Come on. Come on. Your mom says no.'" Grandmothers are known to take pleasure and pride in indulging their grandchildren, but in this case, the grandmother seems not so much to have been trying to give her grandchildren treats as she was trying to antagonize her daughter-in-law. The disagreement over television evident in the Duvall-Brennan network and in the Becker extended family may reflect a shift over time in societal perceptions of the educational and entertainment value of TV, particularly as the number of hours children watch television goes up; the conflict may, as well, reveal family tensions occasioned by upward mobility. Research shows that low-income children watch 50 percent more television than their middle-class counterparts.[29] With television as an example, it is easy to see the conflict that emerges when a family member adopts an opinion counter to the dominant culture, or at least the dominant family culture. The rebel's opinion is contested in the realm of the family, as family settings act as the battlefields for social change.

Juxtaposing the experiences of the Beckers and Duvall-Brennans in selecting network members highlights the importance of child-rearing philosophy in the context of kinship. Kin can be actively marginalized in the care of children. Here, the daughters-in-law operate their networks independently of their mothers-in-law. Although they allow contact between the children and their grandparents, they do not include their mothers-in-law in their networks. This exclusionary practice is strongest among the Duvall-Brennans. Only with respect to Tom Brennan does kinship trump child-rearing values. Despite the cumulative resentment and the many disagreements, Tom cares deeply about his brother and his niece and nephew. He wants to be involved in their lives and he values kinship in spite of his disapproval of the way the children are being raised. He makes himself available and continues to be a network member, although his participation is not without discontent and hard feelings.

Exclusion from Networks

The forces of exclusion are as powerful as those of inclusion: *Not* sharing the anchor's child-rearing philosophy is grounds for exclusion from the network. Although most people within each network share a class position, this does not necessarily mean they agree upon an approach to rearing children. Disagreements about child rearing can create dissonance within marriages and interrupt networks of interdependence. While no one can choose the family they are born into, adults exercise agency in determining with whom they stay in touch and associate. In building networks, parents and guardians act as gatekeepers, strategically selecting some people and consciously excluding others.[30] Michaela Becker made the point that having a strong, select group necessarily means excluding some people: "The other side of the strong family . . . is that it's not completely open to . . . people from the outside. Which seems contradictory to me. Like, there's such a strong sense of . . . family comes first and all of that. And that we all have that so strongly etched into our skin that you know, it would be fine to . . . be more inclusive or whatever. But that's not always the case." The inclusion process, Michaela acknowledged, has an exclusionary dimension: "I think the people that are most readily accepted into our family are people who are not intimidated by ten very vocal, very . . . articulate and strong-willed, [strong-]minded people." Lila Becker considers what this bounded sense of a group has meant for people joining family—currently, marriage and birth are the only ways into the Becker network: "We're probably a pretty formidable group to marry into, . . . a heck of a lot of strong women."

Anchors may exclude people from their networks on the basis of the individuals' personal characteristics, avoiding those they judge incompetent or likely to provide negative role models for their children (e.g., drug abusers or thoroughly self-absorbed individuals) and those with whom they feel no affinity. These purposeful exclusions further narrow the universe of potential network members. Finally, some potential members exclude themselves, either because they have existing commitments to other people and activities or because they consciously opt out of taking on the responsibilities involved in network participation.

Although the discussion here emphasizes the active, conscious character of network building, there is an equally important but more subtle element underlying the decisions anchors make. Across all the networks of care, less conscious, more class-bound factors are at play as the anchors screen potential network members. When they set up thresholds of behavior that others must meet and specify adherence to a particular child-rearing philosophy, the anchors use criteria wrought by their social and economic resources. Upper-class parents like Sarah Aldrich effectively control the people with whom their children have contact by virtue of other decisions they are able to make, thanks to their class location. These include living in exclusive neighborhoods; sending the children to private schools; carefully selecting their after-school activities; and meticulously screening the hired household help. The working-class parents like Patricia Crane observe the way neighbors speak to their children and how they treat them. Patricia notices the value they place on discipline, on education, on responsibility—those qualities she believes to be of the utmost importance in her son's life.

ANCHOR-INITIATED EXCLUSION

AFFINITY. Anchors select people on the basis of their feelings of affinity for the network candidate. Dina Becker did not include her husband, Mark's, family in her network of care because she was uncomfortable with her in-laws' interactive style. Describing the Waldes, Dina said: "They don't hug each other hello or goodbye much. They never say they love each other. Some of them aren't speaking to each other. Like Mark's brother did not speak to his father before he died, and he rarely spoke to Mark's mother, his mother, as well. Now that his father has died, he's speaking to his mother a lot; . . . it's not that they're not nice people. They're just—they're not the same kind of people." Because Mark's family members are "not the same kind of people," Dina excludes them from her network of care.

Sarah Aldrich approaches the problem of affinity differently. She sets high standards for her close friends and for those she hires to help her run the household. She expects members to establish a personal connection with the children and the adults, and to bring expert managerial skills to the network. In emphasizing the importance of screening for "quality people," Sarah expresses the same concerns as Patricia Crane. Sarah, however, must conduct her screening without the benefit of the kind of intimate information that can be acquired from living on the other side of a thin apartment wall from a potential candidate. For inspiration, she recalls the example set by her grandmother: "My experience with my own childhood was that the caregivers weren't really good that my mom found for us. The woman at my grandmother's house was terrific. So that's a part of . . . what drives me." Sarah looks for caregivers who are capable, responsible, dependable, organized, high energy, and, importantly, fun. She applies considerable resources to her quest to retain someone with abundant energy and cultural capital. Across the country, millions of other families also contract out child care and also face the question of quality care. For many, the issue of expense looms large and may push quality beyond reach. Relying on the market to find a highly skilled babysitter gives

Sarah both the power and the authority to fire a person she finds unsatisfactory. Patricia Crane "fires" a person by excluding him or her from the network, an action that effectively removes Robbie from that individual's care.

Sometimes the lack of affinity between an anchor and a potential network member is tied to differences in the way people approach and interact with children. In an extreme case that goes well beyond disagreements over child-rearing style, Patricia excludes her neighbor Luella because she has seen how this woman treats her own children and hears the children's cries at night through the thin bedroom walls. "I don't trust her with my son," Patricia stated firmly. "No, no, no, no. Just the ways she talks to her children, I don't like it." She attributed her neighbor's behavior to mental illness, something beyond Luella's control except when moderated by the effects of medication.

INCOMPETENCE. Occasionally, anchors judge potential network members as incompetent to meet the responsibilities that inevitably accompany caregiving. Fran Crane, in talking about her half-sister's inability to care for their mother, asserted, "Sherry don't know *how* to take care of her." Fran explained Sherry's incapacity as arising from her position as the youngest and therefore least responsible sibling in the family. According to Fran, Sherry is "spoiled," that is, she has never had to pull her own weight in the family: "Sherry never had to cook a meal, and not do nothing. She don't even clean her house. Her husband does. Oh, she does a little bit of housework, but she'll go out in the yard and work. They've got a beautiful home; you'll see it. But she's just been spoiled. . . . I was sixteen when she was born. So she had us older kids, you know? And she was just spoiled. . . . She didn't do nothing, no. She didn't have to. Mother didn't make her do nothing, you know? . . . whatever Sherry wanted, she got. [Laughs.]" In Fran's mind, this form of upbringing left her half-sister ill-prepared to meet the challenge currently at hand and not a good candidate for pitching in with Robbie.

Patricia Crane and Tracy Johnson also consciously excluded individuals with personal characteristics they viewed as dysfunctional, or at least inappropriate for networks involving the care of children. During my first interview with Patricia, Tracy's mother knocked at the door. Patricia shooed her away, saying she had company. Then, in a hushed voice, she told me that Tracy's mother was a heroin addict. She and Tracy tried to keep her away from their children. "We don't use her," Patricia said. Tracy also deliberately keeps her children out of contact with one of her brothers. "I have another brother here; I'm not close to him. Actually, I can't even stand him. Neither can my other brothers, but he's my dad's son. I can't say that's the reason, because my little sister is my dad's daughter. But that doesn't mean a thing to me. I just can't stand him." When I asked if she would ever ask him to take care of her children or help out in any way, she said: "No. Actually, he's greedy. He can eat two steaks, two pork chops, a skillet of potatoes, four eggs, and bread. [Laughs.] And my children could stand there and watch him, and he would never offer them anything. Really, he's greedy." Not only does she dislike this sibling's personality, she also judges him so self-centered as to be incapable of responsibly caring for her children.

NEGATIVE ROLE MODELS. Ryan Becker articulated a dilemma that faced the Becker network regarding his brother Kent's current girlfriend. Because of the importance of kinship to the Beckers, and because of Kent's centrality to the network, the possibility of a long-term relationship with a woman that family members do not like presents a problem for the entire family, not just for Dina. The tension between meddling and giving Kent autonomy in his private decisions was palpable. Ryan opted for meddling: "And to be honest, my brother's dating a woman right now that the rest of my family really doesn't like at all. And I think he's gotta break up with her. It's a disaster. But one of the things I told him is, 'What if Dina is not that excited about having her children hang out at your house with your wife?' I mean, to me that possibility is so frightening that that would be a reason to stop dating somebody."

In effect, Ryan is contemplating both Dina's right to exclude a potential family member she does not trust with the care of her children and the wide-ranging effects such a decision could have on the network as a whole. Ryan knows that the depth of Kent's commitment to the family and his brother's sense of entitlement to their nieces and nephews is so resolute that the argument he put to Kent is likely to be persuasive. At the same time, Ryan himself feels so strongly about the importance of family cohesion and network participation that he cannot imagine entertaining the possibility of a serious romantic involvement with someone his family does not like. Again the family culture operates to dominate and sometimes change individual inclinations that might threaten the group.

SELF-EXCLUSION: OPTING OUT OF NETWORK INVOLVEMENT
Some of the network members I interviewed discussed the power of refusing to give or refusing to receive, both of which fundamentally interrupt network operations and undermine expectations about the likelihood of reciprocity.[31] Undeniably, network participation can be a nuisance. With high commitment comes high involvement, and not everyone finds that desirable or possible. Proximity, and the network involvement it promotes, has its drawbacks. The obligations of involvement can result in an unwanted trade-off with privacy

and autonomy. Kent Becker articulates ways in which being embedded in a cohesive family culture with a highly operational network can be intrusive: "At times it's meddlesome, you know, [laughs] when they constantly call and, 'What are you doing today?' You know, 'What are you up to? What's going on?' I'm like, God [laughs], you know, I'm thirty-two years old, I'm a grownup, you know?" Some potential members purposely exempt themselves from network responsibilities. Kent's sister Michaela, for instance, has deliberately drawn boundaries around her life, creating a zone of privacy, however small, from her kin. "I'm just a little bit more out of the loop than, say, my brothers," she tells me. "I don't show up [at the senior Beckers' house] . . . on a weekly basis, like some people do." Nonetheless, Michaela struggles with ambivalence about her interdependent relationships:

> My dad, you know, helps manage this building. . . . So I see him all the time. Sometimes that's a good thing, and sometimes it's not. Because he'll say, like, "I called you three hours ago. And you haven't gotten back to me. What could you possibly be doing?" He'll leave messages like, "It's eight o'clock at night. Where are you?" You know? . . . I'm thirty-one! I have friends! I have a life! [Laughs.] I'm not necessarily gonna be home every single night. . . . I would never want to live too far away. But, you know, Kent and Ryan are much more [accessible]—and Dina, too, you know. Everyone is, . . . and I try to have a little bit more distance. Because for me, it helps create a balance.

As if to prove her point, when I interviewed her sister Shannon, she relayed a phone conversation with Michaela from earlier that morning. "Right before I came, I called Michaela on the phone; . . . she started saying, 'Oh, you're so lucky I was already awake.' I said, 'Get up! It's almost Christmas! What are you doing?' And so . . . at any given moment, it could cross your mind: 'Gee, I wish that someone didn't wake me up at seven!'" If such a thought fluttered across Shannon's mind, she would never act on it. She knows what she will do when a family member calls. Michaela, however, was the one who said, "You're so lucky I was already awake." She is less willing to have her autonomy hedged and is certainly most upfront about her ambivalence. When I asked Michaela about whether or not her father, the famous price shopper, shopped for her, the question triggered a strong reaction:

> Oh, no! See, that's the kind of stuff where I'm like, "No!" Because if my dad is grocery shopping for me, that's like, way too much information for him. Or my brother used to do laundry at my parents' house, and I'm like, I can't do it. Even though it would be easier and cheap

for me, because now I have to go down to the laundry mat; it's just too much. But I will call my parents, you know, for the littler things. Like if we're going somewhere, I'll call up and say, "Can someone bring me some food?" So someone will make a little lunch for me and bring it or whatever it is. I can't do the laundry thing. To me, that's like, okay, well, you're thirty. You really should be buying your own groceries! Even if it is so much easier to have your dad do it. Like, there are certain things I need to be able to do by myself.

Marking her independence is important, but on a scale of involvements, one could interpret Michaela as very embedded still, deeply interdependent. But for her own sense of self-worth and sanity, she must draw a line. She reserves her right to opt out.

And even among committed network participants, I found that anchors and others periodically opted out of caregiving situations—including those involving their siblings, their nieces and nephews, their friends, or their elderly parents and grandparents. It is impossible to respond to all demands for attention and help. Some individuals, though, try to avoid being drawn into any network of interdependence, citing the demands of employment, or meeting tentative requests for help with silence or withdrawal, or keeping themselves unavailable for recruitment. For example, Sarah Aldrich's friend Kate Farnsworth idealizes network involvement, but purposely excludes herself. The responsibilities of being a part of a network, even a relatively well-defined exchange like a carpool, add more to the complexity of her everyday life than she wants to handle. "I hate carpools," she confessed. "I don't want to deal with other people's kids. One family is enough for me. You know? It's just, I don't want the logistics." She made one exception, for a boy in her son's class whom she loves. But even in that case, "I had kept [the carpooling arrangements] really simple," she said, "because I just don't want more input. I don't want more logistics." Kate deliberately organizes her child rearing in ways that reduce her reliance on and entanglements with other people. As a result, her network participation is minimal—especially in comparison to any one of the Beckers, for example. In that network, it would be impossible for a member *not* to be involved in the logistics of other people's lives. Deciding whether to be involved, how deeply to be involved, and how much information to exchange in the logistical relays are ongoing issues of network participation.

Other kinds of opting out may or may not be intentional, but nonetheless have consequences for anchors. Several subjects with children mentioned their disappointment that their siblings or parents did not take an active role in the lives of their children. Lila Becker's mother-in-law, for instance, developed an aversion to Becker-dominated events and now refuses to attend any event that includes members of Lila's extended family. Occasionally, network members comment on a specific individual's failure to fulfill an idealized kinship role. Maggie Duvall was not alone when she said, "I love [my mother] dearly, but she's not a grandmother." Maggie has a conception of what grandmothers should do, and her own mother falls painfully short. At another point, she observed: "Both my parents are rather distant grandparents, unfortunately for my children. They are not into children, and they are not into really being a part of their lives, which is too bad." A member of the Duvall-Brennan network, Byron Russell, talked in a similar way about his brother, who lives a thirty-minute drive away: "He's not really inclined. I'd like him to spend more time with the kids, but we don't want to push it." The implication is that thrusting children on a reluctant caretaker would be a mistake. And ignoring kinship status remains a means of opting out.

Conclusion

The staging of networks requires careful screening, managing, and ongoing decision making. Anchors purposely review the potential network candidates, assessing the convenience and appropriateness of their involvement. Can they be trusted? Do they share a perspective on child rearing? Does the child feel comfortable with them? All these issues have to be evaluated in the context of the needs of the anchor and the relationship of him or her to the network member. Understanding the intricacies of interpersonal dynamics within the network will subsequently assist in analyzing the meanings of reciprocity— how it is enacted and can be selectively invoked. Through the process of staging networks, anchors winnow out reluctant or inappropriate participants. Indeed, potential members also exclude themselves.

Class contingencies influence the choices parents can make in rearing their children; they shape the contours of the networks parents call upon to help them. As the examples provided in this chapter illustrate, I found a great deal of difference in the *kinds* of expertise individual network members brought to bear on the project of rearing children and in the ways they were valued. Those differences are fundamentally affected by the contingencies of class location. Networks take shape in a culture of expectations about what families should do, participants' realizations about what their specific families can do, and anchors' understandings of the needs of their children in the context of their own work situations.[32] As such, networks not only help working parents, they play a role in reproducing class in the lives of children.

Chapter 7   # The Tangle of Reciprocity

On the evening I arrive to interview Maggie Duvall, her son Scott, three and a half, peers out from behind her legs. Jack Brennan has just taken their six-year-old daughter, Danielle, upstairs to read a story. Minutes earlier, Scott had vomited all over the living room and he is registering a high fever. In a state of despair and determination, Maggie tells me of the impending crisis: Children with fevers cannot go to the child-care center, and both she and Jack have nonnegotiable court appearances the next day. When I arrive, they are feeling the panic of irreconcilably competing obligations.[1] Because Maggie has worked at her job for so short a time, she feels she cannot ask for any favors. And Jack, although he has seniority and administrative authority and typically is the parent who can cover emergencies, feels he has no choice in his work obligation the next day.

Whom can they call? Their initial impulse is to call Jack's brother, Tom, and his partner, Teresa (see Table 4.1). Although they have some flexibility in their schedules, they cannot easily make themselves available on a moment's notice. Jack and Maggie feel reluctant to ask such a big favor, one that would require someone to miss work. Jack's sister lives thousands of miles away, so she is of no use today. Maggie's two close friends from the mother's group work full time and have houses full of children. The couple's former neighbor, Ruth Bergman, is in the midst of chemotherapy treatment, so it seems unfair to approach her. And Byron Russell and Rebecca Hoffman, who have work flexibility, are no longer swimming in the daily stream of Jack's and Maggie's lives. To ask them would feel like a huge, inappropriate imposition.

The Duvall-Brennans have staged a sizable network of care, in fact, a long list of people upon whom they rely for things, including help with child rearing.

155

And they believe in the value of networks and community. The centerpiece of their child care is institutional, which provides stability but lacks the flexibility to care for a sick child. And, because of their jobs as attorneys, neither Jack nor Maggie has the capacity to reciprocate in the day-to-day lives of others or the time to cultivate helping relationships. They cannot effectively stage and mobilize networks that could care *for* their children. Instead, as discussed in Chapter 4, the Duvall-Brennan network is filled with people who care *about* Jack, Maggie, and their children, but whose capacity to give practical help is almost nil. In this situation, with a sick child, immovable work demands, and no one to call, Maggie and Jack are in trouble. Jack says, "We feel like . . . we're totally on our own." They pay for what they can and do the rest themselves, even if this means overwork, fatigue, anxiety, and occasional despair.

Maggie and Jack decide to call the only service that exists in the Bay Area for emergency child care. The service charges fifteen dollars per hour (four dollars more per hour than the rate they usually pay and about 70 percent above the area standard) and offers to provide child care "in a pinch."[2] When they call the agency, they discover that, for the privilege of paying fifteen dollars an hour to have someone they do not know take care of their son, they first need to remit a $250 joining fee. They hang up, but later in the evening call back in a panic, out of options. The office calls them back a short time later, unable to identify a single person who can work the next day. So even with their willingness to pay four hundred dollars for the care of their sick son the next day, Maggie and Jack do not have a solution.

Maggie loses the toss of the coin that determines who will stay home with Scott. Desperate, she contemplates approaching a stay-at-home mom down the street, whom she has not met formally, to watch Scott for an hour so she could at least be in a conference call with the court. The next morning, after a fitful night for the Duvall-Brennans, a woman arrives to clean their house. It was then that Maggie found a way out of her dilemma. This woman agreed to watch Scott for a few hours. In the end, the market saved Maggie, however partially.

The situation of the Duvall-Brennans needs to be analyzed with an eye to the co-anchors' reliance on a market-based model of reciprocity. Reciprocity does not occur naturally, inevitably, or without effort. It rarely evolves spontaneously with biological or socially recognized kin or even members of a network of care. Anchors' resources—including people, time, and money—profoundly shape how and when working parents can create reciprocal relationships to help them rear their children.

Within sociology, the concept of reciprocity generally refers to mutual giving and receiving.[3] In multivariate studies, it is operationalized as giving support and receiving support, but commonly the two are not directly linked.[4] Although researchers disagree about how reciprocity operates and how best to frame it theoretically, they widely agree that reciprocity functions to knit together human beings, creating different degrees of interdependence.[5] Through a tangle of reciprocity, people mobilize networks of care.

This chapter analyzes how anchors set in motion the networks they have developed. As the Duvall-Brennan case vividly illustrates, network members' capacities to reciprocate are predicated on the structure of their employment, the kinship systems of which they are a part, and the social networks they construct. Anchors tap people to become part of their network, which changes over time as children's needs change and adult relationships ebb and flow. This chapter explores the second and third phases of staging networks: linking subjects through reciprocal relations, and mobilizing the obligation that is part of network participation. It analyzes how members perceive and interpret the commonsense understandings of the give-and-take dynamic. Network members evaluate situations and assess each other's commitments, "needs," intentions, reliability, and capacities in light of their own. Through this process of perception, valuation, and interpretation, they negotiate reciprocity.

After reviewing the sociological literature on reciprocity, this chapter compares the Duvall-Brennan's tenuous staging of market-based reciprocity to the vibrant, balanced reciprocity in the Becker network. Comparing the two middle-class networks reveals some critical ingredients in the processes involved in staging networks and negotiating reciprocity. The chapter then turns to the socially constructed dimensions of reciprocity evident in all four networks: evaluating need, constructing balance, and assessing the value of that which is traded in network relationships.

Conceptualizing Reciprocity

Anthropologist Marshall Sahlins, building on the work of Malinowski and others, developed one of the major frameworks currently used to analyze reciprocity. Since the publication of his study of kinship-based societies, his typology that distinguishes between several types of reciprocity has found conceptual resonance across the disciplines. According to Sahlins, reciprocity can only be understood as a continuum, because there are an infinite number of degrees between categories, each difficult to distinguish precisely from another. At one end of the continuum, with *generalized reciprocity*, which typically occurs among kin and household members, there is little expectation of immediate return or return in kind.[6] Sahlins likens generalized reciprocity to a pure

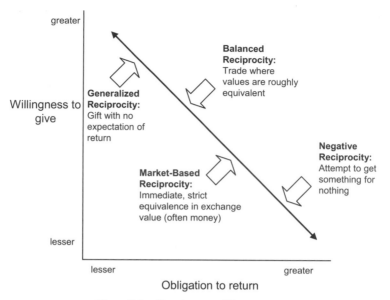

Figure 7-1. Continuum of Reciprocity

gift, if such a thing exists. Traversing the center, *balanced reciprocity* mandates a trade where value is judged as roughly equivalent. Balanced reciprocity marks a "willingness to give for that which is received," but on a more measured basis, with people outside the household (220). According to Sahlins, balanced reciprocal relations cannot "tolerate one way flows" of goods and services; there must be evidence of return over time (195). Balance in reciprocity takes on colloquial meaning in addition to being useful as an analytic concept. To members of these networks, balance implies evenness in give-and-take over the long run. And at the opposite end of the continuum, Sahlins posits the concept of *negative reciprocity*, which is "the attempt to get something for nothing with impunity" (195). The concept of "negative" reciprocity implies a norm of retaliation and a return of injuries.[7]

In this continuum, I fold in *market-based reciprocity* between balanced and negative reciprocity, an important distinction to make for networks operating in a market economy (see figure 7.1). Market-based reciprocity requires immediate, strict equivalence in exchange value. Most commonly, money is exchanged for labor, a service, or a good. The calculation of value is mediated by social convention and sometimes by law. As with other types of reciprocity, market-based exchange shades into other gradations of reciprocity.

Sahlins's conceptual framing continues to be used in research on reciprocity in the United States, although the analysis of how and where each kind

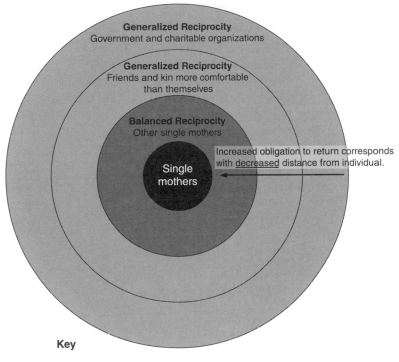

Generalized Reciprocity
Government and charitable organizations

Generalized Reciprocity
Friends and kin more comfortable
than themselves

Balanced Reciprocity
Other single mothers

Single
mothers

Increased obligation to return corresponds
with decreased distance from individual.

Key

Bold Text = Type of reciprocity
Regular Text = Relationship to mothers

Darker circles correspond to relationships
with a higher obligation to return.

Figure 7-2. Reciprocity Relationships in Nelson's Single-Mother Community

of reciprocity works necessarily changes, depending on the cultural and eco-nomic context. Nelson's recent study of single mothers in Vermont, "Single Mothers and Social Support," makes for an interesting point of interpretive comparison because it throws into relief the ways that degrees of social dis-tance and kinship can vary across culture. Nelson analyzed single mothers' reciprocity within three relational contexts, which might be envisioned as con-centric circles (see figure 7.2). The innermost circle consisted of those with similar needs—other single mothers. Among this core, Nelson found balanced reciprocity (in contrast to the generalized reciprocity specified by Sahlins). In the next concentric circle, composed of those kin and friends "more com-fortable" economically than themselves, the single mothers engaged in rela-tions of generalized reciprocity. That is, they were largely the beneficiaries of

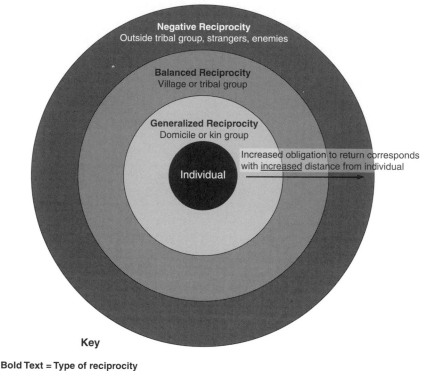

Negative Reciprocity
Outside tribal group, strangers, enemies

Balanced Reciprocity
Village or tribal group

Generalized Reciprocity
Domicile or kin group

Individual

Increased obligation to return corresponds with <u>increased</u> distance from individual

Key

Bold Text = Type of reciprocity
Regular Text = Relationship to individual

Darker circles correspond to relationships
with a higher obligation to return.

Figure 7-3. Reciprocity Relationships in Sahlins's Kin-Based Societies

others' generosity. The mothers saw their benefactors as more fortunate than themselves. From the mothers' perspective, because others could afford to give and because they enjoyed the satisfactions of giving and forging relationships with the children being supported, the mothers did not need to pay back their benefactors in kind. In fact, they could pay back with gratitude. The outer circle consists of institutions and individuals, outside of kin or friends, who give altruistically with no expectation of return. This contrasts dramatically with Sahlins, who found negative reciprocity in the outer circle consisting of strangers outside the tribal group (see figure 7.3).

A key point emerges from a comparison of these two frameworks, which were derived thirty years apart and based on different cultures. The particular cultural and historical context defines what kind of reciprocity can be expected and from whom, and shapes what kind of reciprocity is practiced. Communities privilege different social relationships and expectations of kin. A hierarchy exists in each case, but which relationships fall where within the hierarchy varies by culture and historical moment. Sahlins found that kinship and household relations were privileged, whereas Nelson found that the single mothers organized their reciprocal relations on the basis of a shared condition of circumstance and need; their inner circle consisted of other single mothers. This comparison highlights the usefulness of the multiple conceptions of reciprocity, especially when decoupled from degrees of human intimacy. However, it also points to the shifting expectations of kin and community that unfold with the emergence of a capitalist economy and a welfare state.

The nature of reciprocity has been the subject of ongoing debate. Social exchange theory, the dominant approach to networks and reciprocity in sociology, primarily analyzes exchange dynamics from a utilitarian perspective.[8] Research explores what, how many, how often, and under what conditions things or favors are exchanged. Within a utilitarian framework, rational actors seek to gain from an exchange. As George Homans put it: "Not only does [a person] seek a maximum for himself, but he tries to see to it that no one in his group makes more profit than he does."[9] The economic model assumes scarcity of resources and zero-sum outcomes.[10] Many efforts to capture the concept of reciprocity have similarly relied on metaphors related to commerce and the market, including the notion of debt, a "savings account" of moral capital, or "revolving credit." The very concept of exchange, as Nancy Hartsock points out, is fundamentally based on market logic. She rejects the market as a model for social relationships because it fails to capture human meaning and sociability. However, Hartsock does not reject the idea that rationality or instrumentalism inhere in reciprocal relations.[11]

The question arises: How do these assumptions of bald calculation and self-serving behavior apply in the context of a family raising children?[12] Alvin Gouldner's now classic article, "The Norm of Reciprocity," offers an alternative to the exchange theory approach. He posits reciprocity as a norm that incurs obligation rather than a system of exchange that is profit maximizing and economic in calculation.[13] As a norm, the concept of obligation captures bonds that transcend a transaction, that are rooted in cultural precepts about rights and responsibilities, and that reflect expectations for what constitutes a decent human relationship.

Relations within a network of care for children operate via a culturally specific logic of reciprocity,[14] which is premised on trust, obligation, and mutuality and shaped by historical moment and structural location. A sense of obligation motivates reciprocity, particularly in kin-based networks and friendship networks committed to mutual care.[15] As discussed in Chapter 1, in dominant

U.S. culture, the ideology of independence obscures the practices of dependence and the importance of interdependence, which recent feminist perspectives hold as fundamental to a caring society.[16] Uehara argues that a desire to be independent is not necessarily a rejection of reciprocity. "The individual's desire to be independent or self-sufficient may well explain reluctance to receive assistance in the first place. However, it does not, per se, explain the feeling of compulsion to reciprocate benefit—nor the experiences of greater 'life satisfaction,' 'positive affect,' or 'well-being'" that people report when involved in reciprocal relations.[17]

Because these networks center on children, I argue, reciprocity operates more compellingly than it might otherwise. A child is a person with whom to have a relationship, as well as someone who needs adult attention and supervision.[18] And while the child is symbolically the heart of the network, the absolute center is the anchor—the caretaker, in these cases, the parent. As the symbolic heart, the child can be the invaluable gift that an anchor gives back to network members. However, it is possible for the network member to have a minimal relationship with the child and primarily support the anchor from a distance. Because network members serve at the pleasure of the anchor, if they are too contentious or unreliable, they are out. While the child has some influence in this process, as discussed in the last chapter, the child does not necessarily have the power to exclude someone. The adult relations are key, because if their relationships with the anchor are not copacetic, the network fails to work.

People's perceptions of that relationship and their structural and personal ties shape their calculations of obligation and their sense of reward. People determine the value of what is given according to their own set of needs, assets, and perceptions. That which is given and taken in reciprocal actions is not self-evident or easily measured. Sociologically, it is not just what people count that is interesting, but *how* they count it.

AVERTING A CRISIS: BALANCED RECIPROCITY IN THE CONTEXT OF KIN

The crisis in the Duvall-Brennan network could find no parallel in the Becker family. Simply put, among the Beckers, a sick child would not provoke a crisis. An illness might become an inconvenience, but Dina Becker has an adaptable repertory of people upon whom she can call when she needs help.[19] Dina's network members live conveniently nearby, many of them have flexible work schedules, and all of them want to be involved in the lives of her children. In exchange, Dina is on call for them. When her father cannot pick up her mother at work, she drives over. She shares her photography equipment and gives artistic advice to her sisters. She photographs friends of the family for free.

Reciprocity operates expansively in the Becker network. Dina's sister Shannon Becker explains the family ethos: "We were told when we were little, 'People do favors for you, and you can never repay them in any direct way. And the only way to repay that is to pass the favor on to someone else.'" Reciprocity is not limited to quid pro quo exchange, nor does it benefit only people in the network. The Beckers pass along goodwill and favors. Kent Becker explains:

> We do it . . . for people who aren't family as well, you know, neighbors and friends know that they can always call, and someone in the family will be there. [Laughs] . . . If someone calls and says, you know, "Kent, can you do me a favor?" You know, "Take me to the airport Thursday," and I'm like, "Oh, I'm working Thursday," but I know that Ryan's free or someone else is free. I'll go, "Yeah, yeah, I can do it." You know? And then I'll call them back later after it's kind of been set, and I'll say, "Oh, by the way, you know, I realized I can't do it, but Ryan's more than willing to."

When I asked if Ryan minded when Kent called on him to do a favor for somebody else, Kent said, "No. God, no."

Because of the kind of network the Beckers have developed, Dina's gaps in care do not turn into crises. Importantly, her work is more flexible than either Maggie Duvall's or Jack Brennan's, although she still faces certain imperatives: a wedding photographer cannot miss a person's wedding. The clamber to work and to accommodate children's needs and schedules makes for a flurry of activity, but not a crisis.

Dina's sister Shannon describes an example of the multiplicity of elements traded in the network. She reports on the events unfolding the morning of her interview with me:

> Because my parents live so close by, I dropped by there to drop off a . . . photo dryer, which I borrowed last night because my younger sister helped me yesterday in the photo lab—and I had to take the pictures home and dry them. . . . I had to drop off a bag of clothes. . . . [My niece has] grown out of some stuff, and my parents' former cleaning lady is now a friend; . . . I had been to Caitlin's last week, so dropped off a bag of clothes for Suzanne, and then while I was there, I called Michaela . . . and she said, "Where are you going on your Christmas errands? . . . I need you to go to [the department store] and see how long it takes to engrave things." And I'm like, "But you can call [the department store]." She goes, "Oh, you know, but you're good at this." So, like, the point is that, like—Barbara is helping me with

> my photography, . . . I'm dropping off something for Caitlin, and
> Michaela's calling me to, like, "Can you go downtown for me?" . . .
> And . . . that was, like, the fifteen minutes before I came here.

The operational reciprocity in the Becker network is balanced. It tilts farther toward the generalized end of the continuum than does the Duvall-Brennan network. It is not tit for tat, nor is it restricted to kin, although they are privileged in the system. Middle-class competencies and money to finance higher education shape the talents and resources its members bring to it—knowledge about science, children's literature, medical conditions, photography; highly developed interpersonal skills; and a host of other things. The Beckers have a critical mass of connected, resourceful people, and an active kin network ready and willing to be kin-scripted.

Reciprocity operates within structural constraints and opportunities, most obviously those of employment and kinship. Both the Becker and Duvall-Brennan households have more economic resources than do the majority of U.S. households, yet each can be characterized as anxious about its economic status. The Duvall-Brennans are driven more by professional career demands, the Beckers by the effort to maintain a foothold in the middle class. Work drives them, compels them, motivates them. For the Duvall-Brennans, it is not just employment per se, but the structure of that employment and their commute that diminishes their capacity to reciprocate.[20] Typical of middle-class professionals, they are trapped in a time bind. Because both work in careers that demand so much of their time, like other dual-earner professional couples, they feel stressed by the miniscule number of hours available to attend to family and community needs.[21]

Employment is not the only larger structure that facilitates or impedes people's capacities to care for their children and to reciprocate in a network. All of these network accounts reveal that successful staging is predicated on kinship systems as well.[22] To be effective with practical care, kin need to be geographically close and able to contribute.[23] To provide effective guidance and emotional support, kin need to share values, have the personal aptitude to advise, and feel the impulse or the obligation to give. In the context of employment and kinship structures, in order to stage viable networks to help with care for school-age children, one must engage others in reciprocal relations.

The Process of Negotiating Reciprocity

To initiate the process of reciprocal trades, network members assess and interpret their own situation and that of others, and negotiate what is possible given the circumstances. Reciprocity in the context of rearing children is built on mutuality, trust, and a sense of responsibility and obligation endemic to active kinship. Participation in a network of care for children entails obligation. It may be inconvenient, unpleasant, or unsatisfying, but it is part of the reciprocity covenant, a commitment that has power above and beyond an individual, even though it is individually negotiated. As Gouldner puts it: "The *norm* of reciprocity holds that people should help those who help them, and therefore, those whom you have helped have an obligation to you. The conclusion is clear: if you want to be helped by others you must help them."[24] Network members feel obliged to repay someone who has given them help. One way to recruit someone into helping is to help them first.

Gouldner makes the critical distinction between reciprocity and kinship obligation. If a person is prompted to help because it is incumbent upon them as a kin member, the action can be analytically distinguished from someone hooked into a system by the act of doing a favor. Thus, Gouldner emphasizes that reciprocity creates a *normative* imperative, which is different from a kin obligation.[25] And one of the things I have argued is that kin obligation does not unfold by virtue of blood ties. Like the norm of reciprocity, kin ties have to be activated to be meaningful. A genealogical relationship is worthless to a mother who needs help with her child and finds her own mother estranged from her. Kin relations are socially constructed, as are friendships. However, once activated and socially recognized, kinship comes with a clearer set of agreed-upon rules of behavior and obligation. I am interested in both kinds of obligation, whichever processes link households and prompt someone to care for a nonbiological child.

KIN OBLIGATION

In the realm of kin obligation, Michaela Becker offers a good example of the strength of the coercion to act as a kin member. She reports that she "has to" attend some family events. Her kinship relations create expectations of her that she respects and that are reciprocal, but about which she feels ambivalent: "There's a big trade-off in our family. It's hugely comforting and helpful; . . . I call my siblings up all the time, call my parents up all the time, and I say, 'What do you think about this? I need help with that. . . . Blah blah blah.' And they are always there. . . . But the other half of that is that, you know, you do *have to be there;* . . . when I was younger, it was very pressured for me [emphasis added]." In struggling to do the right thing, but up against her desire for independence, Michaela Becker delineates the obligatory parts of her involvement in the network: "I'm responsible to help out *when it's required of me*, so that, like, if they do call or someone does need me, or the dog needs to be fed or, you know, the kids need to be washed or transported or whatever it is, then I definitely feel like that's . . . a role I need to take on [emphasis added]." In effect, she says, "You do what is necessary to help out" as a member of a socially recognized kin group. Determining what is necessary unfolds as part of an ongoing process. The kinship role is something she recognizes as important.

The nagging pull of obligation tugged at Fran Crane once the family realized her mother had Alzheimer's disease and could not be left alone: "Well, I didn't volunteer. . . . And I've always known that when it came to anyone having to take care of Mother, it would have to be [me]. . . . I didn't volunteer, but it's my duty." In this case, kin care was prompted by a strong sense of duty and no small measure of righteousness.[26] Fran Crane felt determined to take care of her mother, even in the context of their mutual hostility, because as her mother's daughter it was her kin obligation. Fran felt compelled to take responsibility for what she considered a thankless job.

Some people in the networks readily invoked kinship status and its obligation when seeking child-care help. Duvall-Brennan network member Byron Russell does not think leaving his children with his parents imposes on them, whereas an identical request to a friend would be an imposition. "I think we certainly feel more comfortable leaving our kids with family than we do with friends, especially for a long period of time." Byron continues with his explanation: "It's not that we wouldn't trust Jack and Maggie or the Smiths or other friends to take good care of our kids. We would just *feel like it was an imposition* to leave them for our weekend. At least with our parents, I don't feel that it's an imposition. I feel like it's just part of *their roles as grandparents*, and maybe it's because my parents did that with us and I sort of feel like—you got to leave us with your parents, so you ought to be willing to take care of my kids [emphasis added]."

For Byron Russell and his wife, Rebecca Hoffman, the distinction between kinship and friendship is fundamentally important. Asking favors of kin not only relieves Byron and Rebecca of the need to reciprocate because they are merely invoking a kin obligation, but also credits them for the emotional rewards the grandparents derive from the act of fulfilling their kin role. If the grandparents babysit their grandchildren, they are satisfying their expectations of themselves. Their services are not extra, they are part of the bargain of active kinship.

NORM OF RECIPROCITY

Reciprocity of the kind Gouldner outlines can unfold between kin members in a context other than status obligation, just as it can between two nonrelated people. When one accepts a favor or gets involved in an exchange, the expectation of return necessarily shapes the interchange. A person is obliged to accept what is given and give something in return. The Beckers offer a useful illustration. They have a strong sense of kinship obligation but engage in other kinds of reciprocal relations as well. When Dina's father buys his weekly bread at the discount bakery, he expects those he buys for to come quickly and pick it up. The reciprocal obligation here is to accept that which is given, and to retrieve it as a means of acknowledging that it is being given, and also because it is bothersome to have a pile of bread loaves stacked on one's kitchen counter. Dina talks about her internal resistance to following his protocol: "He'll call and say, 'I've got the bread,' and it doesn't bother me if I can't pick it up; . . . I'll say, 'Oh, we'll get it tomorrow,' which my father doesn't like, but I mean, he lives with it. Mark says, 'I'll go get the bread.'" Her husband knows that "I'll get it tomorrow" is the wrong answer, not meeting the obligation to accept the favor on the giver's timetable. Peter Becker will feel displeasure and perhaps some annoyance that his gift is not being appreciated. In delaying, his daughter is not holding up her side of the bargain. Peter is, in effect, exerting an effort to establish his terms of the exchange, in which he succeeds.

Some people use the language of indebtedness to express their sense of obligation and the urgency of creating balance in the relationship. Mark Walde speaks of his debt to his brother-in-law: "We owe him, as I mentioned before, lots." Gouldner argues that this "shadow of indebtedness" exists until the favor is repaid. That debt may not be wrapped in gratitude, but it nevertheless registers deeply. In fact, Gouldner warns us to avoid the "Pollyanna Fallacy." Only Pollyanna would expect recipients to express unqualifiedly their gratitude and appreciation for gifts given and services provided.[27] One need only think of Dina's reluctance to follow the terms of the bread exchange to realize the importance of this point.

To take Gouldner's distinctive definition of the norm of reciprocity to another level of analysis, it is important to understand the microinteractions between individuals as they consider engaging in reciprocal relations and then seek them out. In exploring the social tensions dynamically traversing between obligation, perception, and need, the following discussion reveals the complex ways that network members interpret and negotiate reciprocity through assessing need and capacity, constructing balance, and appraising the value of relationships.

ASSESSING NEED AND CAPACITY

Network members evaluate their own need for help in the context of the needs and capacities of those in the network, including the children. As Gouldner notes, reciprocity is expected "only 'when the individual is able.'"[28] He also cautions that rational individuals may disagree on one's ability, a dynamic at the heart of these negotiations. Network members speak about how well others can handle, or not handle, the ups and downs of daily life. In all four networks, members' perceptions of the needs of others are an important motivating force in their decision to provide help and a modulating force in whether they expect it in return. Factors that shape assessments of needs and capacities include current caretaking responsibilities, health, ages of children, the demands of paid employment, and the constellation of resources of the person helping and the person in need. It is precisely that *should* of helping that can kick a system into gear when it has been sputtering.

An example from the working-class network illustrates the generosity of spirit that can accompany assessments of acute need. When Patricia Crane's mother was hospitalized for lung cancer, Patricia struggled to figure out how to keep her caregiving system going with reduced people power and increased need: "Now it's gonna be put on me to take care of my mom" when she comes home from the hospital. Tracy Johnson observes Patricia fraught with the weight of new responsibilities. Previously, they had passed child care back and forth. Now, Tracy feels more fortunate than Patricia and perceives Patricia as having more pressing needs, even though Patricia has only one child and Tracy has four: "And I'm trying to keep Robbie every weekend, at least one day. Because she needs a break." When I suggest Patricia has a heavy load right now, Tracy responds: "Yeah, and if I can give her that little break, you know— because I used to get it, that little break. And now mine comes at nighttime, which, you know—she does too, but she needs, you know, all day to herself. 'Don't worry about us!' She needs that, and we're gonna give that to her."

In calculating the weight of her own needs, Tracy appraises Patricia's caretaking duties, the age of her son, her current emotional and physical state, and her work situation. Tracy holds Patricia's interests at heart, and she is confident the reverse is true. From Tracy's point of view, Patricia has a problem, and she is determined to be a part of the solution.

This ongoing needs assessment also involves a calibration of the capacity of the network member. Emotional and physical health figure prominently, as does a member's skill with children. Byron Russell reports that his mother finds it challenging to take care of both his children at the same time. So he says, "When possible, we just try to have one." Alex Brolin, separated from Sarah Aldrich, reasons that he can call his in-laws only when he has no other alternative for help: "Their lives are complicated enough as they are, you know. They're more protective of their calmness and serenity because of John's heart condition." In addition, his perceptions filter through his recognition of his new status as a nonresident father.

In assessing their own and others' commitments and current burdens, respondents in the networks try to determine when and whether it is appropriate to ask for help, and when their own need is great enough to overcome any hesitations they might have. Understanding Arlie Hochschild's concept of "feeling rules" is helpful here. She defines feelings rules as those notions that "guide emotion work by establishing the sense of entitlement or obligation that governs emotional exchanges."[29] Hochschild zeroes in "on the pinch between 'what I do feel' and 'what I should feel.'"[30] A parallel disjuncture between what people feel they need, what they think another person can provide, and what they can acceptably ask for reveals what I call the "asking rules" of reciprocity. Asking rules specify the conditions under which a person can ask for help. A request for help has to fit suitably into the proper context of time, place, and circumstance, as judged by the network member and how he or she anticipates another person will interpret the request. Obligation and entitlement centrally influence what network members suppose they can ask for and what the norm of reciprocity will oblige them to repay. The overarching situation and the specific content of the favors both enter into a person's calculation of whether or not to ask, as do the estimated consequences of receiving the help.

Although I would not posit a hierarchy of the rules, one rudimentary asking rule is: Ask only if your request does not impose upon someone. It implies that asking too often or too much constitutes an imposition—inconvenient at least and a major sacrifice at most. So when Dina Becker thinks, "I've asked my parents too many times in a row," she calls a brother to help her. Similarly self-regulating, Jack Brennan considers whether to ask his brother and his partner to babysit the children, "They're interested in seeing them and they will babysit occasionally. We don't impose on them because we're not quite sure how much they really enjoy it. . . . So they do help out, but we kind of try to modulate it so that it's something we're comfortable with and they're comfortable with." Caitlin Becker James talks about arranging coverage for her children while she travels. She incorporates Dina into her plan but tries to do so without imposing: "We try to work her part of it when she already has kids at home, or at least one, because it doesn't quite seem fair if she only has a few hours a day to give her my child during those hours. I might as well give her my child when she already has another child, . . . and she'll be doing child care. And then it helps her, because then they go off and play as opposed to it being a burden." As with other aspects of staging networks and reciprocity, the meaning of "impose" gets negotiated differently in various situations with assorted people. Something that feels easy to one person may be an imposition to someone else.

If someone is overextended, asking that person for a favor amounts to an imposition. Rebecca Hoffman talks about her reluctance to call upon Jack Brennan and Maggie Duvall: "They're working at faraway jobs. They're not working at home, so they feel a little bit more stretched." Ruth Bergman also mentions Jack's and Maggie's commutes and their extreme overwork in considering whether she would ask them to do something for her in return for her babysitting. "I want to be respectful of their time, because given not only their two kids, but given where they work, literally their work location, it's pretty difficult." By not asking, the Duvall-Brennan network members hedge their network involvement. They limit the number of reciprocal obligations they incur. And, by being too busy, the Duvall-Brennans successfully limit what others ask of them.

Another asking rule has to do with the degree of relationship: You have to be close to someone to ask a favor related to child care. The calculation rests on the supposition that caring for children is hard work, people are busy and stressed, and one has to be in a solid relationship before asking. Not surprisingly, several people identify kin as sufficiently close to pass this threshold. As a case in point, Dina Becker favors kinship in her considerations. "Everybody's so stressed that if you were to ask them to fill in in a pinch, it would stress them more. . . . I feel I would have to be so close to them, it'd be like my sister." Consistent with her approach to networking, for Dina, kin constitute close ties. Socially recognized kinship mediates her concerns about imposing. In effect, she worries that a similar request of friends might jeopardize that relationship; she finds it "risky." Amanda Brennan similarly adheres to this asking rule when she recounts a time when her children were little and she was very ill. Her brother, Jack Brennan, was a twenty-year-old who liked children, was good with her children, and came over to help. Amanda talks about his participation as an affirmation of their relationship: "That's how close we were. I could ask him to do it, and he did it." To her mind, that she could ask him to help her when she was sick was a measure of their closeness. It was not just his fraternity that affirmed her entitlement to ask for help, but their strong connection.

In the hierarchy of legitimate grounds for asking for help with children, paid employment and marital work rank high. This points to another asking rule: Ask only if your request falls within the hierarchy of recognized needs in your network. This will vary by network and by gender. In an earlier example, Tracy Johnson recognized Patricia Crane's exhaustion and acted to alleviate it by taking Robbie for a while. However, Mark Walde of the ever-helpful Becker clan does not feel he can ask anyone in the network to babysit while he exercises, which is his main pastime. Although the network members babysit when he works, to him a request to cover time to exercise would be unacceptable. Mark concluded that his network would not see his desire for exercise as sufficiently dire, in contrast to how Tracy Johnson viewed Patricia Crane's need to rest. And yet the Becker network members readily and gladly take care of the children when Mark and Dina go out on a date. This kind of support for pleasure must be understood in the context of what Karla Hackstaff calls a "culture of divorce," where people recognize the prevalence of divorce and act to thwart it by encouraging and facilitating romance in marriage.[31] Virtually all the networks included people who supported others in their attempts to go out and spend time nourishing their marital relationships.

The hesitation that accompanies asking rules makes a person pause and consider the trade-offs. Here reciprocity acts as a regulator, enforcing norms by determining what counts as a need, what gets supported, and what does not. Mark Walde talks about his reluctance to ask for "extra things": "I'd rather do it myself; I'd rather not bother." Essential things are fine, but extra things are not worth it. Without knowing exactly what he would have to give back in the long run in order to balance the trade, he must decide if going for a run is worth the incurred obligation. In this instance, the stakes appear low, but the dynamic points to another asking rule: Do not ask if the price seems too high. Paying back may involve more sacrifice than a person wants to make. This can lead to refraining from asking altogether. Susan Becker ruminates over the choices she made while a young mother, especially when it came to relying on her mother-in-law, with whom she did not have the best relationship: "My mother-in-law would also have come, but I wasn't particularly close to her. . . . I had a feeling that if I had gotten ill and she had to come, she would have come, but she would have [laughs] blamed me for staying out late or [laughs] not putting on a sweater, and getting [sick]. . . . There was a certain judgmentalness . . . that I would have hesitated to call, unless I was on my deathbed."

Another example illustrates the calculations about "price" in a series of trade-offs Byron Russell and Rebecca Hoffman made as they tried joining a babysitting cooperative in their neighborhood. Consistent with the share-care philosophy that hooked the Duvall-Brennans with Byron and Rebecca initially, the babysitting co-op appealed to their childrearing sensibilities. Byron recounts their involvement: "Because we have other people we could use, especially my mother, it didn't seem worth it to us to have one of us away for the evenings. So it was kind of a big price to pay, for having somebody come here another day and then you didn't know the person. . . . It's more stressful when you don't have a relationship, if somebody's essentially a stranger or a bare acquaintance. It's more stressful taking care of their kids and it's more stressful having them take care of yours. So we only did it once." This approach—of using community chits to build a network of helpful acquaintances—is an example of the growing civic engagement movement around the country.[32] However, the overriding issues of familiarity and convenience ended Byron's and Rebecca's desire to make it work, because finally, the price was too high, especially since they have alternative caretaking options available.

In a more extreme example, Fran Crane censored her requests in observing another asking rule: Do not ask if you know your request will be rejected. Fran testified to a lifelong history of rejection in her relationship with her mother. Despite all the time and effort Fran expended taking care of her mother, she insisted that she neither expected nor received anything in return: "I wouldn't ask my mother for nothing. [Laughs] . . . She wouldn't do it, to begin with. I've been told no so many times. Why would I want to waste my breath to ask her anymore? [Laughs.]" She accepts caring for her mother as her kin obligation, her duty. Fran's refusal to ask for anything allows her to set limits on what she gives and on how much she takes of the emotional flack her mother doles out.

CONSTRUCTING BALANCE

Managing to construct a balanced set of relations that both parties perceive as fair is central to maintaining networks.[33] Over time, balance is fairness, and being fair means being balanced. But how people do that and how they interpret fairness and balance varies greatly. Pryor and Graburn raise the issue of the ways perfectly balanced reciprocity operates as a mythical belief, perpetuated in culture and in social science: "A belief in the occurrence of reciprocity makes it unnecessary for close attention to be paid to the exact balance of transactions, and, as a result, balanced exchange may never be achieved."[34] If two or more parties make a commitment to balanced exchange, over the long run, with multiple intangibles valued variably, their shared belief makes reciprocity possible.

Within the context that reciprocity exists, precisely what constitutes an equitable balance must be negotiated. Indeed, as Uehara observes in "Reciprocity Reconsidered," balance is socially constructed, not scientifically calculated. To complicate matters, the literature on reciprocity shows that people want to see themselves as giving more than they get. In part, this is a self-serving deception whereby people account for their own contributions because it is psychologically uncomfortable to be in social debt.[35] In the context of the networks, the anchors all reported the opposite—they see themselves in deficit mode. But they did indeed experience some discomfort about it. That indebtedness is part of the dynamic of reciprocity.

In probing the issue of balance in reciprocity, I got a variety of responses, all of which reflect a careful accounting of the exchanges. When I asked Tracy Johnson, of the working-class network, if she worried about keeping even with Patricia Crane, she said, "No! I've never thought of nothing like that because I don't take advantage of her and she doesn't take advantage of me." That said, although not worrying about being even, she is tracking whether or not advantage is being taken. Their relationship rests on a strong foundation of trust, but it is not without its limits. Tracy attempts to maintain a standard of nonexploitation: "I try not to take advantage of anybody." And along the way, she monitors the comings and goings and exchanges. Some people have exploited her over the years, thereby infringing upon the principles of reciprocal exchange. Those people she has crossed off of her network list.

That striving for balance operated for the professional middle-class network as well and succeeds in part through a strategy of minimizing reliance on the network. When I asked Rebecca Hoffman if she worries about reciprocity in her relationship with the Duvall-Brennans, she said: "No, no, I haven't. Because I feel it all kind of evens out. Yeah, I haven't felt like they're always depending on us, and we're not depending on them or anything like that." Like Tracy Johnson, her nonworry results from her assessment that the system is working, not that she has ignored it. Her response implies that she is monitoring the exchanges for dependency, which in her estimation would be burdensome. For her, dependency implies imbalance and therefore violates reciprocity, which requires equity. Unlike Tracy Johnson, who encourages interdependence, Rebecca avoids it.[36] She thinks that relying too much on someone's assistance means becoming a burden, in effect becoming dependent (as opposed to interdependent). Rebecca's husband, Byron Russell, also talks about keeping even: "We feel like there's reciprocity [when] we know and like the other people who are participating. There has to be some sense that everyone's getting something out of it, no one is being burdened or asked to do more than their share."

Members of the Becker network share the confidence that, in the long run, the balance of favors operates fairly. A family story illuminates the multidimensionality of what can be brought into the calculation of balance in the Becker network. Told to me independently by five members of the network, this story revolves around Caitlin Becker James, one of Dina's younger sisters.[37] Her employment requires that she travel to teach seminars and attend conferences. Because she is still breast-feeding, she has to take her seventeen-month-old along on her travels. She therefore has devised an elaborate system whereby she rotates which family member she takes with her. She pays for their airfare and they care for her daughter while she is teaching or conferencing, and then she can intermittently breast-feed. During a recent commitment to teach two consecutive weekends, her sister Michaela, came on one trip and her husband, Mike, on the other. She plans on teaching two weekends in the Pacific Northwest near her sister Lila, so her brother Kent is scheduled to go with her both times. She chronicles her accounting of the various trade-offs in maintaining a balance in the system when her mother accompanied her to a recent conference:

> That time I made [my mother] pay her own way because [laughs] I can't afford to pay my own way, go to the conference, stay in a hotel for five days—I mean, well, I could, but it's ridiculous. But I get all these free books from publishers when I do this. I have downstairs this year's—fifteen hundred books from this year, you know. Babies to young adolescents—everything published for them. And so . . . we send some appropriate ones to Ireland every year, to this school . . . where my grandmother went. And so they have an improving library. And so it's a gift from my parents to the school, so I said, "You can have the books. It behooves you to keep me on the committee because you get free books to send to Ireland. You don't have to buy books to send to Ireland. So you have to pay your own way to [the conference]" [laughs], and somehow that makes sense.

This system of reciprocity rests on a deeply rooted assumption of common goals, trust, and longevity of the relationships. In the context of the vital ties of active kinship, the Beckers take the long-term view that the balance will be sustained over time. Nonetheless, balance, like value, is not intrinsically self-evident but has to be negotiated based on perceptions and needs.

Importantly, what gets traded for child care varies. Caitlin considers the family help invaluable. With her parents she has found something she can give back, something that they need—books. In her other network relations, she searches for something to give back. She especially worries about what to give her siblings who do not have children. Dina she does not worry about, "because we have the same needs" and they exchange services in kind. Her single siblings pose a more challenging issue of how to give back, as their needs are less obvious. Caitlin says: "Kent can babysit for me and go on trips, and I can't help him out. I mean there's nothing I can do for him that is actually very helpful in his life. . . . I can't trade on days when he wants to have off; . . . I can't go build shelves for his house, because I can't even build them in my own. [Laughs]." She struggles to make sure she does not take advantage of her siblings' goodwill, because "I can't really reciprocate that much. . . . I try to have [my son] make a book about his weekend, because then he gets to put in photographs and what he did with Uncle Kent. . . . And then the thank you becomes a gift of sorts from [him]. . . . They helped me out a lot, and I can never help back, because I just can't. . . . It's not that I can't do anything, but it's not the same practical trade for trade." In addition to the gifts from the children, she offers her husband's advice on financial investments or technology-related issues, as well as her own expertise on children's literature. But in the process, she has qualms because, as Gouldner would predict, she questions whether her return is "appropriate or sufficient."[38] She takes account, worries, juggles, and reaps the fruits of the relationships but tries to create some kind of equivalence in return. Many different things can be substituted in her effort to pay back.

Observing a similarly broad accounting, Patricia Crane feels no compunction about the crossing of categories in a trade with her brother: "I take him to work every morning. Like, he asks me—because he doesn't like going over to his ex-old lady's to get [his son.] He asks me to go over and get him, so I go and get him and stuff. And yeah. It's a mutual." Patricia also strives to assist her brother, Ben, in holding tight to his sobriety. He, in turn, not only cares for Robbie but also backs Patricia unequivocally, validating her as a person, a mother, and a sister. Because they help each other with things they cannot do on their own, they consider themselves even. Patricia notes that she does not expect Tracy to provide equivalent, proportionate babysitting. So one sleepover for Tracy's children at her house does not translate into four overnights for Robbie at Tracy's house. Patricia *does* anticipate getting something back from her involvement with Tracy and her family, but not necessarily babysitting, and not necessarily a specific number of hours or days, and not even, necessarily, from Tracy herself. She may ask Tracy to visit Fran at the hospital, or to pick Robbie up from the school-bus stop on a day when she cannot make it home in time. For her, the return, whatever it might be, comes when it comes; she does not expect it immediately, or even in the near future.

Some people use money to create equity. While this study focuses on the informal networks that people construct, because market relations enter into those networks, it is important to consider what happens to reciprocity when money is exchanged. Patricia Crane occasionally pays Tracy Johnson with cash or groceries. Lila Becker McKendrick has made an unusual arrangement with her neighbor who cares for her two-year-old while she teaches a morning class. Because her eldest daughter sometimes babysits for that neighbor, Lila feels she cannot pay the neighbor less than the neighbor pays her daughter. "But I can't pay her too much, because I get paid so little. . . . I hate giving away everything, so I just split it down the middle." In effect, she gives half of her wages to the babysitter, who exists somewhere in that hazy middle ground between a network member and an employee. She strives for equity and knows that she could not teach if her son was not well cared for, and caring for a two-year-old is never easy.

Sarah Aldrich employs April Miller, pays her well for full-time work, and provides additional job-related benefits. In the process, Sarah sets clear standards for work performance and boundaries around interpersonal relationships. April reigns supreme in Sarah's network of care, as an employee. She reports that neither Sarah nor Alex solicits her advice. In turn, she speaks to them about her problems only when she needs an "outside" opinion. They are not in her network, even though she is the center of theirs. Sarah says she asks advice about children from no one; April is not the exception.[39] April has explicitly conveyed her refusal to mediate Sarah and Alex's separation. When I asked the weekly babysitter, Aidan Macleod, whether she ever sought out Sarah for advice, she said, "No, we haven't had that kind of relationship." Advice is but one form a reciprocal exchange might take; it is a portable asset. Does the exchange of money fundamentally alter the dynamics of reciprocity in a network when a specific sum of money is given for a clear amount of work? In the cases of April and Aidan, the answer is yes. Another compelling question, which this research cannot answer, is: How does it alter the relationship? Feminist scholars debate this question and explore the parameters of commodified relationships in various settings.[40] In this research, the exchange of money per se is less important than the employee-employer relationship. Conditions of equality reign between Tracy Johnson and Patricia Crane; although Patricia has occasionally paid Tracy, the money could just as easily go the other way. For Sarah Aldrich, there is no question about who is running the foundation and who works as an employee.

PERCEPTIONS OF VALUE: REWARDS IN THE EYE OF THE BEHOLDER
Balancing requires assessing value; and rewards exist in the eye of the beholder. Network members detail many kinds of satisfactions and rewards that accrue from participating in a network. They highlight two relational rewards in particular: emotional support and the gift of children.

EMOTIONAL SUPPORT, ADVICE, AND FRIENDSHIP. Supportiveness requires qualities different from those demanded for the practical care of children. Although some people within all four networks had the capacity to be practically helpful and emotionally supportive, the two did not always go together. Nonetheless, one could be exchanged for the other. Unlike practical support, emotional support can be provided from afar. It fuels the "economy of gratitude" that helps perpetuate these elaborate network systems.[41]

Those in the networks who sought support and advice had nothing but effusive appreciation for those who provide it. Jack Brennan boasts about his older sister, who specializes in child-rearing advice and medical knowledge: "She's like, better than a CD-ROM, you know. Yeah, she knows everything. She definitely knows everything." Kate Farnsworth says of her best friend, Sarah Aldrich: "She's just . . . fantastic, I mean a godsend. I mean, Sarah, not only is she so great and so wonderful to talk to, but she's also really smart about things; . . . her question is the hallmark of wisdom as far as I'm concerned." She talked about her stalwart friendship with Sarah, which was at the heart of her commitment to do anything for Sarah whenever she might need it. Gratitude and appreciation are part of what network members give each other.

Maggie Duvall's mothers' group is a perfect example of network members who supply emotional support and advice, but not practical help. Fellow member Lucia Stanley says: "When I think of being part of her support network for her children, I think the main way is through this group. It's kind of like, you know, this therapy session, where one person is going to therapy and it ends up being a support to the whole family." She sees the ripple effects of the support—it enables the recipient to be more capable. Also, she talks about the power of her friendship with the women in the group: "I'll start crying when I think of the support it has been to me." To suggest that such connections do not bring a meaningful resource to rearing children would be wrong. Friends and kin in the networks speak about their ongoing assessments of whom they can believe and trust and who will "be there" when the going gets tough.[42]

RELATIONSHIPS WITH CHILDREN. Relationships with children emerge as a major attractor of participation in a care system. Some people view children as a gift.[43] Since the mid–nineteenth century, within U.S. culture as a whole, children have increasingly been viewed as precious—indeed, sentimentally invaluable.[44] Adult involvement in a network of care can be motivated by a desire to have children in one's life or a fondness for a particular child.

Nelson reports in "Single Mothers and Social Support" that single mothers in rural Vermont use the gift of children to equalize their perception of balance in exchange relations. In other words, in situations where they recognize the unique, seemingly unbalanced benefits they receive, single mothers point to the perceived rewards to the givers of building a relationship with the child. Although rightly pointing to the utilitarian nature of their rationales, Nelson overlooks a key dimension of exchanges focused on children. The kin relations especially, but not exclusively, see themselves as having a vested interest in the children's futures and in the children themselves. The appeal of having a positive role in the life of a child is unquestionably a bargaining chip in negotiations over activities and their relative value.

Shannon Becker speaks at length about her time with young people in the family. She resists calling her time with her nieces and nephews "baby-sitting" because she sees child rearing and teaching as a mission in life, one that our entire society should take seriously:

> I just wouldn't use the same terminology. Like, I never really like to say "babysit" with [my nieces and nephews]. . . . I think babysitting is about paying a teenager, you know what I mean? Like, babysitting is not your family. I watch the children, you know. I spend time with the children, . . . the rewards are totally different. The importance of it is totally different. . . . "Could you go to the grocery store for me and pick up the milk?" is a favor. [Laughs.] I just think kids are a totally different universe of interaction and—it enriches my life. Going to the grocery store to get milk does not enrich my life. . . . Because, for one thing, it's children. It's people. It's an opportunity for me to spend time with them, you know. . . . I think that there's a whole big philosophical thing . . . in our entire society. We have to take care of these children.

I ask Shannon what she gets back from being with the children. A bit exasperated with me, she replies: "What do I get back from them?! You know, I mean, I just love them. What do you get back from being around people that you love? [Laughs.] I don't know. . . . It's just fun with me. You know, the way that any good relationship enriches your life." In our economic system, middle-class children are largely not expected to help with household chores, let alone contribute to the family economy;[45] but they are valued for companionship, pleasure, and their future citizenship.[46]

Involvement in a network of care for children results from connections to the parent via friendship, kinship, employment, and neighbor status. At a minimum it can be a relationship of caregiving convenience. It can result from activating a kin obligation. It can also result from another adult's desire to have children in their lives and a fondness for a particular child, even when that child is not related by kinship. For example, Ruth Bergman, who used to live downstairs from the Duvall-Brennans, said: "I'd just like to hang out with [their daughter, Danielle]; . . . the best was just when she hung out, when she walked the dog with me." Interest in developing relationships with children may prompt engagement in these networks. In a powerful example reflecting the profound importance of children in some people's lives, Patricia Crane's mother, Fran, succinctly voiced her attachment to her grandsons: "He's my life; he really is. Him and [his brother]." In another example, Dina Becker describes herself as currently receiving more than her share in the Becker network. She explains: "It just all balances out. I think because I have the small children, I think I actually get a lot more than I have to give. But they like my children. They don't seem to mind." Like that of the women in Nelson's single-mothers study, her perspective is self-serving insofar as it minimizes the sense of burden she thinks she places on others. That said, her sister Shannon affirms her perspective. She speaks of her devotion to her nieces and nephews: "I think it's a gift to me, to be part of their lives."

Discussion and Conclusion

I argue that the social context of reciprocity must be incorporated into an analysis of networks in order to understand how they operate, what is valued, and what is traded within them. Being part of a network requires being able to give back. Networks constructed to help with the project of rearing children are fundamentally shaped by the relationship between an adult and a child, as well as between the adult and the anchor. What is given and what is received is of an entirely different order than standard economic exchange or simple favor exchanges.[47] Conceiving of reciprocity as a normative obligation in this context seems most theoretically compelling. Many kinds of reciprocity exist in contemporary U.S. society, falling along a continuum bound at one end by a negative, self-interested reciprocity and at the other by a generous, long-term, generalized reciprocity. The kinds of reciprocity practiced by network members in this study fall somewhere in between; a balanced reciprocity based upon mutuality and obligation. Indeed, different types of reciprocity can coexist in the same household, as they do for the Duvall-Brennans, the Aldriches, and the Cranes, or anyone who relies in part on market-based services for child care.

Members of these networks of interdependence constructed around care for school-age children engage in the *process* of staging and mobilizing networks. To negotiate reciprocity, they repeatedly assess the extent to which their needs register on a scale of importance and immediacy, analyze the situation, and evaluate other network members' commitments, needs, and capacities. Their perceptions of value and worth fundamentally define fairness and balance in the situation. Relational satisfactions emanate from reciprocal action, from relationships with other network members and with the children.

Only through ethnographically studying the process of networking is it possible to distinguish profound differences among networks in their ability or inability to negotiate reciprocity. Had the middle-class anchors been surveyed using a closed-ended questionnaire, the structure of their networks would look similar. The Beckers identify eight in their network, as do the Duvall-Brennans. In describing the network of people who care for their children, the Beckers include only kin, while the Duvall-Brennans count only two relatives, one of whom lives three thousand miles away. On the surface, both middle-class networks appear robust, but, in effect, the Becker network is thick and elastic while the Duvall-Brennan's is thin and brittle. The Beckers' web can attract others in order to avert a care crisis, but the Duvall-Brennans' loose association of advisors fails to bring people close enough to engage. All the friends and kin who make up the Duvall-Brennan network work full time, and none live in the neighborhood. Network members deeply care *about* the Duvall-Brennan children but are not situated to care *for* them. When caught with a sick child and intractable work demands—in other words, a crisis of care in part precipitated by a family labor shortage—the Duvall-Brennans attempted to mobilize their network of kin and friends but were limited by circumstances partly of their own making and partly beyond their control. In a pinch, the Duvall-Brennans had to rely on the market, which almost failed them. Fee for services can purchase some things; obligation is not dependably one of them.

The distinction between practical care and advice, or other types of knowledge-based expertise, is important. The Duvall-Brennans have a limited ability to provide hands-on care to others in their network. In contrast, the Cranes have extensive capacity to absorb those who need to be cared for. They, like the Beckers, could avert a child-care crisis if Robbie fell ill. However, their need for legal counsel for Patricia's imprisoned older son cannot be met by members of their network. That kind of a legal crisis the Duvall-Brennans could easily finesse.[48]

Active kinship support can crucially make a difference in the successful staging of networks and negotiating reciprocity. Consistent with findings in other research, the working-class and middle-class network anchors rely more on kin, and the professional middle class and the upper class depend more on friends and paid help. Nonetheless, which kin are identified and mobilized varies. In each of the networks, anchors ignored at least some "blood relations," particularly those who were not active in their lives or those of their children. That said, all networks rely on family—either immediately or "in the last instance." Although both middle-class networks are rooted in highly educated families whose members have skills and resources, the Beckers intentionally live near one another, constitute a critical mass of people, share child-rearing values, and operate using an ethic of reciprocity. The Duvall-

Brennans do not. To be of effective use, kin need to be geographically close and able to contribute, as demonstrated in the last chapter. They also need to share the anchor's child-rearing values. In effect, kinship status is neither static nor fixed but has to be activated and enacted. Active kin can make a substantial difference in the anchors' abilities to cope with crises, because anchors can mobilize the sense of obligation that accompanies kin relations in child rearing, which otherwise has to be cultivated in acquaintances and friends or purchased in the marketplace.

Meeting child-care needs and addressing the labor shortage within families depends on parents' ability to stage a network and mobilize obligatory relations. The language of kinship was not used to describe friends in this study. That did not mean, however, that a feeling of responsibility was absent. Reciprocity as well as kinship has the capacity to invoke a sense of obligation. Indeed, networks are constructed on the foundation of a tangle of reciprocal relationships.

Men, Women, and the Gender of Caregiving

Chapter 8

SOCIOLOGISTS AND ANTHROPOLOGISTS who study domestic networks find men to be peripheral figures. They identify men in the networks, but not as the movers and shakers or the most active participants.[1] When they study kin work and housework, they consistently document the unequal division of labor. Men do less; women do more. Men clean yards and repair cars; women care for children and the elderly and relate to the neighbors. The research clearly shows men's ambivalence toward the interdependence and domesticity necessarily connected to networks of care and rearing children.[2]

The consequence of this consistency in findings is that men's positive contributions to families and networks have been insufficiently studied. While recently some researchers have returned to examine men's contributions to family work and self-provisioning more carefully, others have thrown up their hands.[3] Lareau has gone so far as to argue that resources devoted to research on the daily lives of families would best be spent on interviewing mothers, not fathers. In "My Wife Can Tell Me Who I Know," Lareau finds that while men elaborate their ideological beliefs, they have little to say about children's everyday activities, and what they do say is vague and misleading. Given what social science has established about the cultures of masculinities, the socialization of boys, and the privileges that accrue to men as breadwinners, Lareau's perspective would not strike the informed reader as unreasonable.

In this research, although I had anticipated studying primarily women as kin keepers and caretakers, men actively cared for children in each of the four networks I studied. I found four fathers, four uncles, a grandfather, and a male friend involved in the daily tasks of caring for and caring about children (see

182

Table 8.1
Men in the Networks of Care

Relationship to Child	Network				
	CRANE	BECKER	DUVALL-BRENNAN	ALDRICH	TOTAL
Father	1	1	1	1	4
Friend/Neighbor	—	—	1	—	1
Uncle	1	2	1	—	4
Grandfather	—	1	—	—	1
Total	2	4	3	1	10

Table 8.1). In the first network I looked at, I dismissed my discovery of involved men as an aberration. However, by the third network, after repeatedly encountering men as essential cogs in the caregiving systems, I began to realize that perhaps my assumptions entering the field were ill informed. Or, more precisely, that in attending to the dominant story of the domestic network literature, I had ignored the subsidiary story. Swept up by my critique of the inequality of the big picture—where women do most of the work and take major responsibility for raising children, running kin systems, and caring for the elderly—I made light of the supplementary contributions of men. The people in this study set me straight, emphasizing the significant contribution of men to the networks and to the children.

This chapter does not inventory the gendered division of child care—who does what and how often. However, it does explore what men do in the networks and how they feel about what they do.[4] In this chapter, through probing and thoughtful reflections about their own fathers, their childhoods, and the challenges of how to be a man involved in rearing children, the ten men in this study talk about their relationships with children, the network anchors, and their participation in the networks. Four men are fathers of the children in the study; another four are fathers of other children. All are uncles; one is a grandfather. The chapter also asks how men's assistance meaningfully impacts the women in the networks, particularly the mothers of the children. Women's reactions depend on their gender ideology, their relationship with the men, and their strategy for running their household and caring for the children. In concluding, the chapter explores the gendered orientations of men and women to network involvement and probes how social change is accomplished.

Men's Accounts of Life with Children

Importantly, the men I interviewed are *participants* in the networks. Because I interviewed only those whom the anchors identified as helping in the network, nonparticipants—male and female—are not included in the cases. Therefore, these men actively engage in the lives of the anchors and the children; they are agents who help, not passive beneficiaries of the activism of the networks. Roschelle finds that men's participation in social support networks varies by marital status, race/ethnicity, and class.[5] Married men participate more than single or divorced men. Anglo men are more active participants in networks than men identified as coming from familistic cultures (Afro-American, Puerto Rican, and Chicano men). And the higher their income, the more likely the men are to participate.

This section of the chapter delves into the men's accounts of their lives with children—their activities, their satisfactions, and their travails—as uncles, grandfathers, and fathers. Men do a range of supportive, symbolic, and practical activities with and for the children and the children's parents. And, some men take responsibility, plan, and in one case, co-anchor child-rearing projects.

UNCLES AND GRANDFATHERS

The extant social science research on men in families focuses on men as fathers of children, but largely ignores men as uncles or grandfathers. The exception can be found within anthropology, which studies kinship systems more broadly than does sociology. Sociology's concentration on nuclear family households has led to a general myopia regarding extrahousehold kin involvement, as well as neighborly help. Within anthropology, the mother's brother in particular has been the subject of research and theorizing. Nonetheless a handful of studies in sociology look at grandfathers and uncles.[6] Studies find that grandfathers feel closest to those grandchildren who live nearby. Practically, the tasks they most commonly do for their grandchildren include transportation and care in illness.[7] Interpersonally, they transfer values—regarding religion, family heritage, education, work, and respect for others—to their grandchildren.[8] The sociological and psychological literature tends to focus on uncles as perpetrators of sexual abuse rather than as contributors to family functioning. My intention in examining the role of uncles is not to make light of real problems that exist, but rather to broaden the scope of research to examine positive aspects of uncles' involvement as well.

By placing these relationships between men and children within the broader kinship structure, more is revealed. Uncles are related to children because they are brothers of the children's mothers and fathers. Men have kin responsibilities as siblings in addition to those as uncles. The singular position of the mother's brother in particular, has been a fascination of anthropologists for generations. Also referred to as the "avunculate," the mother's brother in many cultures has rights and responsibilities toward his sister's children. In summarizing the findings of cross-cultural studies, Fox sheds light on the advantages of a kinship system that disperses the many tasks that in the United States are expected of fathers alone. In effect, kinship that honors the avunculate broadens the group of men upon whom a mother can call for teaching her children, provisioning, playing, disciplining, and all those tasks related to child rearing. "The division of labor between the father and the mother's brother . . . made for a much healthier 'male role model' situation than the imposition of all the elements of this role on the father. It also meant that the mother had two males (or sets of males) to call upon *by right* in meeting her and her children's social, economic, and spiritual needs."[9]

For the purposes of kinship in the United States, I would argue that incorporating uncles (and aunts) into a study of rearing children expands the possibilities for understanding networks of care. With decreasing family size, any one household cannot guarantee a mother's brother, or a father's sister, to the children. In this study, significantly, three of the networks have active uncles and two have active aunts as well. The network that has neither, the Aldrich network, is anchored by a woman who has three sisters (no brothers), none of whom live nearby, and who is separated from a man who has a brother that lives thousands of miles away.

In their study of American kinship, Elaine Cumming and David Schneider find evidence of a great deal of sibling solidarity later in adult life.[10] Approaching uncles as siblings, Shelly Eriksen and Naomi Gerstel investigate the role of adult brothers and sisters in each other's lives. Ninety-six percent of men and women in their study report that they have given their siblings help over the past year, 75 percent in the past month. And a vast majority of the respondents feel that their help was reciprocated. Eriksen and Gerstel find that gender is *not* important in the kinds of material and personal tasks that brothers and sisters—uncles and aunts—do for their siblings and nieces and nephews, although in some practical help, such as child care, they find that gender is important and that men are less likely than women to do it.[11]

Symbolically marking their kinship roles, men "watch" children perform in various arenas. Townsend interprets "watching" as a means of expressing "both approval and encouragement" to children.[12] Unlike centuries past where sons in particular would apprentice in the trade of their fathers and learn by watching, men's employment is organized in contemporary society such that children rarely observe it. In a twentieth-century reversal, men watch their children. In this study, men attend important functions in the lives of the children—graduation from kindergarten, dance performances, and Little League games. Sarah Aldrich's son, Jacob, noted that his grandfather has attended virtually all of his Little League games. Sarah interprets his attendance as welcome support for *her,* as well as for Jacob.

The men in this study give numerous examples of the kinds of things they do in the networks, running errands and babysitting especially. And consistent with the research on men and children, the men play.[13] Uncles told stories about playing baseball, going ice skating, and taking hikes in the park to collect autumn leaves for art projects. One uncle recalls the time he provided theme entertainment at his nephew's birthday party: "I dress up as a cowboy, talk to kids about what cowboys do, answer questions, tell them cowboy stories, tell them how to rope, [and] they go to sit on my saddle."

However, the men also provide concrete everyday help—transportation to and from school, babysitting, shopping for groceries. As one uncle puts it, he does "random little things." The Becker grandfather shops weekly for the extended family for discount baked goods and for vegetables and fruit at the farmers' market. His son-in-law mentions that he also monitors the children's health: "When our kids are sick we take them to his house and he gets out his black bag and recommends a hospital or if it's nothing serious, just go back home." While Sarah Aldrich did not name her father as a network member at the beginning of the study, by the end she has revised her assessment of his role and retrospectively says she would include him. She acknowledges that she has come to rely more on her father emotionally since she separated from her husband. Her children expressed no hesitation in putting him on their list of network members. The Becker uncles take kids to their soccer games. Virtually all the uncles in the networks babysit on occasion; in the Crane network, Ben Crane handles a regular part of the week's child-care schedule. Several of the uncles care for the children overnight while their parents go away. Tom Brennan kept his niece for two weeks while his brother and sister-in-law went away to adopt a second baby. When Robbie Crane visits his father, Robert, he stays at the home of Robert's sister and her husband. His uncle regales me with stories about Robbie when I come to interview Robert. He does whatever he can to support Robert's active fathering.

Being part of an interdependent network of care for children has multiple benefits, since many things get traded and many relationships enter into the negotiation process. One consequence of being with children is having fun. Sharing the responsibility and the drudgery of raising children brings with it the joy of being with children. Interestingly, in expressing their feelings about being with children, it is not fathers or mothers in this study who describe themselves as having fun with children, but uncles and aunts. Ben Crane likes to wrestle with his nephew. He takes him on outings, sometimes along with his own son, to go roller skating or to special events in their city. He says: "I'm a big kid myself, so we have a lot of fun. You know, sometimes also being the male figure, I have to get onto him also, but it works out pretty good, actually." Kent Becker takes his nieces and nephews to rodeos, museums, and ball games: "Whenever possible, it's fun to do something interesting, and some kind of kid-centered activity." Men of different kin relations give numerous examples of play: escorting children to a Giants baseball game, attending a circus, fishing, and playing catch. The most rousing account of fun and good times with the children comes from the Becker uncles who sponsored a Superman sleepover party. Everyone wore a Superman t-shirt, fought crime, and made the world safe, well beyond their usual bedtimes.

Another consequence of being part of a network of care is the satisfaction of being needed. Ryan Becker talks about his father, Peter Becker, in this regard:

> I think he gets pleasure from helping other people. You can't tell my father, "Just sit down. Enjoy yourself. Relax." Because he has to be the one who gets up to wash dishes if there are dishes to be washed. And he'd prefer to get up and wash dishes than sit down and relax. Legitimately, he prefers that because that's the way he somehow exists. . . . My father spends all his time doing favors for us also. But to be honest, . . . if we didn't ask him those favors, he would be more unhappy than he is by doing those favors. I think my brother wouldn't mind if I stopped asking him to get my shirts for me [from the cleaners]. . . . But my father, actually, wouldn't know what to do with himself, if he wasn't spending his time being busy taking care of the rest of his family.

Another satisfaction comes from the adoration that children shower upon special adults. Kent Becker also genuinely likes children; he has been babysitting since the age of twelve. He told me with pride about his hands-on involvement with his eight nieces and nephews: "How else are you going to be their favorite uncle? . . . 'Uncle Kent, who's he?' No, it's got to be constant reminders, you know? 'I'm your favorite uncle, and don't you ever forget it.' Ryan can be second, but I'm first." In this case, outperforming his brother has its own rewards. Nonetheless, striving to become the favorite uncle gratifies him to the extent that he organizes much of his nonwork time around achieving that imperative.

Because a multitude of tasks get traded for child minding in the context of networks, and because rearing children requires much more than simply attending to them, women interpret many of the men's activities as support for themselves. For example, Dina Becker construes her brother's willingness to befriend her husband as a kind of support for her child-rearing project. Her brother folds her husband into the extended kin network. Patricia Crane feels grateful for the way her brother shares the worry and the care for their sick mother. And she sees strong men as an essential ingredient in her son's successful upbringing. She expects Ben Crane to help her care for Robbie, not just because Ben is her brother, but also because she helped rear him. She aided him in his quest for sobriety, and he owes her. They have a mutually supportive relationship and expect reciprocity in the long run.

FATHERS

The social science literature uniformly documents the increase in fathers' involvement with children over the past generation, prompted in part by women's increased labor-force participation and hence shared breadwinning.[14] However, the research indicates that men's participation rests in the realm of child tending rather than bathroom scrubbing.[15] Although studies find that the majority of men lag behind women in their contributions to household labor, they find that a subset of men, approximately 20–25 percent of husbands, make equal contributions to child rearing and housework.[16] In seeking to comprehend the positive contributions men make to child rearing, Lareau learns that men contribute entertainment, conversation, and life skills to family life. In *The Package Deal*, Nicholas Townsend reports fathers as important purveyors of masculinity. Some fathers take on the work-family package whole cloth and become "superdads"—in essence, the male equivalent of supermoms.[17]

Regardless of how much men accomplish, social scientists document a sea change in *expectations* about their involvement as fathers.[18] Men are now expected, and indeed, expect themselves, to be active in the lives of their children in addition to being breadwinners.[19] In fact, the involved father has become a new cultural icon for middle-class men.[20] We see television commercials with fathers holding babies, sitcoms with dads pushing strollers, and politicians stepping down from office because of family commitments. It has become honorable, indeed desirable, for men to exhibit an emotional attachment to their children.

In turn, being with children has a marked impact on men's lives.[21] Indeed, some researchers go so far as to say that "fatherhood can profoundly shape the lives of men."[22] As with the other studies on men's involvement with children, these studies tend to be done with fathers rather than other male relatives. The studies show that as fathers grow closer to their children and understand them better, they value that closeness.[23] As a result, they may also come to know themselves better. Fathers are more likely than nonfathers to get involved in civic organizations and religious institutions, as well as to become more attached to employment.[24] Greater involvement of fathers also leads to increased tension and conflict with their wives and their children.[25] Issues that may lie dormant within a division of labor that assigns child-rearing responsibility to women surface when decision making and various tasks have to be shared. More time means more opportunity for conflict and disagreement, as well as more bonding.

Men make different kinds of contributions to these networks of care for children, both directly to the children and indirectly via help to different network members. Consistent with other research on fathers' involvement, this research finds that men participate by attending to the physical needs of children, making decisions about their lives, being available to them, and socializing or endowing, as Townsend puts it, children with important qualities.[26] The fathers do more intimate care than do the uncles and grandfathers. As Robert Holcomb, father of Robbie Crane, says, "Whatever Robbie needs is where I come in." Jack Brennan and Mark Walde bathe their children, supervise homework, cook and feed them dinner, and comfort them when things go wrong. In each of the networks, fathers perform the panoply of tasks associated with rearing children, from waking the children, dressing them, and getting them off to school, to volunteering in their classrooms.

Men's involvement in networks of care for children also has consequences for the women in the networks—most pertinent, for the mothers of children. The women's feelings about men's help vary according to their relationships—structural and emotional—with the men and their expectations of what those men can and should do. Those expectations are profoundly shaped by their gender strategies for rearing children. Research shows that a particular set of expectations unfolds between men and women within marriage. When men share housework and child care, women are much happier in their lives and more satisfied with their marriages.[27] Wives interpret their husband's active fathering as activity that contributes to the marriage and the adult relationship. In contrast, husbands see their wives' mothering as child oriented, not as part of the marital work.[28] Disappointment and resentment can result from this divergence in interpretation.[29]

THE CRANES: "STRUCTURE" AND MALE ROLE MODELS. One male contribution, articulated most loudly and clearly by the men and women in the working-class network, is discipline. Fran Crane, Robbie Crane's grandmother, feels strongly that Robbie's father provides the masculine restraint that her grandson needs, but that she and her daughter cannot provide: "I wish Robert would move up here, just so he could be part of that baby's life. Because he needs the firmness that his dad can put on him. And he'll do it. If I see that he needs it, I'll call Robert and tell him, 'Hey, it's time you take him.'" Fran relayed a contentious discussion with her mother about her daughter Patricia's child-rearing practices. Her mother, who antagonizes Fran much of the time, voiced criticism of both Fran and Patricia, accusing them of spoiling the little boy. The great-grandmother foretold a negative future for Robbie that would land him in jail just like his nineteen-year-old half-brother. Fran retorted, "No, he's not, Mother. He's got a daddy. It'll make a lot of difference." Robert confirmed his own importance in providing "structure" to Robbie's life: "I tell him, 'Hey, man, are you sure you wanna do that?' I'll make him think about these things. You know, 'cause I'm not there all the time and I can't hold his hand all the time." All parties agree that without that structure, Robbie is in danger. As they see it, Robert, as the biological father and a firm disciplinarian, is the only person who can give it to him.

The language of gender-role modeling and the need for fathers laces the working-class women's talk about the adult men in children's lives.[30] Patricia Crane talks about Robert's presence in Robbie's life: "He's the man figure." She also considers her brother Ben's role: As an uncle to Robbie he is the on-site "male figure. He wrestles with him, and all." Tracy Johnson credits her boyfriend of three years with being a "father figure" to her four children and his two. While she has reservations about making him her life partner, she unequivocally says that "he would never let any harm come to my children." She says, "I call him the perfect father figure, because he is. I mean, he's the greatest. There's nothing that he wouldn't do for my kids or his kids. You know, and if they need, if I need, just ask. And it's there." Tracy's expectations evolved in the context of a young marriage that went awry. She now works for pay, rears the children, and takes responsibility for the lot. She laments the absence of her ex-husband from her children's lives because she still adheres to the belief that children need their biological fathers: "I wish their father figure was there. But he's not." According to her, he does not follow through. He contributes child support, which the courts monitor, and he shows up to see the children occasionally. "He's a great person. He was never father-orientated, you know, as far as playing with the kids. He just put up with them, basically. He doesn't do anything." When he shows up, she welcomes him into the house because "he's their dad" and according to her, children need their fathers, regardless of how incompetent or thoughtless.

In contemplating what life skills are important for boys and men, Robert Holcomb is deeply philosophical. He has never been married to Patricia but has an actively supportive, nonromantic relationship with her and acts as a maximally involved parent, with only the limits that a two-hour drive impose. He has his own friend and kin networks that help him with transportation and meeting Robbie's needs. Robert recounts some of his fathering strategies for meeting certain goals,

> I build motorcycles, I make saddles, and do all kinds of things. And [Robbie] really gets involved in all of that. . . . I let him get involved, I mean, you know, these are things I'll pass on to him anyways. But if he's not interested in 'em now, well then, we're gonna find something else to do. I just want him to be interested in something. I don't just want him to be blank out there, walking around following somebody, you know? I want him to be able to fix his own boat, you know? "Don't worry what everybody thinks. You don't have to do that because they do." . . . Robbie, he loves motorcycles. Last year we built three. I had him for a couple of months. And he participated in an actual tear down and reassembly, right down to [starting the engine]. He's quite knowledgeable. He's good. His patience is what I was really after. Let's get that patience under control. Children have *no* patience, you know, but he does. Frustration? "Don't get mad. Set your tool down. Go away, do something else, come back." These things, you know. Things I've had to learn to teach myself, . . . things that aggravate me most in life, man, I don't want him to have to go through that. I don't want him to learn the hard way. But of course, he's a child.

Negotiating the world of tough justice and showing little boys how to be men ranks high on the agenda of the working-class women and men I interviewed, although it went unmentioned by those in the middle-class networks. The class contingencies of working-class fatherhood shape how fathers imagine the world their children will inhabit. Robert teaches his craft to Robbie, mechanical and carpentry skills that will serve him well and that are part of working-class manhood. But Robert goes beyond that, in a break from concerns other studies have identified as associated with working-class masculinity. Based on his own life experience, Robert tries to teach Robbie independence of mind, to spare him the painful mistakes Robert made himself. From his own experience, he knows that "group think" can lead down a delinquent and potentially destructive path. To use Townsend's terminology, Robert is endowing his son with qualities of character that will help him succeed and will simultaneously protect him.

Notable about Robert Holcomb is his strong attachment to children. Robert reflects on his relationship with his stepchildren, with whom he was deeply involved while he and their mother were still married. When they split up, the children disappeared from his everyday life. He acutely experienced his loss of ties with them: "That's a real big void, you know, when you're used to children."[31] In regard to his biological son, Robert Holcomb is the exception to the literature that says fathers who do not share a home with their children do not sustain deep involvement with them, particularly in the absence of a marital relationship.[32] Robert talks about the impact Robbie's birth had on him: "He brought a feeling over me that I'd never experienced. I had his picture but it's packed up. I'd love for you to see it. He's gotta be about five minutes old, and I'm holding him. He just looks up at me, and he puts his arm up like this, and he's just staring at me. I mean, see, this close to my face. [Laughs.] I just—it's a good thing." I probe to find out what it feels like to be a father. I ask Robert if he sees himself as a teacher in Robbie's life.

> I want to be his everything. [Pause.] When things are going good, you know, children hardly think they need much of anything. When things are in perspective. 'Cause they'll just cruise through, too, and enjoy it. When things are rocky, you bet I'm stepping in, that's when he needs me. That's when I'm gonna be there. I'm there twenty-four/ seven, *but*, the times of need I think are the most important. I'm not gonna get on him for stuff. I wanna pick him up and I'm gonna brush him off, and I'm going to tell him *why* this happened. Hopefully he won't do it again.

Robert conveys vividly his fulfillment in his relationship with his son. In a single example, his sense of loss in the aftermath of Robbie's return to his mother becomes palpable: "That's what I missed the most when I got back home, man, I just got so used to hearing, 'Good morning, Dad!' You know, in the house, that's the first thing he'd say while he's stretching, you know? 'Right on, come give me a hug and we'll start this day.' That's important to me . . . we're best friends, man."[33]

Robert prioritizes his relationship with Patricia *because* she is Robbie's mother. "It doesn't matter what I'm doing—she's always been allowed to call me. She's always had a free run in my life. Anything to do with my child has priority. And whoever I'm with at the time, if they don't like it, well, then, 'Bye.' I won't allow anything to come between us." Robert's philosophy is that Robbie is best off when things work well for his mother. What is best for Patricia is best for Robbie. Robert is committed, interested, and ready to step up. He backs up Patricia's decisions, on principle. She knows and appreciates the way Robert prioritizes her parenting needs over anything else in his life. And Robert has extended a standing offer for her to come and live with him. Patricia feels absolute confidence in his steadfast commitment and in his capacity to be a good father and to direct Robbie along the right path. Robert emphatically articulates his passion and commitment to fatherhood. If his account of his participation in his son's life had not been corroborated by the women in the network, I would have perhaps discounted it as the power of ideology or wishful thinking. But everyone in the network provided similar accounts, making Robert an even more compelling figure.

As the father of her child, Robert Holcomb is Patricia Crane's virtual insurance policy that her second son will not end up like her first. She was not so fortunate with her older son. She blames his father for making matters worse rather than better: "When he was in a lot of trouble, when he was a juvenile, I made the mistake of getting ahold of his dad. Because I thought, you know, maybe that's why he's lashing out. So I got ahold of his dad, and he just ruined him. He messed him up, and the father is in prison right now. So that's what I'm dealing with there." She does not believe that just any man who happens to be a child's father will do. Rather, she values a particular kind of father, one who treats his family with respect, supports his child, and lives by a code worthy of emulating. She appreciates Robert as a father to her child and as a partner in parenting.

THE ALDRICHES: MODELING IDEAL CONDUCT. At the opposite end of the economic spectrum, the upper-class father, Alex Brolin, separated from Sarah Aldrich, shares some similarities with Robert Holcomb. He models ideal conduct more gingerly than does Robert, with less active intervention but with equal conviction. He reflects on his own childhood and how his parents taught him values and responsibility: "'You have to figure this out yourself, but, you know, just watch me.' And that was really more how values got instilled. . . . That's probably more how my kids are getting it. It's not because of preaching and sermons and that sort of stuff. . . . I would love to see the kids be very conscious of their societies and contribute as best they can. . . . And that'll be a learned-by-watching kind of thing." To elicit a set of desired behaviors, this upper-class fathering approach looks remarkably like that of the working-class father, insofar as it involves modeling ideal conduct and acting on one's values. (Conversely, it does not include "getting on" the children nor threatening to do so.) And his sense of appreciation and affection for his children infuses his conversations about them. "The kids are both so wonderful." He brags about them and celebrates the pleasures of being with them.

Some women in the upper-class network take charge of the home front, using a supermom gender strategy within marriage, with low expectations of men's involvement. For example, Lydia Dunn talks about her children's lives as though her husband does not exist. They share a residence, but as an individual parent, he is outside her networking system. In her accounts of educational planning, pickups, and summer camps, Lydia fails to mention him. How this imbalance in child rearing and household management impacts their marriage is not revealed in the interview. In relation to constructing a network of care, her husband is noticeably absent, although she calls upon male babysitters to help with her three sons.

In contrast, Sarah Aldrich, similarly executive in organizing the household, includes her separated husband, Alex Brolin, in her network. She expects Alex to contribute to their child-care system. And, like a small percentage of divorced fathers, Alex spends more time with the children as a separated father than he did while he lived with the family.[34] From her position as the virtual president of the family foundation, Sarah delegates tasks to Alex as she does to others. Like Patricia Crane and Tracy Johnson, she exercises control but sees the virtues of involving the children's father. She perceives him as a powerful, positive, and loving force in their lives. Because she has April Miller as her main care provider, she does not call on Alex as much as she otherwise might for the practical aspects of care. However, he purposely lives nearby, and now that he works closer to home, he is more easily available to be involved in the children's lives and their daily transportation; Sarah views his accessibility as a valuable asset to her and the network.

THE BECKERS: "BABYSITTING" VERSUS "PARENTING." The fun of fathering can come at the cost of other kinds of fun. When fathers intensively parent their children while they are employed full-time, like women, they risk "work overload."[35] Kerry Daly reports: "An analysis of the meanings of family time for fathers suggests that men believe in the priority of 'spending time with their children' but at the same time lament that 'making' time for family is 'costly,' fixed in amount, and largely beyond their control to change due to the demands of their paid work."[36] Fathers' involvement means they have less free time to socialize with friends.[37] And, as Dina Becker's husband, Mark Walde, would attest, fathers bemoan the demands of their wives' paid work.

One study finds that men "do time" with their children, rather than enjoy the time.[38] While for the vast majority of men I interviewed this perspective did not hold, it rang true for Mark Walde. Stuck in his ambivalence about the transition to parenthood, Mark feels reluctant about the sacrifice of free time that being a father entails. He belongs to a father's group that goes on outings together, often with the children. In the group, Mark has not confided in any of the fathers about how he feels. But he keeps his antennae out for clues to help him: "I know that these dads, . . . as I hear from the moms and my wife, that they also take duties with their kids. I mean, just as much probably as the moms. . . . But in terms of working all week as I do and then the weekends come and I know Dina's working, it's like she'll say, 'Well, I was working too,' but it's like, I don't know, I haven't totally [laughs] accepted that role." He gropes for ways to convey his predicament. He inquires whether I watch *Ally McBeal* on television and I regretfully report my ignorance. He describes an episode about a man who struggled to balance work and family with his employed wife:

> He had joined a chauvinist pigs' men's group and realized he joined it because he wanted to get over being a chauvinist pig. But then he eventually separated from his wife because he realized that he didn't *want* to end being a chauvinist pig [laughs] and he wanted his wife at home. You know, they had kids and so on; and I'm *not* in that category, but I also have not totally accepted . . . the paternal role. Although I know I'm a parent, she's a parent, we're equal, but . . . maybe it's just having kids and never really . . . accepting the responsibility totally. . . . Okay, my life is done.

He has reluctantly relinquished the freedom of his premarital life, but not his zest for it. He feels imprisoned. He resents his domestication and lack of autonomy, he speaks of "my life," not the family life, not family needs. And his life is over. From his perspective, he has little ability to do whatever he wants, like watch football with his friends or feel endorphins pumping after working out. He recognizes the appeal of a stay-at-home wife, although he does not want to be a male chauvinist pig. Unspoken is the fact that if Dina stopped doing photography, the household income would drop considerably. Mark does not have a job that pays a family wage that would sustain their current standard of living. Furthermore, while Dina has flexible work, "her work interferes with the weekends. I mean, photography is great for her, and I'm sure she maybe talked about this, because it's a stay-at-home kind of job, and I can help her out."

Dina and Mark agree that Mark plays a supporting role, one that is essential to Dina's ability to work, to run the network of care, and to rear their children. He "helps her out"; child rearing is not his job. He does not plan or organize the children's schedule. Nor does he mobilize members of the network to take over, except in rare instances. However, they disagree about how much he does and how to frame it—babysitting or parenting. Recall the conversation in Chapter 5, when Dina recounted that she would take off to photograph a wedding, hand the children over to Mark, and he said, "I'm babysitting *again?*" She retorted, "No, you're parenting." In his mind's eye, helping excuses him from taking responsibility. The distinction becomes more irksome when Mark says, "Sometimes I think I do more." He acknowledges that she "works incredibly hard and she stays up later than me." Consistent with other studies, he gets more sleep than she does.[39] He concedes, "When I think about those things, then I would have to say that she perhaps does more, even considering the times in the weekend when I take care of the kids." Yet in the end his ambivalence shows through: "I'd say probably fifty-fifty, although during the day, again, she doesn't have the kids anymore because they are in school and she does do carpool. I don't have to do that, but again, I would like to have during the day some free time to do stuff as well, which I think she could do if she was caught up, but she's not caught up yet. Who knows when, and if then, that will happen." In essence, he blames her lack of free time on her own disorganization. He envies her unrealized capacity to have free time during the day, resentful that she does not use it. If she did, he would gain ground from which to bargain. Previous conflict between them informs the discussion about who does more. Mark says: "I think it would be an interesting conversation if we really kind of objectively looked at it instead of at times, it's like, okay, 'Oh, I do more work.'. . . 'No, I do more,' and it becomes, like, you know, who is sacrificing more, which is such a silly concept." He realizes the futility of the language of sacrifice and one-upping. He and Dina are, after all, rearing children together. And he wants to be a father, he loves being part of an extended family, but he resents the workload and his lack of free time.

Dina Becker and Mark Walde differ in their gender strategies, but in practice, their child rearing is virtually fifty-fifty. Dina wants to share; she has a sharing strategy that she thinks is only fair because Donalyn and Aaron are Mark's children too. But Mark signed up to be a father, not a babysitter, and not a "parent" in the way Dina defines it. His version of fatherhood does not include full-time responsibility for the children.[40] But rather than adjust to the reality, he continues to fume, resenting his lack of free time and occasionally his wife for putting him in this position. For their marriage, the differences mean conflict. Without her husband's willingness to engage in the split-shift work arrangement, Dina would not be able to sustain her business as a freelance photographer. Without her extensive network of men and women to bolster the marriage and to buttress the child rearing, she could easily be in a situation similar to Sarah Aldrich's, but without the resources to deal with it. To Dina Becker, the involvement of men means being surrounded by reliable, safe, fun brothers on call all the time, and a husband who will do the work, even against his better judgment.

THE DUVALL-BRENNANS: FIFTY-FIFTY EXHAUSTION. Like Mark Walde, Jack Brennan suffers from overwork, but unlike Mark, he accepts it. Like the fathers interviewed by Townsend, he anticipated the drudgery of rearing children and sought "fun" before settling down to marry and have them. Townsend's fathers "assume that 'fun' is incompatible with the day-to-day work of raising children."[41] Jack Brennan's account reveals a fervent commitment to equity in parenting and a determination to create a good family life. Yet it is heavily marked by resignation and, at times, despair. When I inquired about whether or not he and Maggie might adopt more children, Jack replied, lowering his voice:

> God help me. Two is a tough enough choice. I think, having three kids—I might as well jump out that window and commit suicide right now. It would definitely be more efficient. You know, I think—we decided after a lot of thought and talking and struggling to try to have a second child, and for fairly specific reasons (I'm glad we did and I would make the same decision again), but. . . . Unless one of us had our salary doubled so the other one could quit, or we hit the lottery, we'd just—for us, it would be totally transactional. . . . The biggest thing we sigh to each other about over the table is that we don't give our kids time. We don't give them individual private time. You know, it's like today. You know, I come in, I give them a bath, I give them dinner. You know, I sit down at the dinner table with them and I talk to them in the bathtub. While I clean up, they do blocks next to me. This is, like, as intimate as it gets. And it's like, you know, three kids? I'd have to put them in a cage or something. No.

In part his exhaustion comes from still having a preschooler, one he and Maggie have designated a "spirited child." At this developmental point in their family life, it overrides the other aspects of parenting. When I asked Jack if there was anything else I should know about how he and Maggie make their system work, Jack responded:

> Well, I have no idea. I wonder every day as I stand over the sink doing dishes and making lunches for next day, and the kids are asleep. . . . Tonight, I thought, "Well, gotta get the kids in bed by nine. I'll see Karen for an hour. Then I gotta get that stuff from the basement. Then I've gotta do this for tomorrow." And it's kind of like you have this window for forty minutes or half an hour. At the end of each day, it's like a dog and a bone. Seriously, and beyond that, . . . I was looking at Scott today. . . . I'm gonna be bending over to pick things up with him until I can't stand anymore, so I'd better adjust to this. When I look at the longer term, it's daunting: financially,

transactionally, emotionally, physically. And . . . we are not gonna complain about it. We are well-to-do people in a nice home. We have two beautiful kids. We both have jobs. But it's still daunting.

When I ask if he and Maggie have time to have fun in all of that, he answers: "Yeah, but less fun. I mean, yeah. Less sex, fewer hikes, you know. Venice by fifty—did we share that with you? Venice by fifty? If that doesn't happen, the other side of fifty would be fine too. But you know, obviously you make choices. But it's harder." Jack's account of his fathering is about the minutiae of everyday life, the work of raising children, the effort, the exhaustion. A deeply thoughtful man, he has sorted through the choices he has made, the constraints he is up against, and the wealth of resources at his disposal. These resources do not make him *feel* life is easier. For him, fatherhood means responsibility, a deep-rooted commitment to his children, and endless work.

Women involved in parenting partnerships hold high expectations of men, equivalent to those they set for themselves. Along with their friends Rebecca Hoffman and Byron Russell, Jack and Maggie come closest to a full fifty-fifty sharing of the work of child care and mobilizing a network. They split the drop-offs and pickups and then take turns working late. Once a week, they hold a meeting to plot the week's schedule. They divide the labor and share equally in their intensive involvement with the children. Together, they consciously prefer the co-parenting strategy; and both recognize and appreciate each other's efforts, unable to imagine rearing children alone.

Some women who adopt a co-parenting strategy are jarred into a rude reality when they discover their partners share the belief but do not deliver in practice. Maggie's friend Lucia Stanley is a case in point. She and her husband believe in peace and justice in the world and equality at home. They structure the week as close to fifty-fifty as possible. Lucia's husband has designed an elaborate table that charts driving and caretaking responsibilities, which they amend regularly. "Monday, Friday, I'm responsible for dinner and, kind of, clean up," Lucia says. "Tuesday and Thursday, [my husband] is for clean-up. Wednesday, it's [date night.]." Each night they take turns putting their three children to bed. "One of us puts the girls to bed, one puts [our son] to bed. And whoever puts [our son] to bed, since that's usually the easier one since you don't have to read stories and all, also has to make lunches for the next day. After a while, it's like, this is so unromantic that you know it's working." They similarly schedule drop-offs and pickups at school with equity in mind. But in spite of divvying things up, Lucia says, "I think it's not equal, that I take more of it." And she resents her husband because they share an egalitarian gender ideology and strive for fairness. When she does not feel angry, she can see and appreciate his involvement. But she works full time, commutes three hours a day when she goes into the office, and feels that the conceptual details of the children's life fall to her. "I'm the one that, you know, is kind of on top of the appointments, and 'What do they need to bring to school that day?'" Her husband rebuts her complaints with the "I do a lot more than most guys" justification, and she concedes that is true. In spite of her resentment, which causes some real tension in their marriage, she says, "It's really pretty good. And I try as much as possible to look at it in that light." But they have not yet reached full equity in child rearing and network mobilizing, and she resents it.

Unlike Lucia Stanley, Maggie's friend Brenda Emerson genuinely appreciates her husband's involvement, which on its face appears about the same as Lucia's husband's. Like Lucia, she and her husband evenly divide pickup and drop-off times. Compared to her mother's generation, she sees that her husband is "really involved and he's very interested in the kids." And Brenda does not aspire to a fifty-fifty strategy, nor does her husband. He is involved with the children, and she manages the schedule and the household. "I'm behind the scenes running things about lunches and dinners, you know, doing some kind of detailed stuff that he doesn't do. But otherwise, we share pretty much everything in terms of child rearing." She explains her strategy of accommodating family needs: "I have put my career, definitely, on a slower pace in order to have more sanity at home." This compromise has meant a four-day workweek and a job for a public institution rather than for a demanding corporation. For Brenda, this is a workable solution. And perhaps because her expectations for her husband's involvement are lower, she does not feel the umbrage that Lucia does.

For all these middle-class parents, professional demands are unrelenting; in the face of family needs, overwork and exhaustion appear to be the inevitable outcomes. But within the marital partnerships, there are varying expectations. All the men contribute more than their fathers did before them. From their perspective, their workload has increased. All the women work in the paid labor force more than their mothers did before them. From their perspective, their workload has increased. Both are correct that contemporary work-family arrangements for middle-class professionals have increased the work hours and decreased the family labor supply. The restructuring of the economy and of kinship arrangements has created new tensions within marriages and families, some of which have prompted greater male participation in child rearing, if not housework. Does it create other kinds of opportunities? How women feel about men's involvement depends on their kinship relation, their own gender strategies and gender identity, and their expectations of the men.

How Do Men Get Involved with Children?

BECOMING INVOLVED FATHERS

Most of the fathers in this study practice a form of involved fatherhood. Not all sought to be this kind of father, but life circumstances, marriage, and partnership have pushed them in this direction. At a more profound level, that men share the work of hands-on child rearing transforms fatherhood in this culture. Involved fatherhood does not exclude breadwinning, but adds to it numerous relational and caretaking tasks historically deemed female.

For men, becoming involved fathers means treating children differently than their fathers treated them. Echoing the respondents in Daly's "Reshaping Fatherhood," the fathers in this study search about unsuccessfully for role models. And like many of the men interviewed by Townsend for *The Package Deal* and Gerson for *No Man's Land*, they reject the distant and authoritarian fathering by which they were reared, and hence their own fathers' practices. In turn, they create new ways of being fathers for themselves.

The men in my study look to an older generation to get a handle on what it means to be a father. But sometimes what they find spurs them in an opposite direction. The example of the upper-class father, Alex Brolin, illuminates what an awkward process this can be. Alex grew up in the Midwest with a full-time corporate father and a full-time homemaker mother. He recalls a painful attempt to connect emotionally with his father about their shared kinship status:

> Dad and I were fishing in Idaho and we were, you know, camping out with a bunch of guys. It was a very nice thing, and we went to bed and we were lying there talking a little, and I said, "Dad, tell me. What was it like being a dad?" You know? And my motivation for saying that was kind of to start some conversation, but I'm trying to find something we really have in common. You know, there's fishing and all that, but let's kind of a little bit more—you know, I thought, "We're both dads. What was it like being a dad?" He blew up. He just said, "What kind of stupid question is that? Oh, Alex, what are you talking about? Come on!" It was off the wall. I was blown away. . . . That gives you an example—he's not a big sharing-type kind of guy. It's true that . . . his parents sent him away to boarding school when he was in fourth grade—fourth grade. Not only did they send him away to boarding school. . . . They sent him to Canada, sent him to a different country.

In his effort to connect, Alex used a vocabulary of feeling that was not just unfamiliar to his father, but taboo. Like the men in Daly's study, Alex's father thinks "fatherhood should be done and not talked about."[42] Alex's quest to be a "good enough" involved father relies on others in the culture, his female friends, what he reads, and his own inspiration to make his relationships with his children different than his own with his father. He says, "I'd like to believe that we relate better, me to the kids and my kids to me, than I did with my parents, whether it's listening to the same music or doing the same kinds of things." He makes an effort to connect on their terms.

Jack Brennan's father died when he was seven and his brother Tom was nine, before they had a chance to observe critically or ask questions about fatherhood. Their father had minimal contact with the children, "unless there was serious discipline, all that stereotypical fifties dad [stuff]." Like Alex Brolin, Jack is purposely motivated to transform fathering so that his children's experience of him is different than his was of his father:

> That's been really important to me, . . . to be involved with my kids. And to establish a personal relationship with them, to understand them, give them an opportunity to understand me. That, you know, I didn't have with my dad because I didn't get it when he was alive, then the bastard up and died on me, so I didn't have the chance later. I'm very aware of that. I think I'm also acutely aware of bringing to my parenting the limitations of my upbringing; . . . for all my volubility as an attorney or an interviewee, . . . I learned, you know, you control situations more through passive aggression than . . . something direct. . . . All of those things have been incorporated in my personal way of interacting and my own emotional vocabulary. I'm constantly aware that's how I parent . . . and I have to take out the motherboard and do some readjusting; . . . that's obviously a lifelong process, but I'm particularly aware of it in the context of parenting.

Not only is Jack involved in a completely different way than his father, he is evaluating how he thinks about himself as a father, how he understands his emotional life, as well as how he relates to his children. His brother, Tom Brennan, already has grown children who he reared as a single divorced parent. As an uncle and a brother, Tom is anxious to lend a hand and offer advice to Jack, who is unwilling to accept it. They have reached a stalemate of sorts, in part because while they share their rejection of the fathering they received, they differ on their sense of what the new father model should be.

Like Jack and Tom Brennan's, Ben Crane's father was virtually absent in his childhood. By age eleven, Ben was living with his older sister and helping her raise her infant son. At seventeen, when Ben went to live with his biological father, he did not find the father he imagined. He found an alcoholic who had little to offer him. Now Ben, a divorced father, tries to actively parent his four-year-old son, who is in his ex-wife's custody. Like Jack, Ben takes pride in being a father. But because his father was not in the picture, he does not have a wealth of observation or experience from which to draw. He was raised, as he puts it, "the old-school way," where fathers exercised a firm, authoritarian hand. His most extensive experience caring for small children was with Patricia's older son, who, only eleven years younger than Ben, was a brother/nephew. His sense of how to be an uncle and a father derives from that experience. He relies heavily on his sister to help him negotiate child rearing with his ex-wife and to set standards of behavior for his son. He tries to spend "quality time" with Paulie and do "whatever's good for his best interests," including taking him to church every week.

Another example similarly involves an uphill battle, but for different reasons. Robert Crane's father was a truck driver in the agricultural heartland of California who also brought Robert up in the "old school," as he calls it. Robert reflects on his struggles to adapt to the world his six-year-old son inhabits. In his narrative, becoming a father has been life transforming, in the most positive of senses. "I really try hard since he's been born, to be a lot more flexible, you know. And open, I guess, to things that I never have been open to before." He zealously makes himself available to Robbie "twenty-four/seven." Robert's metamorphosis, only a glimpse of which the reader sees here, stems from fatherhood and also from the accident that left him with paraplegia. The challenge of fathering from a wheelchair is not one about which the culture gives much guidance.[43] At this point, mobility seems the least of Robert's worries, because he manages to live independently so well. His disability does not diminish his authority but rather enhances it. Robert comes across as a man who could surmount any obstacle. He is determined to teach his son fortitude and courage, which he has learned the hard way.

For Robert and other men, becoming fathers provides an opportunity to relate to their children differently than their own fathers related to them. They universally feel positively about this. Peter Becker raised eight children by purposely embarking on a new kind of family venture. He forged a pact with his wife to worship together in the same church (which his own mother and father had not done). They aspired to have many children and to build a congenial, family-centered culture. And Peter Becker has devoted his life to the project of family.

His two sons, the Becker uncles, are the only exceptions in my research to this pattern of rejecting the model of their own fathers. They expressly want to be like their father, whom they depict as a helper and extraordinary caretaker. Their parents' gendered division of child rearing aside, both men describe Peter Becker as available and present in their upbringing. The two uncles have a strong orientation toward children and their extended kin; they are "family men," as Coltrane would put it. They point to a model of fatherhood that is typically not assumed to have great emotional depth or much contact with children. In a household with a full-time working father and full-time stay-at-home mother, these two men grew up immersed in an ethic of family solidarity and connection to their father. In relying on their father as a role model and as a kin member, these adult men are reproducing a particular kind of manhood they find appealing.

MEN'S RELATIONSHIP TO THE LABOR MARKET

One method men use to become involved fathers is to alter their relationships to the labor market. In contrast to the women, men did not articulate the same kind of family imperatives that trumped work, which is not surprising given the importance of breadwinning to conceptions of masculinity.[44] Nonetheless, the transformation of gender relations in the past thirty years has accompanied a shift not just in how men think about their families and their fathering, but, for some, the degree to which they are attached to traditional workplaces and breadwinning.[45]

In this vein, each of the four central fathers in this study has made changes in his employment to accommodate family life in some way. Alex Brolin moved his office closer to home and the children's schools so he could be more available and not commute two hours each day. The move allows him to see his children more and be involved in their activities. As head of his department, Jack Brennan regularly arrives at the office around 9:30 or 10:00. He interprets his position of authority as having some flexibility to facilitate his family responsibilities. As a schoolteacher, Mark Walde has a job considered more compatible with child rearing. In addition, he has markedly reduced the number of hours he devotes to his own athletic training and feels he has sacrificed a great deal to be with his family. Robert Crane does not have a position in the formal labor force; nonetheless, he works as a mechanic and rearranges his life when his son is with him. He tries to teach Robbie by absorbing him as an apprentice into his work. In sum, each of these fathers has struggled with how to be an effective family member and a worker at the same time.

Like the middle-class mothers, the middle-class fathers, Jack Brennan and Mark Walde, speak with some anxiety about work. Their anxieties center on their perception of their own less-than-optimal performance at work.[46] At the men's place of employment, their families are invisible; the men are there to be productive workers. Both feel the internal clutch of knowing they could do more and better, but not if they are going to remain active in their children's lives. They seek to be good providers, but they want to be involved fathers at the same time. They are making trade-offs and incorporating family life into their work equations in a way their fathers did not. Their choices leave them feeling uncomfortable and worried about the precariousness of their employment.

Discussion and Conclusion

To the question about what men positively contribute to networks of care, we now have some answers. These accounts of men give us insight into what child-related activities they do, what that means to them, and how they interact with the women in negotiating reciprocity and help. The men love, express affection, and demonstrate emotional involvement. They support their partners, daughters, brothers, and sisters in various ways. Collectively, they also cook, clean, play, worry, plan, and discipline. Men step up to fill partly the family labor shortage. Some contribute reluctantly, others enthusiastically. Regardless, they provide an important source of labor for the practical and emotional chores of child rearing and for the support to parents.

Significantly, fathers are not the only men involved with children. Emotionally and logistically, uncles and grandfathers figure prominently as well. In this research, grandfathers watch children's athletic events and theatrical performances; they drive carpools; they shop. Uncles babysit, play, advise, and cover in scheduling emergencies. Involvement in the lives of children is important to these men, as well as to the women. Nonetheless, grandfathers and uncles also emphasize their willingness to rearrange their lives to accommodate the logistics of rearing their nieces, nephews, and grandchildren. These men experience fun and satisfaction as well as despair and frustration. Being a part of a network means being needed and being able to trade on reciprocal relations. And their accounts detail the complex processes involved in forging a "new fatherhood" in the face of few role models of their own. In these networks, class does not appear to differentiate either involved fatherhood or participation in a network of care. Men are involved across the class spectrum. The cases also show that men do not need to live with children to love them, to help care for them, or to be engaged in their lives. Resident fatherhood is not essential for men's involvement in the lives of children.

That the vast majority of men in the networks were related to the anchors raises the question: Do men need to be kin to be recruited into the networks? The accounts in this chapter consider men in their kin context. Only one man of the targeted ten male network members, Byron Russell, is a friend of the family. And I discuss him here only in relation to his own wife and children, not in relation to his friends, Jack Brennan and Maggie Duvall. In fact, he was recruited into the network by Jack and Maggie as part of a co-parenting team (with his wife Rebecca). Because he shared their child-rearing philosophy and had children of his own, he became a trusted network member. Without these markers of fatherhood and feminist commitment, would he have been recruited via the staging process? It was not a question I directly asked my subjects, but the exclusion of other nonrelated men speaks volumes. Notably, the same high threshold does not apply to women in the networks. Many female network members are friends of the anchors, although only one is not also a mother.

While this chapter explores how these particular men reproduce fatherhood differently than their fathers did, the question remains, how do these men come to be network members in a society that prefers female caregivers? The intractable gendered division of labor in the household and in the economy assigns women the work of caregiving and lays the responsibility for it on the shoulders of women.

To link this question to an overarching issue of the book, it is possible to see the tension between the *interdependence* of network participation and involved kinship, and the *autonomy* and *individualism* ideologically celebrated about men in U.S. culture. This tension operates on at least two levels—the community/network level and the household level. This chapter reveals that men may be willing to give up the advantages of individualism on one level but not on another.

At the community/network/kinship level, the Cranes, the Aldriches, and the Beckers have no trouble with interdependence. As networks, they connect, get involved, give up time (and money) to be involved in children's lives. A conscious philosophy of connection can push an individual or a family toward involvement with others. The Cranes recognize the interdependence of kin, neighbors, and friends; it is a fact of life. They also believe in a kind of Christian altruism that prompts them to reach out to others. Robert Holcomb counts his blessings in being alive and in the miracle of his child. He sees his life as infinitely enriched by the presence of his son. The Aldriches have a philosophy of philanthropy that means they reach out to others through giving. In regard to their network, they trade among a community of relative equals. They have no qualms about their reliance on others, their embedded interdependence—through employing people and through friendship. The Becker commitment to family solidarity motivates its members toward helping and interdependency. The gender-neutral ethos of "we help" (as opposed to "my wife helps" or "my sister helps") removes the stigma from helping and support work. In contrast, the Duvall-Brennans have a political belief in comwmunitarianism, but their commitment to professional work interferes with their ability to put it into action. So they are the ones who resort to household self-sufficiency the most, and rely least on their community and network.

At the household level, the tension works in more complicated and more visibly gendered ways. As I discussed in Chapter 1, the internal household practice of interdependence counters the ideology of individualism in the culture as a whole. It is a contradiction that occasionally creates tensions, but that women, and to a lesser extent men, largely accept[47]—particularly in regard to child rearing. Family members at different stages of their lives go through periods of dependency, childhood being the most relevant here. Internal to the household, that interdependence between members over the life course operates in the context of an economically and socially gendered division of labor. Historically, the tasks of caring for dependents have fallen primarily to women and have been seen as women's work (whether or not men did them). And these tasks—such as child rearing—are the precise ones that create women's economic dependence on men. Janet Finch and Dulcie Groves note that women's dependent status as mothers, housewives, or daughters "is not absolute, but is conditional upon their being simultaneously depended upon by others. Thus, for many women, being a dependant is synonymous not with receiving care, but with giving it." They further argue that "for women, economic dependency and poverty is the cost of caring."[48]

For men, the cost of independence in the marketplace is dependence on women in the home. The ideology and the consequences operate differently for men, even though their circumstance is based on the same foundation of gendered work. As the historical breadwinners, men have depended on women to care for them; that is part of the breadwinning bargain. To be "independent" wage earners, men have relied on women to cook for them, clean their houses, provide sexual services, bear their children, and the like. The dependence that their independence has been built upon has been invisible.

In the shift to households with two breadwinners, men have had to come to terms with the invisible labor, and suffer its absence when their partners do not have the time or inclination to continue the support services. In addition, the men have had to become supporters of their partners, who as breadwinners also need help. Therefore, not only do the men lose services, but also they must become the invisible caregivers to their partners. If the couple has children, both man and woman must do the family labor to rear those children.

So when Robert Holcomb, in the opening passage in the book, declares himself to be self-sufficient and independent, he is looking at the world as a male breadwinner. Those support services that make his life possible, that enable him to be mobile and to live independently, are invisible. Because he is a man, they are assumed and necessarily unseen. When pushed, Robert acknowledges them, because he recognizes that behind his presentation of self lies a network of people caring for him—not a wife or partner, but an entire network that enables him to care for his son. While his life circumstances are more extreme than those faced by most men, the themes are no different from theirs.

Jack Brennan and Mark Walde have handled this shift to caregiving partners and fathers in different ways. The philosophy of feminism and equity between men and women motivates Jack to share the work of parenting. While Jack and Maggie do not parent in the context of extended kinship, they share an ideology of equality. With a commitment to co-anchoring the child-rearing project, Jack's involvement in his children's lives means sharing the emotional challenges of parenting and the attendant exhaustion. And along the way, the egalitarian approach requires rethinking his approach to life and parenting differently than he was parented; as Jack puts it, he is readjusting his motherboard. He does this individually and with Maggie, but not in a context of family solidarity. Their partnership enhances their marriage, even if in the short term it depletes them as individuals.

Mark Walde is a different sort of man with a different kind of marriage. He has become an egalitarian reluctantly and is not sure that is where he wants to end up. He struggles with giving up his autonomy for fatherhood and partnership. Not brought up in the Becker family, his ideology of individualism clashes with the family practice of collectivism and solidarity at the household level. Even though he likes the interdependent trappings of extended kinship at the community level, he has not made the full transition to involved fatherhood at the household level. Mark's conception of his responsibilities as father and the kind of partnership he desires make his time and labor feel like unfair burdens. Unlike Jack Brennan, he is not committed to fifty-fifty parenting, let alone fifty-fifty exhaustion. Therefore, his lack of free time and the lack of a wife in a supporting role grate on his nerves and rankle his marriage.

The context of the two networks is illuminating because their respective networks offer different things. The Duvall-Brennan network offers emotional support and advice, whereas the Becker network makes the child-rearing and marital arrangement possible. The Duvall-Brennans get sympathy, but no help. The Beckers get help, but at the same time the network eases the tensions of Dina and Mark's marriage, it simultaneously facilitates Dina's absorption in her work, which in turn creates more conflict with Mark.

It is important to continue to analyze the accounts of men's life with children from a feminist perspective. Because most fathers are found to be helpers rather than sharers in housework and parenting, the responsibilities for women rearing children are enormous. Women may judge the help inadequate, but they recognize it as better than nothing, sometimes very much so. Because men's contributions vary, situating what they do and whom they help becomes essential for evaluating the impact. When men help women or share in a child-rearing project, women have a lighter load—practically and psychologically. This is no small thing. Even when men provide back-up help, women's tasks become easier. Patricia Crane sees the involvement of her son's father as the salvation of his future. Robert Holcomb brings interest and passion to fathering and he opens a door for Robbie to viable adult manhood. To Patricia, Robert's involvement means the difference between her success and failure as a mother.

Conclusion

IN MAPPING THE lives that intertwine in the project of rearing school-age children, this book has explored the not-so-nuclear *practice* of interdependence with kin and friends in the context of a cultural *belief* in the independence of nuclear families. It has considered the conundrum that even though most people say family is important, they simultaneously think extended families are not sufficiently available, amenable, or stable to help their members. And yet, the stories of the people interviewed for this book fly in the face of this widespread perception. Raising children, an enterprise largely cast as an individual or nuclear family endeavor in postindustrial, postmodern U.S. culture, retains important collaborative dimensions.

Economic Restructuring and Creative Family Solutions

Families are suffering a labor shortage. It is not just poor families that need help rearing children; it is families across the economic spectrum. From the perspective of single female–headed households, this seems obvious. However, importantly, nuclear heterosexual households with two wage earners face this problem as well. Structurally, the problem exists for all households trying to rear children and earn a living wage at the same time. The dilemma is not simply about a shortage of time, which strains family resources in and of itself, it is about needing multiple sets of hands to help care for children.

This case-study approach to networks provides a unique opportunity to investigate how agency on a household and neighborhood scale dovetails with restructuring in the larger economy. The families profiled here, like families across the country, seek financial solvency in the context of economic shifts and the decline in male wages. And, in the face of decades of economic change and dramatic alterations in family structure, in order to raise children, they craft networks of care. Through these richly textured accounts of everyday bartering and caretaking, we see how individuals and families adapt to the conflicting commitments of working for wages and rearing children, while creatively constructing networks of interdependence.

Negotiating these work-family tensions is not new in the United States; it has a long history. Working-class women like Patricia Crane, and her mother and grandmother before her, have always had to find paid employment and care for children in their absence. This has also been true historically of immigrant women, African American women, and other women of color. With the family labor shortage at the turn of the twenty-first century, middle-class women of the privileged racial group have had to follow in their steps. Over time, women have created alternative family structures and relied on both kin and nonkin to care for children.

These networks are invisible to academics, policy makers, and the public in general. The enduring mythology of American self-sufficiency and independence interferes with a willingness to recognize the centrality of networks of care and to eliminate the obstacles to facilitating them. Research that documents interdependence has not translated into the reformulation of theories of families. In the plea to decenter theoretically the white nuclear middle-class family and accept "all kinds of families" on their own terms, scholars must keep in mind that not only household structures are multiple and varied, but also arrangements for rearing children.

Networks are not merely the products of deficits, although they spring up in response to the family labor shortage. Nor are they outcomes exclusively of privilege, although without sufficient resources anchors have difficulty constructing and sustaining effective networks. Having a pool of potential members from which to draw, identified via friendship or kinship, creates an essential kind of wealth for parents as they rear children. If potential network members make themselves inaccessible because of work commitments, geographic distance, or lack of interest, that wealth is diminished. If network members care *about* the children but cannot care *for* them, or vice versa, then anchors must continue their recruitment efforts: The ideal network of interdependence includes members who are capable of meeting both these criteria. Moreover, maintaining networks and network relationships requires time and effort. The net effect is not that networks save time for the anchor, but rather that they shore up the household labor pool.

While networks solve some family labor-force problems, they do not solve them all. These networks of care can operate as a safety net for families and their children, but not necessarily under all conditions. Most crises of care could be handled by the Cranes, for example, because someone would step forward and take responsibility for Robbie. However, their network members' capacity to help is subject to their current job requirements and the state of their health. In contrast, in the Duvall-Brennan network, short of a catastrophe such as sudden death or an earthquake, Maggie Duvall and Jack Brennan are largely on their own.

Classic social tensions surface in the networks between autonomy on the one hand and communal interdependence on the other. Network involvement, because it obliges one to others, comes at a social cost that some people do not want to pay. Those in a position similar to Dina Becker's are heavily indebted. Network involvement may also hedge one's privacy, as the Becker siblings complained; in their case, other network members became concerned about their personal business and expected to know where they could be found at all times of the day and night. And the number of logistical challenges under consideration increases with participation, which is precisely what drives Kate Farnsworth away from carpools. Ultimately, although anchors may increase the household-care labor force by staging and mobilizing networks, their time will diminish because others now have a claim on it. As this research shows, when people anchor networks, they must perform endless work to develop and sustain them.

Kinship and the Enduring Power of Class Contingencies

Importantly, parents are constrained by the contingencies of their class location. In conceiving of class as a complex relationship with overlapping economic and social dimensions, I posit that ideologies and experiences are linked to class location but are not determined by it. Subjects in different networks articulate their own ideas about the appropriate contributions of friends and family, and they privilege different social relationships. Their class-situated beliefs in interdependence build the foundation for their preferences. Interdependence is something with which the working-class women and some middle-class women feel more comfortable, in part because it is based on mutuality and commonality of circumstance. Interestingly, the upper-class women also felt comfortable with interdependence, but did so in the context of a clear hierarchy of decision making and control. In contrast, the middle-class professional women seek independence and indeed seem reluctant to engage in interdependent relationships. But is their aversion to asking for help a belief? Or is it a survival strategy?

All the women and men in this study differentiate between kinship and friendship in how they construct and observe the asking rules of reciprocity. Consistent with the ideology of kinship, the subjects of my research generally accepted the principle that kin are interdependent with other active, identified, known kin, particularly in relation to child rearing. Some think grandparents have an obligation to care for grandchildren; others extend this principle to include uncles and aunts, in their belief that family comes first and that family members should help each other, regardless of competing obligations. Still others reject this idea but fall back on the notion that family can be counted upon in the last instance.

Structural forces—the robustness of the economy, educational achievement given early schooling, job availability given skill level, the number of hours people need to work in order to keep their jobs, and the like—profoundly shape the situation in which parents find themselves and the resources at their disposal. Not only does employment determine monetary resources, but also the conditions of the workplace influence the health of workers and how much energy and attention they can devote to family and community life. To be part of a network, one has to be able to reciprocate, over the long run. Not being able to reciprocate hobbles one's ability to construct a network. Workplace policies and conditions, however, are forged on an ideology of the individual worker, promoting an ethos of success and competition.

The structure of work can likewise make involvement in a network of care easier, as with Kent Becker, whose chunks of time off work made him available to help others in his network. More commonly, work constraints hinder involvement. In the workplace, women have fewer benefits and less flexibility in their jobs, as do poor people in general. As Margaret Nelson and Joan Smith put it, women are more likely to work in "bad" jobs than "good" jobs—defined as jobs with "decent wages, permanent work, and secure benefits."[1] Ironically, good jobs that pay decent wages, such as those of attorneys and other career professionals, similarly lack flexibility. For the Duvall-Brennans, both lawyers, not just employment per se but the structure of their employment and the commuting it entails diminish their capacity to reciprocate.

Jobs are structured to maximize productivity and profit, not to accommodate family or community commitments. Workers must decide to accept the conditions of employment, lose their jobs, or collectively organize to change those conditions. For those with careers, diminishing aspirations or opting for a shorter workweek can stigmatize and even derail them. Careers demand focused attention and copious time. In an era of corporate downsizing, too great or visible a commitment to family can target one's position for elimination altogether.

Even with structural constraints, all people have some agency in the decisions they make. In myriad ways, anchors, through their choices, strategically construct networks. They decide where they can live, given their means; whom they recruit into their network based on who they trust; how much energy they commit to being part of a network in the context of their kin and work commitments; what kinds of jobs they can get; and then, which job to accept.

The working-class and upper-class women demand that their employment accommodate caregiving needs. For Patricia Crane, paid work is contingent on the exigencies of her family life. Her options are limited to low-paying, low-skilled jobs; nevertheless she chooses carefully, identifying bosses who recognize the primacy of her family commitments and the quality of her work contributions. Just as employers think of low-wage workers as interchangeable, Patricia considers her low-wage jobs interchangeable. While she contemplates her options, she thinks about her two part-time service-sector jobs that offer no benefits. She imagines life at a nearby factory, a job she applied for and never got, but that promised health insurance and a higher salary. And she takes into account the essential backdrop of the state allowance that pays her to be a home health-care provider for her ailing mother. Although working from a completely different context, Sarah Aldrich chose a path similar to Patricia Crane's after she separated from her husband and recognized the need to be home more with her children: She dropped half her board commitments to reduce her workload. Both women made work decisions contingent on family needs. And for neither of them did these decisions threaten downward mobility.

In contrast to the working-class and upper-class women, the women with middle-class jobs made family needs contingent on work. They feared an economic tumble. In these anxious economic times, they struggled to hold onto their class position, sacrificing family time if necessary. Dina Becker stuck with a niche photography business even though it impinged extensively on family time. Her insistence on framing her business in a particular way had consequences for her schedule, her level of stress, and the anxiety she brought to family life. Trying a different route, the Duvall-Brennans left higher-paying jobs for lower-paying and less demanding ones to have more time with their children. Nevertheless, still locked into law careers, they found that the slack their more adaptive jobs cut was not enough. They still had little time to be with their children, and even less time to engage in the kind of reciprocal community relations that would help them establish a more fully functioning child-care network. Class contingencies shape not just the location one is in, but where one is trying to go. In this vein, the middle-class network members had the least advantage, because they had little psychological autonomy from work. They were trying desperately to hold onto their careers, their middle-class incomes, and their social position.

The structural constraints of employment are coupled with those of the kinship system into which one is married, born, or adopted. The limitations can be as entrenched as those of the workplace. Kin commitment and resources are enforced not just by cultural beliefs, but also by laws and federal policies that endorse a particular configuration of kinship. Federal policies support a heterosexual *nuclear* family with a breadwinning husband and stay-at-home wife if a family is middle class; they demand an employed mother if the family is poor. These policies ignore demographic realities and defy family needs for more resources in time, money, and labor power.[2]

The constraints and opportunities of kinship are systemic. While sociologists recognize that kinship operates as a system of obligations and statuses, they less commonly explore the ways that people face the constraints of their extended families. No one has control over their family of origin—its beliefs, capacities, resources, or personalities. While the anchors in this study have some ability to influence their children's behavior, they are faced with the fait accompli of the number of their siblings, the attitudes or character of their parents, and the health status of their grandparents. Having relatives in the vicinity guarantees neither their availability nor their interest in one's child.

And yet, as with the workplace, people exercise agency within that structure. People construct active kinship ties much as they construct friendships and community involvements, or shape workplace conditions. They entice select kin and enlist their active participation, while they discourage or ignore others. Parents act as gatekeepers to the kin domain, edging some out, recruiting others. Maggie Duvall might have constructed a more kin-based network had she been born into the Becker family. As it is, she has relatives who are not that interested in her children and who strongly disapprove of her child-rearing philosophy. And most parents are unwilling to spend much time persuading others to value and be involved with their children. Nonetheless, networks of care for children have a kin advantage over other kinds of networks, because parents can mobilize kin obligation to help in their child-rearing project, as well as stage reciprocal relations with family and friends. The kin cushion makes a difference in care, as does the friend cushion, although as I have demonstrated, neither is a guarantee of secure, reliable care of one's children. In other words, kin are not a fixed resource that a person can simply tap into when the need arises. Nor are friends and neighbors.

The labor force of nuclear families, which consists of one or two working parents, is insufficient to cover the care needs of the family as a whole. Parents need help and they wisely turn to others for it. Because they largely manage to care for their children, despite many mishaps and occasional tragedies, the current situation is seen by the general public as working. Yet parents need both informal and formal social supports.

Framing Future Studies of Families

Just as a focus solely on the nuclear family misses "other mothers," aunties, grandmothers, and child-care workers, so too it misses uncles, grandfathers, and male friends.[3] Instead of starting with the assumption, for example, that men are at best marginal figures in networks, I followed the lead of the anchors, tracking the many people who moved in and out of the children's lives, and found men. An inductive approach allowed me to explore where the networks took me, rather than assume a gendered division of network labor that would have led me to miss important processes. And this case-study method enabled me to study the networks in their entirety.

Networks that form to provide the care for and about children often spill over into arenas outside child care. Thus, for working parents, constructing a network is in effect a means of community building. A network constructed around care for children can quickly, but not necessarily or automatically, broaden to a system of sharing and trading. Future research must ask: What are the limits of that expansion? How precisely does the conversion unfold?

Does the fact that these networks center on children make them different from other kinds of networks? Probably, but future research should study this issue in a comparative context. Does the fact that the subjects are largely white, and that the anchors are white, make a difference in the construction of the networks? This is another question that can be answered only in the context of comparative study.

Implications for Social Policy

To my mind, Robert Holcomb's strategy for supporting his son's mother can act as a model for U.S. family policy. Robert helps Patricia Crane raise their son by endorsing her parenting decisions, helping to build her self-confidence, offering her housing, and supporting her kin activities and employment to insure that she can make the most of the monetary and people resources at her disposal. His position is: Whatever works best for Patricia works best for his son.

The government should take a similar approach to supporting families. What works for the mothers and fathers of the children works best for the children. Informal practices must go hand in hand with formal social policies.

State-supported services are important because not every parent has a network, and by themselves, informal networks are typically not enough to meet all the needs of parents and care for school-age children. Only the state has the capacity to collectivize the costs of child care and make it available to all, regardless of individual family resources. Only a multitiered, multifaceted system of care can assure parents of the safety and well-being of their children. The balance of choices and constraints has to help parents make the most of the options for care, so they can in addition continue to support their families financially.

State and federal governments need to provide support for families in their various configurations. Without state support for certain social programs, families are in jeopardy. Universal health care would shore up the family labor force, helping to insure its good health and capacity to care for itself and others. Without state-supported medical care, Patricia Crane risks her own long-term health, and she is forced to make no-win judgments about medical treatment for her son. Other kinds of family-income supports need to be funded—those that help families in crisis, and those that help poor families on an ongoing basis. Had California not financed some home health-care wages for Fran Crane in the midst of her health crisis, Patricia Crane could not have quit her jobs to care for her convalescing mother and still put food on the table.

Formally, parents need high-quality, affordable options that range from institutional day care to before- and after-school programs to neighborhood family day care to kin care. Until parents' workdays precisely match the length of their children's school days, holidays, and vacations, there will be gaps in care for school-age children. After-school program hours critically supplement school hours, but programs often end at six o'clock, with no wiggle room, making them inadequate to the schedules of parents who work longer days, swing shifts, or weekends.[4] After-school programs, an essential building block of school-age care, need to serve all school districts and offer more hours of coverage. Flexibility is key. Whenever arranging child care, parents state clearly that they have to trust the people that care for their children. Should they settle for anything less?

On the work front, parents also need flexibility in the organization of their tasks and schedules to accommodate the care for children.[5] Workers need legal guarantees that their employers will not punish them if they miss work to manage a family crisis. They need *paid* family and medical leave. Workers in general need workplace accommodation for their substantive ties to others that may not be defined by formal, legal kinship, but that make an essential difference in others' well-being. Shifts in workplace culture need to accompany those policies to make them viable options for workers.[6]

Supporting the caretakers of children in whatever way possible creates the best possible circumstances to enrich children's lives—through paying a living wage; insuring affordable, quality childcare; providing universal health care and affordable housing; and offering income supports to families where necessary. Children are a public good, as Nancy Folbre puts it, as well as a private treasure or a gift.[7] A good society encourages its citizens to invest in children, to recognize their collective responsibility for rearing children, and to become personally involved in the lives of children who are not their own. A good society facilitates participation in networks of care for children.

The work of caregiving for children and for adults requires recognition, honor, and respect. That work is best shared within households and across networks. This revaluation and redistribution will insure that the gender of caregiving in the future will not be always and forever female. The concept of interdependence emphasizes an important reality, removes the stigma of dependency, and challenges the fallacy of independence. Recognizing the interdependence of family, kin, and network members means acknowledging the sociality of humans and honoring the work of life.

Appendix

Name Index

Aldrich, Jane, mother of Sarah Aldrich (Aldrich network)

Aldrich, Sarah, anchor (Aldrich network)

Becker, Barbara, sister of Dina Becker

Becker, Dina, anchor (Becker network)

Becker, Kent, brother of Dina Becker (Becker network)

Becker, Peter, father of Dina Becker (Becker network)

Becker, Ryan, brother of Dina Becker (Becker network)

Becker, Shannon, sister of Dina Becker (Becker network)

Becker, Susan, mother of Dina Becker (Becker network)

Becker-Walde, Aaron, child of Dina Becker and Mark Walde

Becker-Walde, Donalyn, child of Dina Becker and Mark Walde

Bergman, Ruth, former neighbor (Duvall-Brennan network)

Brennan, Amanda, sister to Jack Brennan (Duvall-Brennan network)

Brennan, Jack, co-anchor (Duvall-Brennan network)

Brennan, Tom, brother of Jack Brennan (Duvall-Brennan network)

Brolin, Alex, separated husband of Sarah Aldrich (Aldrich network)

Brolin, Jacob, son of Sarah Aldrich and Alex Brolin

Brolin, Kimberly, daughter of Sarah Aldrich and Alex Brolin

Clark, Teresa, coresident partner of Tom Brennan (Duvall-Brennan network)

Crane, Ben, brother to Patricia Crane (Crane network)

Crane, Brendan, nineteen-year-old son of Patricia Crane

Crane, Fran, mother of Patricia Crane (Crane network)

Crane, Louise, grandmother of Patricia Crane

Crane, Patricia, anchor (Crane network)

Crane, Paulie, son of Ben Crane, cousin to Robbie Crane

Crane, Robbie, six-year-old son of Patricia Crane

Crane, Sherry, half-sister of Fran Crane and grandmother of Robbie Crane
Dunn, Lydia, mother of Jacob Brolin's best friend (Aldrich network)
Duvall, Maggie, co-anchor (Duvall-Brennan network)
Duvall-Brennan, Danielle, child of Maggie Duvall and Jack Brennan
Duvall-Brennan, Scott, three-year-old child of Maggie Duvall and Jack Brennan
Emerson, Brenda, friend from mother's group (Duvall-Brennan network)
Farnsworth, Kate, best friend of Sarah Aldrich (Aldrich network)
Hoffman, Rebecca, former neighbor (Duvall-Brennan network)
Holcomb, Robert, father of Robbie Crane (Crane network)
James, Caitlin Becker, sister of Dina Becker (Becker network)
Johnson, Tracy, friend and neighbor (Crane network)
MacLeod, Aidan, babysitter (Aldrich network)
McKendrick, Lila Becker, sister of Dina Becker (Becker network)
Miller, April, nanny of Aldrich children (Aldrich network)
Ramsey, Lee, manager of Hacienda Apartments, where Patricia Crane lives
Russell, Byron, former neighbor (Duvall-Brennan network)
Stanley, Lucia, friend in mother's group (Duvall-Brennan network)
Walde, Mark, husband of Dina Becker (Becker network)

Notes

Preface and Acknowledgments

1. Reflexivity in qualitative research inevitably prompts autobiographical musings. See Hertz, *Reflexivity and Voice*.
2. It was California's commitment during the 1960s to excellent, affordable education at all levels that made it possible for me to continue my education beyond high school. Bankrolled by scholarships and financial aid, I not only earned an undergraduate degree but also went on to attend graduate school and receive my doctorate from one of the finest universities in the world—the University of California, Berkeley.
3. I did have a car, which gave me independence, as well as the power to leave campus and sustain ties to my family and boyfriend.
4. My sister's three daughters, whose ages cluster around mine, lived with us periodically. They called my father "Daddy" instead of "Grandpa" because he was the primary father figure in their lives.
5. By most standard definitions we were. My parents earned only slightly more than the minimum wage. And by the time I was working as a waitress, at the age of eighteen, my hourly wages (plus tips) were higher than theirs.
6. Richard Sennett and Jonathan Cobb talk about the way working-class families discourage reading in *The Hidden Injuries of Class* (New York: Knopf, 1972).
7. Childers, "'Parrot or the Pit Bull,'" 203.
8. Baltzell, *The Protestant Establishment Revisited*; DiLeonardo, "Female World"; Schneider and Smith, *Class Differences in American Kinship*.
9. Baltzell, *The Protestant Establishment Revisited*, 99.
10. Childers, "'Parrot or the Pit Bull.'"
11. U.S. Census Bureau, *Statistical Abstract*.
12. See Keister, *Wealth in America*. Class location cannot be understood in its full social, psychological, and even economic dimensions without studying families. Social mobility studies repeatedly identify parents' characteristics (education and occupation, in particular) as the strongest predictors of an individual's economic trajectory. Baltzell argues that the very essence of upper-class status "refers to a group of *families*" (*The Protestant Establishment Revisited*, 30, emphasis added). Nevertheless, he and most other researchers who study the upper classes focus largely on economic, political, and volunteer activity, *not* on family practices or child-rearing philosophies (see Baltzell, *Puritan Boston and Quaker Philadelphia*; Daniels, *Invisible Careers*; Domhoff, *Who Rules America?*; Mills, *The Power Elite*; Ostrander, *Women of the Upper Class*). Those who write about class from a personal perspective acknowledge its powerful effects on family experience and life

consequence (e.g., Childers, "A Spontaneous Welfare Rights Protest"; Steedman, *Landscape for a Good Woman*; Zandy, *Liberating Memory*). Social scientists who pay attention to the details of family dynamics discover the systematic ways that social location shapes how families live and how parents rear their children (DeVault, *Feeding the Family*; Lareau, *Unequal Childhoods*; L. Rubin, *Worlds of Pain*).

13. Reinharz, "Who Am I?"
14. Nancy Naples's observation regarding the "ever shifting and permeable social locations" of insiders and outsiders as they are interactively constructed is an insightful addition to the insider-outsider debate in sociology (Naples, "A Feminist Revisiting," 71).

Chapter 1   Networks of Interdependence in an Age of Independence

1. All names and place names in the book are pseudonyms.
2. Casper and Bianchi, *Continuity and Change*.
3. Glenn, "Creating a Caring Society."
4. On male wages, see Casper and Bianchi, *Continuity and Change*; Faludi, *Stiffed*; Townsend, *The Package Deal*.
5. In 1958, for example, 7.5 million of the married or formerly married women (the census defines the second group as "separated, divorced, and widowed") in the labor force had children under eighteen (Lajewski, "Working Mothers," 8). In 2000, 22.7 million had children under eighteen (U.S. Census Bureau, *Statistical Abstract*, Table 577).
6. U.S. Census Bureau, "Who's Minding the Kids?" PPL Table 3A.
7. On economic sectors with longer work hours, see Jacobs and Gerson, "Who Are the Overworked Americans?"
8. U.S. Census Bureau, "Who's Minding the Kids?" Table 3A. The question of what parents prefer is harder to sort out. The data speak to what people do, but to characterize these actions as evidence of choices or preferences strikes me as wrong. Until there is a full range of options that are not constrained by economic imperatives, social scientists should attend to what people say they prefer, not take their behavior as reflecting their preference.
9. Kaplan, *Not Our Kind of Girl*.
10. Thorne, "Pick-up Time." Thorne uses the term "patchworked," which aptly captures the hodge-podge nature of the caretaking arrangements.
11. In sociology, the enduring pervasiveness of the functionalist theoretical approach shapes the ideology of families. Functionalists argue that the nuclear family form is an adaptive response to economic circumstances (Goode, *World Revolution and Family Patterns*; Parsons and Bales, *Family, Socialization, and Interaction Process*). That is, they maintain that families dropped the extended ties that had helped sustain agricultural life to enhance their ability to respond effectively to the new conditions imposed by industrialization. Despite historical evidence that nuclear households pre-dated industrialization and that the industrial revolution did not alter household structure, the functionalist perspective has continued to influence U.S. sociology (Laslett, *Household and Family*). As early as 1961, social scientists challenged that portrait. Elaine Cumming and David Schneider wrote: "The ideal American family is a nuclear family, but the real American family is often an extended one" ("Sibling Solidarity in American Kinship," 499). Feminists have criticized the gendered and ahistorical assumptions of functionalism and pointed to its mythic qualities but have not succeeded in supplanting the

functionalist paradigm in the practice of family sociology (Collier, Rosaldo, and Yanagisako, "Is There a Family?"; Stacey, *Brave New Families*).

12. D. Smith, "The Standard North American Family." Feminists discuss SNAF and its ideological power using various terminologies. Thorne calls it the "monolithic family" (Thorne, "Feminism and the Family"). Stacey calls it the "modern family" (Stacey, *Brave New Families*). And, stressing its ideological power, Collier, Rosaldo, and Yanagisako call it "The Family," while Pyke calls it the "normal American family" (Pyke, "'The Normal American Family.'"

13. One need only consider the hotly contested issue of same-sex marriage to see the depth of this assumption. Lehr, *Queer Family Values*.

14. Stacey, *Brave New Families*, 251–271. Given the ubiquity of the SNAF ideal, it is interesting to note that historians find extensive evidence of nuclear families embedded in extended kin networks, evidence largely ignored by sociologists in conducting contemporary research (Hareven, *Family Time and Industrial Time*). In keeping with the Standard North American Family ideal, this nuclear structure and ideology have been interpreted as a sign of greater self-sufficiency and a measure of success.

15. Whether women in these groups shared the preferences of the dominant culture is a matter of debate. For example, see Blewett, *Men, Women, and Work*; Hansen, *A Very Social Time*; Jones, *Labor of Love*.

16. Roschelle, *No More Kin*, xi–xii. Research shows that those of working-class, immigrant, African American, Latino American, and Asian American origins more frequently privilege kin relations (Lan, "Subcontracting Filial Piety"; Roschelle, *No More Kin*; L. Rubin, *Worlds of Pain*).

17. Engels, *The Origin of the Family*; Zaretsky, *Capitalism*.

18. Historically, family members were considered the private property of the male head of household. That ownership gave men dominion over their wives, children, and servants. In other words, male heads of households had ultimate say in decisions, financial or social, and discretion in how they spent their own time and money and in how they directed others to spend theirs. Even with women's increased economic independence that accompanied wage earning and the passage of the married women's property acts of the mid-nineteenth century, the structure of labor markets and the differential legal status of women and men in marriage have continued to undercut women's equality within families as well as outside them (Basch, *Eyes of the Law*; Salmon, *Women and the Law*). Although women in the twenty-first century are no longer men's private property, the legal situation of children is more contested. Children remain under the legal jurisdiction of their fathers and mothers; how much "voice" they have in their treatment and futures is debated (Beck, "Democratization of the Family").

19. In the nineteenth century, the male head of household's discretionary power was circumscribed by his neighbors and extended kin; the community monitored heads of households to curb their excessive use of force in dealing with family members. Over the course of the twentieth century, the increase in single-family dwellings, the geographic dispersion of kin, and the growth of urban/metropolitan areas have rendered the community irrelevant as a control for internal household behaviors. Scholars debate the degree to which state control over family activities has increased apace through laws designed to prevent the exploitation and abuse of children, and laws regarding public education, the welfare state, "child saving" agencies, and so on. In spite of the shift from social to legal control, the importance of the privacy of the household has not diminished ideologically; indeed, it has grown (D'Emilio and Freedman, *Intimate Matters*; Gordon, *Heroes of Their Own Lives*).

20. Fischer, "Just How Is It That Americans Are Individualistic?" 4. Historians debate the degree to which Euro-American households in the colonial period and the nineteenth century were in fact economically self-sufficient (see, for example, Ulrich, "Housewife and Gadder"). Nonetheless, they tend to agree that westward expansion, the development of industrial capitalism, and the growth of consumerism over the course of the nineteenth century fostered beliefs in self-sufficiency and the capacity for individuals to make it alone (Fischer, "Was There a Moment?").

21. Fischer notes that there are different types of individualism—political, economic, and familial. His review of debates about individualism points to contradictory cultural impulses that coexist with a focus on the self. It is precisely those contradictions that can produce a belief that families are self-contained units that can go it alone ("Was There a Moment?" 10; also see Bellah et al., *Habits of the Heart*).

22. Fischer points out that beliefs in individualism vary by sphere, so although Americans, in comparison to people in other countries, may express a more individualist set of beliefs about government and the economy, they tend to articulate more collectivist values in regard to families ("Was There a Moment?"). Thorne notes, for example, that families have been associated with the values of nurturance and community ("Feminism and the Family").

23. This portrait of dependence is challenged by the new debates about care among feminists (see Fraser and Gordon, "A Genealogy of Dependency"; Garey et al., "Care and Kinship"; Kittay, *Love's Labor*). See also Kittay and Feder, *The Subject of Care*.

24. Daly, *Families and Time*, 133.

25. Hays, *The Cultural Contradictions of Motherhood*, 4.

26. Garey, *Weaving Work and Motherhood*.

27. Hofferth et al., "National Child Care Survey, 1990," 201–248.

28. Gerstel, "The Third Shift"; Hofferth et al., "National Child Care Survey, 1990"; Hunts and Avery, "Relatives as Child Care Givers"; Kibria, *Family Tightrope*; Michel, *Children's Interests/Mothers' Rights*; Nelson, *Negotiated Care*; Roschelle, *No More Kin*; Stewart et al., "Staying and Leaving Home"; Wellman, "The Place of Kinfolk" and *Networks in the Global Village*.

29. Weston, *Families We Choose*.

30. Clark and Ayers, "Friendship Expectations and Friendship Evaluations"; Hofferth et al., "National Child Care Survey, 1990"; Stack, *All Our Kin*; Trimberger, "Friendship Networks and Care"; Weston, *Families We Choose*.

31. Pyke, "'The Normal American Family;'" D. Smith, "The Standard North American Family"; Thorne, "Feminism and the Family."

32. Schneider, *American Kinship*; Wellman and Wortley, "Different Strokes from Different Folks; Weston, *Families We Choose*.

33. Minow, "Who's In and Who's Out."

34. Caplow et al., *Middletown Families*; Fischer, *To Dwell among Friends*; Roschelle, *No More Kin*.

35. G. Rubin, "The Traffic in Women."

36. Abel and Nelson, *Circles of Care*, 4–34; Glenn, *Unequal Freedom*, 1–17; Hansen, *A Very Social Time*, 103–109.

37. Hochschild, with Machung, *The Second Shift*, 15.

38. DeMott, *The Imperial Middle*; Wolfe, *One Nation, after All*.

39. Newman, *Falling from Grace*; Zweig, *The Working Class Majority*.

40. Mishel et al., *The State of Working America*, 277–307. In 1998, the top 1 percent

of the population owned 38.1 percent of the wealth, while the bottom 40 percent owned but .2 percent (Wolff, "Recent Trends in Wealth Ownership," 300).

41. McCall, *Complex Inequality*.

42. Newman, *Falling from Grace*, 34.

43. These figures are adjusted for inflation to 1997 dollars (Center on Budget and Policy Priorities, "Pulling Apart," www.cbpp.org/pa-statelist.htm).

44. Casper and Bianchi, *Continuity and Change*, chapter 10; Goldin, *Understanding the Gender Gap*, chapters 2, 5.

45. Coontz, *The Way We Never Were*.

46. Goldin, *Understanding the Gender Gap*, 10–57.

47. Lajewski, "Working Mothers," 10.

48. U.S. Census Bureau, "Who's Minding the Kids?" PPL Table 3A.

49. Casper and Bianchi, *Continuity and Change*; Gornick and Meyers, *Families That Work*; Heymann, *The Widening Gap*; Hochschild, with Machung, *The Second Shift*.

50. Collins, *Black Feminist Thought*; DiLeonardo, "The Female World"; Philipson, *Married to the Job*; Putnam, *Bowling Alone*.

51. Oliker, "Examining Care at Welfare's End."

52. Williams, *Unbending Gender*.

53. Goldin, *Understanding the Gender Gap*.

54. Heymann, *The Widening Gap*, 13.

55. Hofferth et al., "National Child Care Survey, 1990."

56. Bundy, "Out of School Time Survey."

57. By this, I do not mean to suggest that families have not experienced labor shortages in other time periods under different economic systems, but rather that the one this country is facing now is uniquely shaped by historical circumstance and particular expectations about gendered behavior.

58. Other gendered organizations of labor in different historical moments created needs also, but I would posit such needs are not identical to current ones, although they may have prompted people to engage in networks.

59. Coontz, *The Way We Never Were*.

60. Lajewski, "Working Mothers," 11. In practice, this figure probably was higher. The 1958 survey required respondents to identify only one type of child-care arrangement, regardless of how many were in place. This mutually exclusive forced choice means that the 1958 data point to the *primary* care arrangement, which was not necessarily the only one. Respondents had the choice of identifying "Other" from the list, which was one way of resolving cases where children had multiple caretaking arrangements.

    I am purposely not discussing fathers here, because I want to emphasize the caretakers outside the nuclear family. That said, fathers were the second most common category of caretakers, after "other relatives." In 1958, fathers constituted 16.6 percent of the caretakers for school-age children, compared to 24.4 percent in 1999 (Lajewski, "Working Mothers"; U.S. Census Bureau, "Who's Minding the Kids?" PPL Table 3B).

    Note, however, that the Census Bureau has changed its categories slightly since 1958. The 1958 census reported on children age five to eleven; the 1999 report grouped children six to fourteen. For simplicity's sake, here I refer to the two groups as grade-school children or school-age children, while acknowledging that the statistics for 1999 reflect a broader category of children.

61. U.S. Census Bureau, "Who's Minding the Kids?" PPL Table 3B. Acknowledging the prevalence of a patchwork approach to child care, for the 1997 survey, the U.S. Census Bureau changed the way it collects data (K. Smith, "Who's Minding

the Kids?" 7). It now allows for multiple arrangements all to be coded and counted. This means that all categories of caregivers can be identified, and therefore the statistics no longer reveal the *primary* care arrangement. The data in 1958, 1997, and 1999 do not specify the amount of time a child spends in each type of care, leaving the statistical puzzle incomplete. Other research documents that extended kin, especially grandmothers, are often involved (Hofferth et al., "National Child Care Survey, 1990"; Hunts and Avery, "Relatives as Child Care Givers"; Presser, "Child Care Provided by Grandmothers").

62. Interestingly, the proportion of nonrelatives (babysitters, friends, and neighbors) caring for children in the child's home has declined from the fifties. *Nonrelative care in the child's home* was provided to 10 percent of the children whose mothers worked full time in 1958 (Lajewski, "Working Mothers," 11) compared to 3.6 percent in 1999 (U.S. Census Bureau, "Who's Minding the Kids?" PPL Table 3B).

One of the biggest changes in the forty-year period is in the area of group-care and day-care centers. Very few day-care centers and after-school programs existed in 1958; therefore, *group care* accounted for a miniscule 1.0 percent of school-age children whose mothers worked full time (Lajewski, "Working Mothers," 11). In 1999, 17.6 percent of grade-school children were involved in organized care or at a day-care center before and after school (U.S. Census Bureau, "Who's Minding the Kids?" PPL Table 3B).

In 1958, the remaining children were either in "self-care" or in some combination of caregiving situations that were not easily placed in the census categories. The issue of "self-care" sparked controversies in the fifties. Legislators, psychologists, and PTA members debated the wisdom of allowing "latch-key children" to be at home without on-site adult supervision. The controversies surrounding this issue are many, and the challenge of counting is huge. No less controversial today, this category of care appears to have increased dramatically. In 1958, 12.8 percent of children five to eleven were identified as being in self-care. The comparable figure for 1999 is 20.6 percent (U.S. Census Bureau, "Who's Minding the Kids?" PPL Table 3B). This may be due simply to the inclusion of older children (twelve- to fourteen-year-olds) not included in 1958. For an insightful demographic analysis of self-care, see Casper and Smith, "Dispelling the Myths."

63. Casper and Bianchi, *Continuity and Change.* That said, after-school programs are more likely to exist in urban areas and be used by mothers who work part-time versus full time. Full-time working mothers rely more on kin because they provide greater flexibility (Brandon and Hofferth, "Out-of-School Childcare Arrangements," 139). According to a study by the Urban Institute, after-school programs are used more frequently by higher-income families than lower-income families, regardless of household structure (Sonenstein et al., *Primary Child Care Arrangements,* 7.

64. Knowledge of this stress makes mothers reluctant to ask for help and kin members reluctant to say yes. But they do.

65. Scholars have pursued the question of how networks impact the lives of their members—in psychological as well as financial ways (Belle, "The Social Network"; Domhoff, *Who Rules America?*; Fischer, *To Dwell among Friends*; Stack, *All Our Kin*; Wellman, *Networks in the Global Village.* Research shows that network relations change when women are employed full time (Gerstel, "The Third Shift"). In the context of families, networks are shown to have positive effects that include the reduction of stress and depression, mitigating the isolation of

women in nuclear families, creating a cushion from poverty, and increasing positive outcomes for children (Belle, "The Social Network"; Barrett and McIntosh, *The Anti-Social Family*; Stack, *All Our Kin*; Marshall et al., "It Takes an Urban Village." This research shows that networks act to alleviate crises in child care and provide a kind of kin cushion. Research also reveals some negative effects of networks: They can increase stress for some, and if the families are poor, domestic networks can hinder economic mobility (Belle, "The Social Network"; Stack, *All Our Kin*).

66. Bott, *Family and Social Network*; Fischer, *To Dwell among Friends*; Hofferth, "Kin Networks"; Hogan, Hao, and Parish, "Race, Kin Networks, and Assistance"; L. Rubin, *Worlds of Pain*; Young and Willmott, *Family and Kinship*.

67. Roschelle, *No More Kin*, 81.

68. Ibid., 174.

69. For example, in an attempt to assess the importance of culture versus immigrant status, both identified as sources of motivation for network development, Menjivar designed her comparisons across immigrant groups, contrasting those moving to the United States from Vietnam, El Salvador, and Mexico (Menjivar, "Kinship Networks among Immigrants"). To look at the role of class and the way it affects network formation and operation among African American single mothers, McAdoo studied their networks, comparing those of the middle class to the working class (McAdoo, "Black Mothers"). More recently, Brewster and Padavic have investigated employed black mothers' reliance on kin, comparing women over time by class, household structure, and geographic region (Brewster and Padavic, "No More Kin Care?").

70. For an exception, see Stacey, *Brave New Families*. In one sense, this is not at all ironic. In general, "whiteness" is associated with middle-class status. Until researchers released the findings of studies conducted in the early 1990s, the middle classes were assumed *not* to have extensive kin networks.

71. Hogan, Hao, and Parish, "Race, Kin Networks"; Roschelle, *No More Kin*.

72. Eggebeen and Hogan, "Giving between Generations"; Roschelle, *No More Kin*; White and Riedmann, "Ties among Adult Siblings."

73. Roschelle carefully maps the debate: Those taking the structural-economic theoretical approach have argued that class and relative scarcity in resources lead poorer people to share what they have (Baca Zinn, "Family, Feminism, and Race"; Wilson, *The Truly Disadvantaged*). In contrast, others argue that ethnic culture, shaped by historical processes, prompts minority families in the United States (primarily African American and Latino) to be more family oriented, to be more involved with extended kin, and to live in extended households (e.g., Hays and Mindel, "Extended Kinship Relations").

74. Brewster and Padavic, "No More Kin Care?"; Roschelle, *No More Kin*.

75. Brewster and Padavic, "No More Kin Care?"

76. Newman, *Falling from Grace*; Wilson, *The Truly Disadvantaged*.

77. Roschelle, *No More Kin*.

78. E.g., Stack, *All Our Kin*; Brewster and Padavic, "No More Kin Care?"; Hogan, Eggebeen, and Clogg, "The Structure of Intergenerational Exchanges"; Roschelle, *No More Kin*.

79. Faludi, *Backlash*.

80. Daly, *Families and Time*; Jacobs and Gerson, "Who Are the Overworked Americans?" Jacobs and Gerson analyze the differences between various sectors of the labor market and how much time they work.

81. Annie E. Casey Foundation, "Care for School-Age Children."

82. Tronto, *Moral Boundaries*; Ungerson, "Why Do Women Care?"
83. My focus on informal networks has meant not analyzing the racialized division of labor as it affects the formal, institutional caretaking of children, an important investigation that others have undertaken (Uttal, *Making Care Work*; Wrigley, *Other People's Children*).
84. Osnowitz, "Constructing Opportunity and Choice"; Wellman, "The Place of Kinfolk."
85. Nelson, "Single Mothers and Social Support"; Pryor and Graburn, "The Myth of Reciprocity"; Uehara, "Reciprocity Reconsidered"; Weinberg, "Reciprocity Reconsidered."
86. The purpose of a study tends to shape the definition of "network" that is used. So, for example, McCallister and Fischer define a "core network" as "the set of people who are most likely to be sources of a variety of rewarding interactions, such as discussing a personal problem, borrowing money, or social recreation" (McCallister and Fischer, "Procedure for Surveying Personal Networks," 135). This definition results in the identification of rather large networks. In contrast, Belle defines a social network as a "list of important others," and its average size as seven to eight people (Belle, "Social Ties and Social Support," 135–136). Stack defines a "domestic network" as "the smallest, organized durable network of kin and non-kin who interact daily, providing domestic needs of children and assuring their survival" (Stack, *All Our Kin*, 31). Hogan et al. create a quantitative variable for "support network": "A mother is counted as participating in a support network if she (a) lives in an extended family situation (with one or more adult kin other than a husband, (b) receives half or more of her income from someone other than her husband, or (c) gets unpaid child care" (Hogan, Hao, and Parish, "Race, Kin Networks," 801). This definition, however, ignores all the other dimensions of support given to families, even within the range of child rearing and child care.
87. I used a stratified purposeful sampling method (see Miles and Huberman, *Qualitative Data Analysis*, 28). I recruited the anchors by activating my own networks of friends, kin, and colleagues to search for working couples in different class locations, guaranteeing at least two degrees of separation from me. Rather than seek people who fit a profile of an average working person in each particular class, if such a thing exists, I sought people whom I could locate within a class context, and who were in a sense randomly contacted by me. The bulk of my energy in screening potential subjects occurred in my discussions with contacts who had suggested them. Once I had determined that the person fit my criteria (a working person who had at least one child in elementary school, who fell within one of the three class categories, and who had a partner in child rearing), my contact would raise the possibility of participation in the study with that person. If s/he agreed to be approached, I called and proposed scheduling an interview. *Everyone* I called agreed to participate in the study. I did not further screen or reject any of the subjects I contacted. Once I had found anchors in different economic locations, I stopped recruiting.

    After some fits and starts, I realized the value of leaving open the option of whether or not the anchor's partner in parenting lived with the anchor. With the divorce rate so high in California, as in the nation as a whole, many households are headed by single women. I therefore decided to include single heads of households as they got referred to me. The most challenging anchor to find was the working-class one. Most working-class candidates suggested to me were either immigrants or women of color. Since I was determined not to repeat the errors of previous research that conflate class and race/ethnicity difference, I continued to search for a white working-class woman who had an active partner in parenting her child(ren). Part of the challenge had to do with the nature of my professional and friendship networks, which were largely middle class, and part had to do with the racial stratification of the labor force in northern California. Urban centers act as magnets for immigrants, but white working-class couples have found it increasingly difficult to afford housing in the cities and have opted to move farther out into semi-rural areas. Finally, it was through activating my own family networks and moving beyond the metropolitan area that I was able to identify a white woman, working in sanitary maintenance, on a waiting list for a better-paying job at a nearby factory, who also had a partner in rearing her child.

88. Classic network studies include Bott, *Family and Social Network*; Young and Willmott, *Family and Kinship*.

89. I use Ostrander's definition of the upper class: "That portion of the population that owns the major share of corporate and personal wealth, exercises dominant power in economic and political affairs, and comprises exclusive social networks and organizations open only to persons born into or selected by this class" (Ostrander, *Women of the Upper Class*, 5). Domhoff points to the importance of attending upper-class schools, belonging to certain social clubs, and being listed in the *Social Register*. My definitions of occupation are based primarily on the conditions of work (see Wright, *Classes*; Zweig, *The Working Class Majority*). So, for example, I define a working-class job as one that demands low skill, offers little power or autonomy in the workplace, and pays low wages; a middle-class job is defined as one that requires a college education and tends to be managerial and white collar. Given the broad range of middle-class jobs and the even broader range of incomes scholars have defined as middle class, I distinguish two layers of the middle class: the middle class, and the more affluent, professional middle class (Ehrenreich, *Fear of Falling*, chapter 1; Newman, *Falling from Grace*, 15). Like all jobs, upper-class jobs are strongly gendered (Daniels, *Invisible Careers*; Ostrander, *Women of the Upper Class*). For men in the upper echelons, this translates into ownership (of the means of production), economic leadership, and political authority. For women, it means leadership in the community and typically no recompense; indeed, volunteer work is a marker of upper-class status.

90. Keister, *Wealth in America*; Townsend, *The Package Deal*.

91. Garey, *Weaving Work and Motherhood*, 53–54. I avoid using the term "social capital" because it has been so imprecisely applied that it has come to mean everything and nothing. I prefer Garey's term, "constellation of resources."

92. See Holloway and Valentine, *Children's Geographies*.

93. Boulding, "Nurture of Adults by Children"; Christensen, "The Social Construction of Help"; Fogel and Melson, *Origins of Nurturance*.

94. Pitfalls of this methodological approach include problems with confidentiality among interview subjects.

95. Hochschild, with Machung, *The Second Shift*; L. Rubin, *Worlds of Pain*; Stacey, *Brave New Families*; Townsend, *The Package Deal*; Weston, *Families We Choose*; Zavella, *Women's Work and Chicano Families*.

96. U.S. Census Bureau, *Census Summary File 3: Sample Data*, http://factfinder. census.gov/servlet/DDTable?_ts=52586425717 (total U.S.); http://factfinder. census.gov/servlet/DDTable?_ts=52586976429 (California).

97. Hispanics and other people of color disproportionately work at the lower ends of the economic ladder (Amott and Matthaei, *Race, Gender, and Work*; Cancian and Oliker, *Caring and Gender*; Glenn, "The Dialectics of Wage Work"; Romero,

Maid in the U.S.A.). In the 1990s, people employed to care for children, staff nursing homes, and clean homes and offices were more likely to be of Hispanic origin than white or black (Amott and Matthaei, *Race, Gender, and Work*; Hondagneu-Sotelo, *Doméstica*). In the context of these similarities and differences, if one were to study the institutional care for children, this racial stratification would emerge as important to the analysis. However, this study focuses on *informal* care that operates selectively in more homogeneous environments.

98. Hertz and Ferguson, "Childcare Choice and Constraints"; Hofferth et al., "National Child Care Survey, 1990."

99. Hunts and Avery, "Relatives as Child Care Givers." However, the comparative importance of these factors is debated in the sociological literature. For example, Hunts and Avery (ibid., 327) find "none of the variables measuring child characteristics, time, or financial resources of the family were significant in explaining the use of a relative for child care in the sample." And yet Peter Brandon and Sandra Hofferth find that degree of economic disadvantage influences the choices parents make (Brandon and Hofferth, "Out-of-School Childcare Arrangements").

100. Mills, *The Sociological Imagination*.

101. Ausdale and Feagin, *The First R*, emphasis in original, 21. They refer to Karl Marx, *Die Grundrisse*, ed. David McClelland (New York: Harper and Row, 1971), 77.

102. See Ferguson, "Kin Keepers and Gatekeepers."

Chapter 2   *The Cranes: An Absorbent Safety Net*

1. The place names in the book are fictional.

2. Top occupancy for a one-bedroom apartment is four people. Renters must pay extra for each additional person, although less for children.

3. It was not until Brendan's last year in high school that he was found to have attention deficit hyperactivity disorder (ADHD), too late to be of any use in improving his academic experience.

4. Passed in 1994, California has a "three strikes, you're out" law that carries mandatory sentencing for people found guilty of three felonies. California Penal Code Section 667 (b)–(i).

5. To visit this state prison, people must fill out a form and receive prior approval. It takes approximately four to six weeks to have their application approved, at which point they may schedule an appointment to visit.

6. Her truck-stop employers assured Patricia that her job would be waiting for her when she was ready to return, even though she had been working there only three months. While the area's low unemployment rate must have been working in her favor, Patricia strikes me as a hard worker and a very responsible person.

7. When I ask about Sherry's occupation, Patricia seems unsure, first saying that her aunt is a teacher, but then amending that: "Well, she's not a teacher. She works with computers. I guess, yes. She must be a teacher or something, because she works with kids." Patricia's confusion about her aunt's middle-class job does not strike me as unusual. For those who are unfamiliar with the educational bureaucracy, and for those who do not label people by the kind of work they do, an individual's specific job is less important than the place where the work is done.

8. Steinbeck, *The Grapes of Wrath*.

9. Although Fran is living with Louise, when I interview her, she sees the situation as temporary.

10. Not long ago, her ex-husband took Tracy to court in an attempt to get partial custody of the children. He didn't succeed; instead, the court increased his contribution to child support.
11. Connell, *Masculinities*.
12. There have been reprisals, however. Returning home after she had been away one weekend, Lee found one of her dogs poisoned.
13. See, for example, L. Rubin, *Worlds of Pain*.
14. Stack and Burton, "Kinscripts," 410.

Chapter 3   *The Aldriches: A Family Foundation*

1. Sarah's household includes other workers, but they are not part of her network of care for her children. She has household cleaners, gardeners, accountants, and the like, who work on a weekly basis.
2. Lareau, *Unequal Childhoods*.
3. Daniels, *Invisible Careers*; Kendall, *The Power of Good Deeds*; Ostrander, *Women of the Upper Class*.
4. Baltzell, *Puritan Boston and Quaker Philadelphia* and *The Protestant Establishment Revisited*.
5. I make this claim based on anecdotal evidence. I have not been able to find anything in the academic literature about family compounds. The major works on upper-class cohesiveness focus on private clubs and public service, not on family life. See, for example, Domhoff, *The Bohemian Grove*.
6. Ostrander, *Money for Change* and *Women of the Upper Class*.
7. On middle-class overscheduling, see Lareau, *Unequal Childhoods*.
8. Hackstaff, *Marriage*.
9. Arendell, *Fathers and Divorce*; Kurz, *For Richer, for Poorer*.
10. Ferguson, "Kin Keepers and Gatekeepers"; Hertz and Ferguson, "Kinship Strategies and Self-Sufficiency."
11. Ostrander, *Women of the Upper Class*. This forthrightness is something upper-class women share, in a different form, with working-class women.
12. By "imported food," she means that she purchased prepared foods cooked by a store or catering company.
13. Macdonald, "Working Mothers and Mother-Workers."
14. Ostrander, *Women of the Upper Class*.
15. This feeling is consistent with that reported by other upper-class people who grew up in fancy big houses. Aldrich, *Old Money*; Ostrander, *Women of the Upper Class*.
16. Macdonald, "Working Mothers and Mother-Workers."
17. Lareau, *Unequal Childhoods*.
18. Research is needed to explore the child-rearing approaches of upper-class mothers. In her seminal book, Ostrander finds a pattern of do-it-yourself mothering that is similar to that of Kate Farnsworth and differs greatly from that of Sarah Aldrich. Based on her data, Ostrander says: "It appears to be a myth that upper-class women leave the raising of children to hired caretakers" (*Women of the Upper Class*, 71). Admittedly, I am basing my analysis on a handful of people, and Ostrander interviewed thirty-six women. Nonetheless, I think it is possible that the differences are a result of a generational divide rather than the idiosyncrasy of my cases. Ostrander's subjects reared children largely in the 1950s, a unique time in child-rearing history in the United States. It is possible that in the long-term trajectory of upper-class child rearing, the generation she interviewed is the

exception rather than the rule. Sarah Aldrich is a baby boomer and looks to the example set by her grandmother for guidance in child rearing.

19. Arendell, *Mothers and Divorce*; Kurz, *For Richer, for Poorer*.
20. Baltzell, *Philadelphia Gentlemen*, 174.

Chapter 4 The Duvall-Brennans: A Loose Association of Advisors

1. Pierce, *Gender Trials*.
2. Garey, "Constructing Motherhood on the Night Shift"; Thorne, "Pick-up Time."
3. Thorne, "Pick-up Time."
4. Brandon and Hofferth, "Determinants of Out-of-School Childcare Arrangements."
5. Hughes, "Informal Help-Giving." Uttal finds the identical problem in child-care centers for younger children: "Staff scheduling effectively functioned to prevent communication with mothers." *Making Care Work*, 85.
6. Social science research consistently shows the gendered dimensions of practicing law and the discrimination women face because they are female, or because they have families (Epstein, *Women in Law*; Pierce, *Gender Trials*).
7. For a discussion of constructed kinship, see Weston, *Families We Choose*.
8. Disproportionate numbers of women work in government practice, for a variety of reasons, including nondiscriminatory hiring practices and more contained work hours. The pay is generally lower than in corporate law, however (Epstein, *Women in Law*; Nelson, "Futures of American Lawyers").
9. Epstein et al., *Part-Time Paradox*.
10. Ibid.
11. Ibid.
12. Blair-Loy, *Competing Devotions*, 49.
13. Later signals from my informants indicated that the Duvall-Brennan's neighborhood situation improved around the holidays after I interviewed them, as they got to know more people better.
14. Based on their analysis of the Survey of Income and Program Participation data from 1999, Brandon and Hofferth report that "schoolchildren with two employed parents are three times more likely to be cared for by parents and 75% less likely to be cared for by other relatives than schoolchildren living with one employed parent" ("Out-of-School Childcare Arrangements," 130).

Chapter 5 The Beckers: A Warm Web of People

1. Newman, *Falling from Grace*, chapters 1, 2.
2. Hertz and Charlton, "Making Family under a Shiftwork Schedule; Presser, "Shift Work and Child Care."
3. Average home price in 2000 was slightly over $400,000.
4. Hochschild, with Machung, *The Second Shift*.
5. Hertz and Charlton, "Making Family under a Shiftwork Schedule"; Presser, "Shift Work and Child Care."
6. He found a similar kind of creative self-expression only in the noneconomic pursuits of running or cycling, neither of which he had much time to do anymore.
7. Townsend, *The Package Deal*.
8. Boydston, *Home and Work*; Oakley, *The Sociology of Housework*.
9. Detinger and Clarkberg, "Informal Caregiving and Retirement Timing."
10. Waters, *Ethnic Options*.

11. Hays, *The Cultural Contradictions of Motherhood*; Lareau, *Unequal Childhoods*.
12. On issues of relative poverty, see Kaplan, *Not Our Kind of Girl*.

Chapter 6 *Staging Networks: Inclusion and Exclusion*

1. Uttal finds this to hold true for parents searching for child care for preschool children as well (*Making Care Work*, chapter 1). Research shows that the highest-quality care is provided to children at the highest and lowest ends of the income spectrum (Hofferth et al., "National Child Care Survey"). At the high end are people like Sarah Aldrich and Alex Brolin, those who can afford to pay for child-care expertise and offer enticing working conditions. At the low end are people who send their children to government-sponsored programs (such as Head Start) that set high standards because they have a social agenda and are regulated by law (unlike many family day-care centers).
2. Lareau, *Unequal Childhoods*.
3. Bott, *Family and Social Network*; Roschelle, *No More Kin*; Schaffer and Wagner, "Mexican American and Anglo Single Mothers"; Young and Willmott, *Family and Kinship in East London*.
4. Schneider and Smith, *Class Differences in American Kinship*; Weston, *Families We Choose*.
5. Walker, "Always There for Me." Walker finds stay-at-home mothers in the middle class are the exception to the middle-class friendship norms. These women tend to have friendship patterns and exchanges more similar to those of working-class women.
6. L. Rubin, *Just Friends*; Walker, "Always There for Me."
7. The parallel here to findings among low-income women is striking. In a study conducted on out-of-school time, a group of researchers at Wellesley Center for Research on Women found that among low-income women, "the determinant of employment" was "the availability of child care from another adult in the household" (Miller et al., "I Wish," 4). Although Lydia and Sarah do not live in the same household, they live near one another and have cars, so transportation presents a negligible barrier.
8. Oliker, *Best Friends and Marriage*; Walker, "Always There for Me."
9. Roschelle, *No More Kin*; Wellman, *Networks in the Global Village*; White and Riedmann, "Ties among Adult Siblings."
10. Fischer, *To Dwell among Friends*; Hofferth, "Kin Networks"; Logan and Spitze, *Family Ties*; Roschelle, *No More Kin*; Wellman, *Networks in the Global Village*.
11. Daly, *Families and Time*.
12. Fischer finds that in the core metropolitan area 18 percent of kin live less than five minutes away. Fischer, *To Dwell among Friends*, 159.
13. Americans also do not move as often as presumed (Fischer, "Ever More Rooted Americans").
14. Cochran, *Extending Families*; Hunter, "Counting on Grandmothers"; Hunts and Avery, "Relatives as Child Care Givers"; Logan and Spitze, *Family Ties*.
15. Fischer, *America Calling*; Wellman, "Are Personal Communities Local?"
16. Gerstel, "The Third Shift"; Jacobs and Gerson, "Who Are the Overworked Americans?"; Schor, *The Overworked American*.
17. Hochschild, with Machung, *The Second Shift*.
18. Fried, *Taking Time*; Gerstel, "The Third Shift"; Nelson and Smith, *Working Hard and Making Do*.
19. See, for example, Garey, *Weaving Work and Motherhood*, on hospital workers.

20. Newman, *Falling from Grace*, 246.
21. Hertz, *More Equal Than Others*, 5.
22. Osnowitz, "Marketing Expertise."
23. Wellman, "The Place of Kinfolk."
24. Macdonald, "Working Mothers and Mother-Workers"; Uttal, *Making Care Work*.
25. In reflecting on the process of screening kin, friends, neighbors, and hired help to assist in raising their children, the subjects of this study talk about values and practices they adhere to while rearing their children. It is important to remember, however, that people's accounts of their beliefs and practices in raising children are not necessarily accurate portrayals of their actual *behavior*. My subjects' statements must be understood as their own constructions.
26. Lareau, *Unequal Childhoods*.
27. Ostrander, *Women of the Upper Class*, 70. There is little academic literature on the child-rearing practices of the upper classes.
28. Lareau, *Unequal Childhoods*.
29. Condry, "Thief of Time, Unfaithful Servant"; Levin and Carlsson-Paige, "Developmentally Appropriate Television."
30. Ferguson, "Kin Keepers and Gatekeepers."
31. Given that my research focuses exclusively on people who participate in networks, *all* the respondents whose actions and opinions I discuss are engaged at some level, even members who place limits on what they do or are selective about with whom they associate.
32. Hunter, "Counting on Grandmothers."

Chapter 7 *The Tangle of Reciprocity*

1. This kind of family emergency is fairly common. "In a given month one out of four families experiences a breakdown of child care or a child's illness, causing a parent to lose at least a day of work" (Hofferth et al., "National Child Care Survey, 1990," 427).
2. The child-care market in the greater Bay Area is segmented, based on neighborhood and parent occupation and income. While it was possible to find those who pay less than the minimum wage for babysitting, in more affluent neighborhoods parents regularly paid ten to twelve dollars per hour.
3. Hogan, Eggebeen, and Clogg, "The Structure of Intergenerational Exchanges"; Nelson, "Single Mothers and Social Support"; Weinberg, "Reciprocity Reconsidered."
4. Fischer, *To Dwell among Friends*; Nelson, "Single Mothers and Social Support"; Roschelle, *No More Kin*.
5. Gouldner, "The Norm of Reciprocity"; Herrmann, "Women's Exchange"; Moore, *Injustice*; Simmel, *The Sociology of Georg Simmel*; Uehara, "Reciprocity Reconsidered"; Wellman, *Networks in the Global Village*.
6. Sahlins, *Stone Age Economics*, 199. Succeeding citations of this book appear as page numbers in parentheses in the text.
7. Gouldner, "The Norm of Reciprocity," 172. Similarly, "negative reciprocity" has a colloquial meaning different from that which Sahlins intends.
8. Blau, *Exchange and Power in Social Life*; Coleman, "Social Capital"; Homans, "Social Behavior as Exchange."
9. Homans, "Social Behavior as Exchange," 606.
10. Ferber and Nelson, "Introduction."
11. "The form of interaction may vary; it may be nurturant, instrumental or ratio-

nal; it may take the form of domination, force, persuasion, bargaining, or expression of love. In every case, however, what is at stake is the very existence of a relation with another, the existence of community" (Hartsock, *Money, Sex, and Power*, 6).

12. The economists' answer to this question is to apply economic assumptions to families and households (Becker, *A Treatise on the Family*). A storm of feminist criticism has followed, for example, see Folbre, *The Invisible Heart*; and Ferber and Nelson, *Beyond Economic Man*.

13. Uehara argues that scholars have ignored this distinction, which was, in fact, one of Gouldner's great insights. According to Uehara: "Social support is as much invested with symbolic as economic significance" ("Reciprocity Reconsidered," 486).

14. Nelson, "Single Mothers and Social Support."

15. Trimberger, "Friendship Networks and Care"; Uehara, "Reciprocity Reconsidered."

16. Meyer, *Care Work*; Nelson, "Single Mothers and Social Support"; Tronto, *Moral Boundaries*.

17. Uehara, "Reciprocity Reconsidered," 492.

18. Ruddick, "Care as Labor and Relationship."

19. Hertz and Ferguson, "Kinship Strategies and Self-Sufficiency," 204–206.

20. Gerstel, "The Third Shift"; Hertz, *More Equal Than Others*; Nelson and Smith, *Working Hard and Making Do*.

21. Jacobs and Gerson, "Who Are the Overworked Americans?"

22. Because the networks I studied all included some kin, I cannot speak to the phenomenon of networks entirely devoid of kin, which do exist, flourish, and successfully help rear children as well. The research on "families we choose" suggests that caregiving networks set up a system of obligation and reciprocity based on principles of friendship, romance, commitment, longevity, and the like (Trimberger, "Friendship Networks and Care"; Weston, *Families We Choose*).

23. Fischer, *To Dwell among Friends*, chapters 7, 13; Stewart et al., "Staying and Leaving Home," 6–7.

24. Gouldner, "The Norm of Reciprocity," 173.

25. Gouldner emphasizes the importance of the *norm* of reciprocity. He sees it as a fundamental critique of a functionalist perspective (as articulated by Parsons and Malinowski) on society, because it indicates the capacity to assemble and disassemble social relationships, as opposed to their existence a priori to serve the larger system. For a good discussion of contemporary kin obligation in England, see Finch and Mason, *Negotiating Family Responsibilities*.

26. Fran Crane also set bounds on her mother's attempt to give the appearance of meeting a kin obligation. When she was in intensive care at the hospital, she refused to let her mother visit her. She said she was concerned about her mother throwing a fit and drawing attention to herself. But she also implied that a gesture like being visited in the hospital is a symbol of concern and fulfills a kin obligation. Fran did not accept this as genuine on the part of her mother and resented the impression her mother would create in visiting her, which was false.

> And when I was in the hospital, I wouldn't let them bring her up there. I made it very clear. She don't like me. I don't want her up here bugging everybody and causing a scene. 'Cause I know what she done with my sister, my other sister who died of the same thing. I know what she done for her surgery, and I didn't want her up there causing no damn problems and no scenes. Because she wasn't getting no attention. Because my mother has to

be the center of attention. And I told them, "Don't you bring her up here." And they did not; . . . she don't like me, so why do you wanna come up and make a scene? Now, that's what I said to her. And she asked somebody how come I felt that way. . . . Sherry told her. She said, "Mother, it's true. She knows you don't like her." "Well, I do too!" "Well, you don't show it, you know? It's just the way she feels and we're going by her wishes."

The relationship has many complex twists and turns. In her decision to deny her mother the ability to visit her in the hospital, Fran is setting boundaries. She is not letting Louise profit from symbolic kin entitlements that she did not earn. Hostility between mother and daughter in part is about those boundaries, and also about dashed hopes and previous hurt that are part of their relationship.

27. Gouldner, "The Norm of Reciprocity," 164.
28. Ibid., 177.
29. Hochschild, *The Managed Heart*, 56.
30. Ibid., 57.
31. Hackstaff, *Marriage in a Culture of Divorce*.
32. Sirianni and Friedland, *Civic Innovation in America*.
33. Finch and Mason, *Negotiating Family Responsibilities*; Neufeld and Harrison, "Reciprocity and Social Support"; Weinberg, "Reciprocity Reconsidered."
34. Pryor and Graburn, "The Myth of Reciprocity," 236.
35. Weinberg, "Reciprocity Reconsidered."
36. This attempt at independence and seeing friends as facilitating independence rather than undermining it is among the qualities found by Walker in middle-class friendships ("Always There for Me").
37. That five of the network members told me about this system of kin-scription indicates that it is unusual. However, it is consistent with their conception of themselves as helpers, pitching in to make the lives of their kin work better.
38. Gouldner, "The Norm of Reciprocity," 177.
39. In contrast, Sarah Aldrich and Kate Farnsworth exchange ideas and confide in one another. And Lydia Dunn freely offers logistical consulting. Both Lydia and Kate come to the board of trustees with equal social and economic status.
40. They explore what happens to caring relationships in the context of commercialization by studying child-care workers, home-health-care workers, party planners, domestic workers, sex workers, and the like (Hochschild, *The Commercialization of Intimate Life*; Macdonald, "Working Mothers and Mother-Workers"; Tuominen, *We Are Not Babysitters*). As Uttal says: "Exchanging money for child care is distasteful because market exchange relationships seem inconsistent with caring relationships" (*Making Care Work*, 20).
41. Hochschild, with Machung, *The Second Shift*; Nelson, "Single Mothers and Social Support."
42. Walker talks about a similar language for the strength of friendships ("Always There for Me").
43. Maus, *The Gift*; Nelson, "Single Mothers and Social Support."
44. Gillis, *A World of Their Own Making*; Zelizer, *Pricing the Priceless Child*.
45. Children who live on farms and immigrant children continue to help their families make a livelihood. See Thorne, "Pick-up Time."
46. See, for example, Folbre, *The Invisible Heart*; Stack, *All Our Kin*; Stack and Burton, "Kinscripts"; Zelizer, *Pricing the Priceless Child*.
47. Uehara, "Reciprocity Reconsidered"; Weinberg, "Reciprocity Reconsidered."
48. My thanks to Claude Fischer for bringing this strength to my attention.

Chapter 8   Men, Women, and the Gender of Caregiving

1. Roschelle, *No More Kin*; Stack, *All Our Kin*.
2. Kathleen Gerson explores men's childhoods and expectations for adulthood and finds that the larger culture that celebrates autonomy and independence leads some men to reject fatherhood and domestic involvements (*No Man's Land*).
3. Gerstel, "The Third Shift"; Nelson, "Men Matter."
4. My research does not address the question of how important fathers or uncles are to children. Some social scientists also make arguments for men's involvement in child rearing because of the benefits that accrue to children, ranging from higher educational achievement to greater self-esteem (see McLanahan and Sandefur, *Growing up with a Single Parent*). A heated political as well as academic debate rages about the importance of fathers in the lives of children (see Biblarz and Raftery, "Family Structure, Educational Attainment"; McLanahan and Sandefur, *Growing up with a Single Parent*; Popenoe, *Life without Father*; Stacey, *In the Name of the Family*).
5. Roschelle, *No More Kin*, chapter 7.
6. Eriksen and Gerstel, "A Labor of Love"; Kivett, "Grandfathers and Grandchildren." Studies that look at custodial grandparents are not relevant to this study. Also, studies of grandparenthood that may be interesting do not elaborate on the distinctions of grandfatherhood (versus grandmotherhood) or its gendered dimensions in relationship to grandchildren, for example, Baranowski, "Grandparent-Adolescent Relations"; Cherlin and Furstenberg, *The New American Grandparent*.
7. Kivett, "Grandfathers and Grandchildren," 569.
8. Waldrop et al., "Wisdom and Life Experience."
9. Fox, *Reproduction and Succession*, 137.
10. Cumming and Schneider, "Sibling Solidarity."
11. Eriksen and Gerstel, "A Labor of Love," 844, 846, 847.
12. Townsend, *The Package Deal*, 71.
13. Coltrane, *Family Man*; Russell, *The Changing Role of Fathers*.
14. Coltrane, *Family Man*; Gerson, *No Man's Land*; Hochschild, with Machung, *The Second Shift*; Townsend, *The Package Deal*.
15. Studies that examine the division of household labor consistently find that men do less than women (Bianchi et al., "Is Anyone Doing the Housework?"). Women now do approximately two-thirds of household work and men do one-third. Using 1965 as a baseline, Bianchi et al. find that husbands now do more household work, and wives do less. They conclude that what appears to be greater equality on the surface is in fact a reduction in the overall amount of housework being done. Some proportion of it is outsourced to paid workers and some part of it is simply not being done. The work men tend to do is more episodic and seasonal than routine housework, and therefore social scientists have tended to discount its value. In a thought-provoking study, Nelson ("Men Matter") rethinks men's tasks, such as yard work and home repairs, in the context of households run by single women. Simultaneously, more children are reared outside of marriage, either because of divorce or out-of-wedlock childbearing. This results in a parallel trend where men are less involved with their children, in part because they do not live in the same household.
16. Coltrane, *Family Man*; Hochschild, with Machung, *The Second Shift*; Risman and Myers, "As the Twig Is Bent."
17. Cooper, "Being the 'Go-to Guy'"; Hochschild, with Machung, *The Second Shift*.
18. Coltrane, *Family Man*; LaRossa, *The Modernization of Fatherhood*; Marsiglio,

"Contemporary Scholarship on Fatherhood"; Messner, "Changing Men and Feminist Politics."

19. Coltrane, *Family Man*; Townsend, *The Package Deal*.

20. Messner, "Changing Men and Feminist Politics." The logic informing men's involvement is based on a concern about equity. It is only fair, this perspective goes, that men share the work related to children, given that women share the work of breadwinning (see Hertz, *More Equal Than Others*; Hochschild, with Machung, *The Second Shift*). Furthermore, some argue, equity at home is the only way to free women from primary responsibility for the "second shift" that hampers, ideologically and practically, their capacities as wage earners in the workplace (England and Folbre, "The Cost of Caring"). Feminists have made claims that involvement with children will lead to kinder, more empathic men.

21. See Eggebeen and Knoester, "Does Fatherhood Matter for Men?"; Russell and Radin, "Increased Paternal Participation."

22. Eggebeen and Knoester, "Does Fatherhood Matter for Men?" 392.

23. Russell, *The Changing Role of Fathers*.

24. Eggebeen and Knoester, "Does Fatherhood Matter for Men?"; Gerson, *No Man's Land*.

25. Russell and Radin, "Increased Paternal Participation."

26. Coltrane, *Family Man*; Lamb, *The Father's Role*; Russell and Radin, "Increased Paternal Participation"; Townsend, *The Package Deal*. As Townsend argues, fatherhood has to be understood as a set of interrelated activities and ideologies. Assessing a man's involvement does not mean simply measuring time or direct contact with his offspring, but rather placing fatherhood in the larger context, one that men understand as a "package deal": "having children, being married, holding a steady job, and owning a home" (*The Package Deal*, 2). In the eyes of the men Townsend studied, competence at breadwinning, the most important aspect of fatherhood, demonstrates their devotion—emotional as well as material—to their children. They do not earn a living *instead of* fathering, they do it *because* they want to be good fathers. Breadwinning is fathering for them. As fathers, they also strive to protect their children, in part through adequate breadwinning; to endow their children with the qualities that will make them successful; and to be close to them, even though that closeness can be mediated through the children's mothers (53).

27. Coltrane, "Research on Household Labor"; Cowan and Cowan, *When Partners Become Parents*; Frisco and Williams, "Perceived Housework Equity."

28. Cowan and Cowan, *When Partners Become Parents*.

29. There is less research that addresses men's contributions to family life outside of marriage as friends, neighbors, or boyfriends. Nelson ("Men Matter") attends to male contributions to self-provisioning. Nelson and Smith define it as "the efforts that household members make to provide, through their own labor (and for themselves), goods and services they would otherwise have to purchase in the (formal or informal) market" (*Working Hard and Making Do*, 10). In households with school-age children, self-provisioning might take the form of car repair, home maintenance, or yard work. Nelson finds that single women rely on fathers, brothers, and former husbands. See also Hertz and Ferguson, "Kinship Strategies and Self-Sufficiency."

30. This language reflects an ideology, directed at poor and single women in particular, about the importance of men in children's lives. This point of view is promoted vociferously and sometimes coercively by the state in various ways (see Hertz, "The Father as an Idea"; Schnitzer, "He Needs His Father"). It is impor-

tant to note that their adopted language, "man figure," "father figure," and the like, distances the actual man. Robert is important not just because he is the biological father, but because he brings a symbolic male presence to Robbie's life. Ben Crane also used this terminology about himself in Robbie's life. Interestingly, Tracy Johnson talks about the importance of her children's "father figure," who is in fact their biological father. Again, this language privileges the symbolic presence of the father, not just the father himself. Those in the Crane network have come to accept the ideological analysis that men qua men are desperately needed in children's lives.

31. Studies find that, especially for stepfathers, "once men step away from coresidence, the transforming power of fatherhood dissipates" (Eggebeen and Knoester, "Does Fatherhood Matter for Men?" 391).

32. Cooksey and Craig, "Parenting from a Distance"; King, "Nonresident Father Involvement."

33. Although Robert sets clear boundaries of authority, he also imbues Robbie with more adult attributes than he can possess as a child. In her study of coparenting, Diane Ehrensaft finds involved men to be effusive fathers who describe their relationships with their children as "intimate," in contrast to women who describe their own relationships as "nurturant." Ehrensaft interprets this as men's "quest for a close and all-encompassing emotional relationship" (*Parenting Together*, 132).

34. Arendell, "Best Case Scenarios"; Gerson, *No Man's Land*.

35. See Russell and Radin, "Increased Paternal Participation."

36. Daly, *Families and Time*, 165.

37. Eggebeen and Knoester, "Does Fatherhood Matter for Men?"

38. LaRossa and LaRossa, *Transition to Parenthood*.

39. Hochschild, with Machung, *The Second Shift*.

40. Using Hoschschild's (ibid.) framework for understanding this situation, Mark and Dina's relationship is caught in a transitional ideology—Dina's gender ideology is egalitarian, Mark's is traditional. Although Mark's practice is egalitarian, he adopted it reluctantly and resists acknowledging that the shared parenting is fair.

41. Townsend, *The Package Deal*, 40.

42. Daly, "Reshaping Fatherhood," 523.

43. See Gerschick and Miller, "Coming to Terms."

44. Coltrane, *Family Man*; Gerson, *No Man's Land*; LaRossa, *The Modernization of Fatherhood*; Potuchek, *Gender and Breadwinning*; Townsend, *The Package Deal*.

45. Gerson, *No Man's Land*; Lamont, *The Dignity of Working Men*; Potuchek, *Gender and Breadwinning*.

46. This feeling of inadequacy is wholly consistent with what Hochschild describes about male careers; see "Inside the Clockwork of Male Careers."

47. Gerson, *No Man's Land*.

48. Finch and Groves, Introduction, 24–25.

Conclusion

1. Nelson and Smith, *Working Hard and Making Do*, 14.

2. In assuming nuclear families as the sole domain of child care, the U.S. government legislates to privilege nuclear families, at the cost of extended kinship. As Robin Fox puts it: "In promoting the self-sufficiency of the nuclear family unit, the state is in effect attacking the essence of kinship." Federal court decisions regarding custody and visitation in divorce and foster care provide but one sort of evidence of this phenomenon. "The paradox then is that, in promoting the

nuclear family, the state (or church) is paring kinship down to its lowest common denominator while appearing to support basic 'kinship values'" (*Reproduction and Succession*, 144). It is undermining the potential bases of networks of care.

3. See, for example, Collins, *Black Feminist Thought*; hooks, "Revolutionary Parenting."

4. See Brandon and Hofferth, "Out-of-School Childcare Arrangements."

5. Gornick and Meyers, *Families That Work*; Meiksins and Whalley, *Putting Work in Its Place*.

6. Fried, *Taking Time*; Hochschild, *The Time Bind*.

7. Folbre, "Children as Public Goods."

Bibliography

Abel, Emily K. *Hearts of Wisdom: American Women Caring for Kin, 1850–1940*. Cambridge: Harvard University Press, 2000.

Abel, Emily K., and Margaret K. Nelson, eds. *Circles of Care: Work and Identity in Women's Lives*. Albany: State University of New York Press, 1990.

Aldrich, Nelson W., Jr. *Old Money: The Mythology of America's Upper Class*. New York: Knopf, 1988.

Amott, Theresa, and Julie Matthaei. *Race, Gender, and Work: A Multi-Cultural Economic History of Women in the United States*. Boston: South End Press, 1996.

Annie E. Casey Foundation. "Care for School-Age Children" ("Kids Count" brochure). Baltimore, Md.: Annie E. Casey Foundation, 1998.

Arendell, Terry. "'Best Case Scenarios': Fathers, Children, and Divorce." In *Families in the U.S.: Kinship and Domestic Politics*, edited by Karen V. Hansen and Anita Ilta Garey, 387–401. Philadelphia: Temple University Press, 1998.

———. *Fathers and Divorce*. Thousand Oaks, Calif.: Sage, 1995.

———. *Mothers and Divorce: Legal, Economic, and Social Dilemmas*. Berkeley and Los Angeles: University of California Press, 1986.

Ausdale, Debra Van, and Joe R. Feagin. *The First R: How Children Learn Race and Racism*. Lanham, Md.: Rowman and Littlefield, 2001.

Baca Zinn, Maxine. "Family, Feminism, and Race in America." *Gender and Society* 4, no. 1 (1990): 68–82.

Baltzell, E. Digby. *Philadelphia Gentlemen: The Making of a National Upper Class*. Philadelphia: University of Pennsylvania Press, 1989.

———. *The Protestant Establishment Revisited*. New Brunswick, N.J.: Transaction, 1991.

———. *Puritan Boston and Quaker Philadelphia: Two Protestant Ethics and the Spirit of Class Authority and Leadership*. New York: Free Press, 1979.

Baranowski, Marc D. "Grandparent-Adolescent Relations: Beyond the Nuclear Family." *Adolescence* 17, no. 67 (1982): 575–584.

Barrett, Michele, and Mary McIntosh. *The Anti-Social Family*. London: Verso, 1982.

Basch, Norma. *In the Eyes of the Law: Women, Marriage, and Property in Nineteenth-Century New York*. Ithaca, N.Y.: Cornell University Press, 1982.

Beck, Ulrich. "Democratization of the Family." *Childhood: A Global Journal of Child Research* 4, no. 2 (1997):151–168.

Becker, Gary S. *A Treatise on the Family*. Enlarged ed. Cambridge: Harvard University Press, 1991.

Bellah, Robert N., Richard Madsen, William M. Sullivan, Ann Swidler, and Steven M. Tipton. *Habits of the Heart: Individualism and Commitment in American Life*. Berkeley and Los Angeles: University of California Press, 1985.

Belle, Deborah. "The Social Network as a Source of Both Stress and Support to Low-Income Mothers." Paper presented at the Society for Research in Child Development, Boston, 1981.

——. "Social Ties and Social Support." In *Lives in Stress: Women and Depression*, edited by Deborah Belle, 133–144. Beverly Hills, Calif.: Sage, 1982.

Bianchi, Suzanne M., Melissa A. Milkie, Liana C. Sayer, John P. Robinson. "Is Anyone Doing the Housework? Trends in the Gender Division of Household Labor." *Social Forces* 79, no. 1 (2000): 191–228.

Biblarz, Timothy J., and Adrian E. Raftery. "Family Structure, Educational Attainment, and Socioeconomic Success: Rethinking the 'Pathology of Matriarchy'." *American Journal of Sociology* 105, no. 2 (1999): 321–365.

Blair-Loy, Mary. *Competing Devotions: Career and Family among Women Executives*. Cambridge: Harvard University Press, 2003.

Blau, Peter. *Exchange and Power in Social Life*. New York: Wiley, 1964.

Blewett, Mary H. *Men, Women, and Work: Class, Gender, and Protest in the New England Shoe Industry, 1780–1910*. Urbana: University of Illinois Press, 1988.

Bott, Elizabeth. *Family and Social Network: Roles, Norms, and External Relationships in Ordinary Urban Families*. New York: Free Press, 1957.

Boulding, Elise. "The Nurture of Adults by Children in Family Settings." *Research in the Interweave of Social Roles* 1 (1980): 167–189.

Boydston, Jeanne. *Home and Work: Housework, Wages, and the Ideology of Labor in the Early Republic*. New York: Oxford University Press, 1990.

Brandon, Peter D. "An Analysis of Kin-Provided Child Care in the Context of Intrafamily Exchanges: Linking Components of Family Support for Parents Raising Young Children." *American Journal of Economics and Sociology* 59, no. 2 (2000): 191–216.

——. "Determinants of Self-Care Arrangements among School-Age Children." *Children and Youth Services Review* 21, no. 6 (1999): 497–520.

Brandon, Peter D., and Sandra L. Hofferth. "Determinants of Out-of-School Childcare Arrangements among Children in Single-Mother and Two-Parent Families." *Social Science Research* 32 (2003): 129–147.

Brewster, Karin L., and Irene Padavic. "No More Kin Care? Change in Black Mothers' Reliance on Relatives for Child Care, 1977–1994." *Gender and Society* 16, no. 4 (2002): 546–563.

Bundy, Andrew. "National School-Based Out of School Time Survey." Boston: Parents United for Childcare, 1998.

Cancian, Francesca, and Stacy Oliker. *Caring and Gender*. Thousand Oaks, Calif.: Pine Forge Press, 2000.

Caplow, Theodore , Howard M. Bahr, Bruce A. Chadwick, Reuben Hill, and Margaret Holmes Williamson. *Middletown Families: Fifty Years of Change and Continuity*. Minneapolis: University of Minnesota Press, 1982.

Casper, Lynne M., and Suzanne M. Bianchi. *Continuity and Change in the American Family*. Thousand Oaks, Calif.: Sage, 2002.

Casper, Lynne M., and Kirstin E. Smith. "Dispelling the Myths: Self-Care, Class, and Race." *Journal of Family Issues* 23, no. 6 (2002): 716–727.

Center on Budget and Policy Priorities. *Pulling Apart: A State-by-State Analysis of Income Trends*. Center on Budget and Policy Priorities, 2000. Cited March 18, 2003. Available from www.cbpp.org/pa–statelist.htm.

Cherlin, Andrew J., and Frank F. Furstenberg, Jr. *The New American Grandparent: A Place in the Family, a Life Apart*. New York: Basic Books, 1986.

Childers, Mary M. "'The Parrot or the Pit Bull': Trying to Explain Working-Class Life." *Signs* 28, no. 1 (2002): 201–220.

———. "A Spontaneous Welfare Rights Protest by Politically Inactive Mothers: A Daughter's Reflections." In *The Politics of Motherhood: Activist Voices from Left to Right*, edited by Alexis Jetter, Annelise Orleck, and Diana Taylor, 90–101. Hanover, N.H.: University Press of New England, 1997.

Christensen, Pia Haudrup. "The Social Construction of Help among Danish Children: The Intentional Act and the Actual Content." *Sociology of Health and Illness* 15, no. 4 (1993): 488–502.

Clark, M. L., and Marla Ayers. "Friendship Expectations and Friendship Evaluations: Reciprocity and Gender Effects." *Youth and Society* 24, no. 3 (1993): 299–313.

Cochran, Moncrieff, Mary Larner, David Riley, Lars Gunnarsson, and Charles R. Henderson, Jr. *Extending Families: The Social Networks of Parents and Their Children.* New York: Cambridge University Press, 1990.

Coleman, James. "Social Capital in the Creation of Human Capital." *American Journal of Sociology* 94, issue supplement: Organizations and Institutions (1988): S95–S120.

Collier, Jane, Michele Rosaldo, and Sylvia Yanagisako. "Is There a Family? New Anthropological Views." In *Rethinking the Family: Some Feminist Questions*, edited by Barrie Thorne, with Marilyn Yalom, 31–48. Boston: Northeastern University Press, 1992.

Collins, Patricia Hill. *Black Feminist Thought: Knowledge, Consciousness, and the Politics of Empowerment.* 2d ed. New York: Routledge, 2000.

Coltrane, Scott L. *Family Man: Fatherhood, Housework, and Gender Equity.* New York: Oxford University Press, 1996.

———. "Research on Household Labor." *Journal of Marriage and the Family* 62 (2000): 363–389.

Condry, John. "Thief of Time, Unfaithful Servant: Television and the American Child." *Daedalus* 122 (1993): 259–278.

Connell, R.W. *Masculinities.* Berkeley and Los Angeles: University of California Press, 1995.

Cooksey, Elizabeth C., and Patricia H. Craig. "Parenting from a Distance: The Effects of Paternal Characteristics on Contact between Nonresidential Fathers and Their Children." *Demography* 35 (1998): 187–200.

Coontz, Stephanie. *The Way We Never Were: American Families and the Nostalgia Trap.* New York: Basic Books, 1992.

Cooper, Marianne. "Being the 'Go-to Guy': Fatherhood, Masculinity, and the Organization of Work in Silicon Valley." *Qualitative Sociology* 23, no. 4 (2000): 379–405.

Cowan, Carolyn Pape, and Philip A. Cowan. *When Partners Become Parents: The Big Life Change for Couples.* Mahwah, N.J.: Lawrence Erlbaum Associates, 2000.

Cumming, Elaine, and David M. Schneider. "Sibling Solidarity: A Property of American Kinship." *American Anthropologist* 63 (1961): 498–507.

Daly, Kerry J. *Families and Time: Keeping Pace in a Hurried Culture.* Thousand Oaks, Calif.: Sage, 1996.

———. "Reshaping Fatherhood: Finding the Models." *Journal of Family Issues* 14, no. 4 (1993): 510–530.

Daniels, Arlene Kaplan. *Invisible Careers: Women Civic Leaders from the Volunteer World.* Chicago: University of Chicago Press, 1988.

D'Emilio, John, and Estelle Freedman. *Intimate Matters.* New York: Harper and Row, 1988.

DeMott, Benjamin. *The Imperial Middle: Why Americans Can't Think Straight about Class.* New York: Morrow, 1990.

Detinger, Emma, and Marin Clarkberg. "Informal Caregiving and Retirement Timing among Men and Women: Gender and Caregiving Relationships in Late Midlife." *Journal of Family Issues* 23, no. 7 (2002): 857–879.

DeVault, Marjorie L. *Feeding the Family: The Social Organization of Caring as Gendered Work.* Chicago: University of Chicago Press, 1991.

————. "Personal Writing in Social Research: Issues of Production and Interpretation." In *Reflexivity and Voice*, edited by Rosanna Hertz, 216–228. Thousand Oaks, Calif.: Sage, 1997.

DiLeonardo, Micaela. "The Female World of Cards and Holidays: Women, Families, and the Work of Kinship." *Signs* 12, no. 3 (1987): 440–453.

Domhoff, G. William. *The Bohemian Grove and Other Retreats: A Study in Ruling-Class Cohesiveness.* New York: Harper and Row, 1974.

————. *Who Rules America?* Englewood Cliffs, N.J.: Prentice-Hall, 1970.

Eggebeen, David J., and Dennis P. Hogan. "Giving between Generations in American Families." *Human Nature* 1 (1990): 211–232.

Eggebeen, David J., and Chris Knoester. "Does Fatherhood Matter for Men?" *Journal of Marriage and Family* 63, no. 2 (2001): 381–393.

Ehrenreich, Barbara. *Fear of Falling: The Inner Life of the Middle Class.* New York: Pantheon, 1989.

Ehrensaft, Diane. *Parenting Together: Men and Women Sharing the Care of Their Children.* New York: Free Press, 1987.

Engels, Frederich. *The Origin of the Family, Private Property, and the State.* New York: International, 1972.

England, Paula, and Nancy Folbre. "The Cost of Caring." *Annals of the American Academy of Political and Social Sciences* 56, no. 1 (1999): 39–51.

Epstein, Cynthia Fuchs. *Women in Law.* 2d ed. Urbana: University of Illinois Press, 1993.

Epstein, Cynthia Fuchs, Carol Seron, Bonnie Oglensky, and Robert Saute. *Part-Time Paradox: Time Norms, Professional Life, Family, and Gender.* New York: Routledge, 1999.

Eriksen, Shelley, and Naomi Gerstel. "A Labor of Love or Labor Itself? Care Work among Adult Brothers and Sisters." *Journal of Family Issues* 23, no. 7 (2002): 836–856.

Faludi, Susan. *Backlash: The Undeclared War against American Women.* New York: Crown, 1991.

————. *Stiffed: The Betrayal of the American Man.* New York: Perennial, 2000.

Ferber, Marianne A., and Julie A. Nelson. "Introduction: The Social Construction of Economics and the Social Construction of Gender." In *Beyond Economic Man: Feminist Theory and Economics*, edited by Marianne A. Ferber and Julie A. Nelson, 1–22. Chicago: University of Chicago Press, 1993.

Ferguson, Faith. "Kin Keepers and Gatekeepers: Kinship and Family Identity among Single Mothers by Choice." Ph.D. diss., Brandeis University, 1999.

Finch, Janet, and Dulcie Groves. "By Women for Women: Caring for the Frail Elderly." *Women's Studies International Forum* 5, no. 5 (1982): 427–438.

————. "Introduction." In *A Labour of Love: Women, Work, and Caring*, edited by Janet Finch and Dulcie Groves, 1–30. Boston: Routledge and Kegan Paul, 1983.

————, eds. *A Labour of Love: Women, Work, and Caring.* Boston: Routledge and Kegan Paul, 1983.

Finch, Janet, and Jennifer Mason. *Negotiating Family Responsibilities.* New York: Tavistock/Routledge, 1993.

Fischer, Claude. *America Calling: A Social History of the Telephone to 1940.* Berkeley and Los Angeles: University of California Press, 1994.

————. "Ever More Rooted Americans." *City and Community* 1, no. 2 (2002): 175–193.

————. "Just How Is It That Americans Are Individualistic?" Paper presented at the American Sociological Association, Washington, D.C., August 2000.

———. *To Dwell among Friends*. Chicago: University of Chicago Press, 1982.

———. "Was There a Moment (When Americans Became Individualists)?" Paper presented at the American Sociological Association, Anaheim, Calif., August 2001.

Fogel, Alan, and Gail F. Melson, eds. *Origins of Nurturance: Developmental, Biological, and Cultural Perspectives of Caregiving*. Hillsdale, N.J.: Lawrence Erlbaum Associates, 1986.

Folbre, Nancy. "Children as Public Goods." In *Families in the U.S.: Kinship and Domestic Politics*, edited by Karen V. Hansen and Anita Ilta Garey, 831–836. Philadelphia: Temple University Press, 1998.

———. *The Invisible Heart: Economics and Family Values*. New York: New Press, 2001.

Fox, Robin. *Reproduction and Succession: Studies in Anthropology, Law, and Society*. New Brunswick: Transaction, 1993.

Fraser, Nancy, and Linda Gordon. "A Genealogy of Dependency: Tracing a Keyword of the U.S. Welfare State." *Signs* 19, no. 21 (1994): 309–336.

Fried, Mindy. *Taking Time: Parental Leave Policy and Corporate Culture*. Philadelphia: Temple University Press, 1998.

Frisco, Michelle, and Kristi Williams. "Perceived Housework Equity, Martial Happiness, and Divorce in Dual-Earner Households." *Journal of Family Issues* 24, no. 1 (2003): 51–73.

Garey, Anita Ilta. "Constructing Motherhood on the Night Shift: 'Working Mothers' as 'Stay-at-Home Moms'." *Qualitative Sociology* 18, no. 4 (1995): 415–435.

———. *Weaving Work and Motherhood*. Philadelphia: Temple University Press, 1999.

Garey, Anita Ilta, Karen V. Hansen, Rosanna Hertz, and Cameron Macdonald. "Care and Kinship: An Introduction." *Journal of Family Issues* 23, no. 6 (2002): 703–715.

Gerschick, Thomas J., and Adam Stephen Miller. "Coming to Terms: Masculinity and Physical Disability." In *Men's Lives*, edited by Michael S. Kimmel and Michael A. Messner, 392–406. Boston: Allyn and Bacon, 1998.

Gerson, Kathleen. *No Man's Land: Men's Changing Commitments to Family and Work*. New York: Basic Books, 1993.

Gerstel, Naomi. "The Third Shift: Gender and Care Work outside the Home." *Qualitative Sociology* 23 (2000): 467–483.

Gillis, John. *A World of Their Own Making: Myth, Ritual, and the Quest for Family Values*. New York: Basic Books, 1996.

Glenn, Evelyn Nakano. "Creating a Caring Society." *Contemporary Sociology* 29, no. 1 (2000): 84–94.

———. "The Dialectics of Wage Work: Japanese-American Women and Domestic Service, 1905–1940." *Feminist Studies* 6 (1980): 432–471.

———. *Unequal Freedom: How Race and Gender Shaped American Citizenship and Labor*. Cambridge: Harvard University Press, 2002.

Goldin, Claudia. *Understanding the Gender Gap: An Economic History of American Women*. New York: Oxford University Press, 1990.

Goode, William J. *World Revolution and Family Patterns*. New York: Free Press, 1963.

Gordon, Linda. *Heroes of Their Own Lives: The Politics and History of Family Violence, Boston, 1880–1960*. New York: Penguin, 1988.

Gornick, Janet C., and Marcia K. Meyers. *Families That Work: Policies for Reconciling Parenthood and Employment*. New York: Russell Sage Foundation, 2003.

Gouldner, Alvin. "The Norm of Reciprocity: A Preliminary Statement." *American Sociological Review* 25, no. 2 (1960): 161–178.

Hackstaff, Karla. *Marriage in a Culture of Divorce*. Philadelphia: Temple University Press, 1999.

Hansen, Karen V. *A Very Social Time: Crafting Community in Antebellum New England*. Berkeley and Los Angeles: University of California Press, 1994.

Hansen, Karen V., and Anita Ilta Garey, eds. *Families in the U.S.: Kinship and Domestic Politics.* Philadelphia: Temple University Press, 1998.

Hareven, Tamara. *Family Time and Industrial Time: The Relationship between the Family and Work in a New England Industrial Community.* New York: Cambridge University Press, 1982.

Hartsock, Nancy C. M. *Money, Sex, and Power: Toward a Feminist Historical Materialism.* Boston: Northeastern University Press, 1983.

Hays, Sharon. *The Cultural Contradictions of Motherhood.* New Haven, Conn.: Yale University Press, 1996.

Hays, William C., and Charles H. Mindel. "Extended Kinship Relations in Black and White Families." *Journal of Marriage and the Family* 35, no. 1 (1973): 51–57.

Herrmann, Gretchen. "Women's Exchange in the U.S. Garage Sale: Giving Gifts and Creating Community." *Gender and Society* 10 (1996): 703–728.

Hertz, Rosanna. "The Father as an Idea: A Challenge to Kinship Boundaries by Single Mothers." *Symbolic Interaction* 25, no. 1 (2002): 1–31.

———. *More Equal Than Others: Women and Men in Dual-Career Marriages.* Berkeley and Los Angeles: University of California Press, 1986.

———, ed. *Reflexivity and Voice.* Thousand Oaks, Calif.: Sage, 1997.

———. "Working to Place Family at the Center of Life: Dual-Earner and Single-Parent Strategies." *Annals of the American Academy of Political and Social Science* 562 (1999): 16–31.

Hertz, Rosanna, and Joy Charlton. "Making Family under a Shiftwork Schedule: Air Force Security Guards and Their Wives." *Social Problems* 36, no. 5 (1989): 491–507.

Hertz, Rosanna, and Faith I. T. Ferguson. "Childcare Choice and Constraints in the United States: Social Class, Race, and the Influence of Family Views." *Journal of Comparative Family Studies* 27, no. 2 (1996): 249–280.

———. "Kinship Strategies and Self-Sufficiency among Single Mothers by Choice: Post Modern Family Ties." *Qualitative Sociology* 20, no. 2 (1997): 187–209.

Hertz, Rosanna, and Jonathan B. Imber. "Introduction." In *Studying Elites Using Qualitative Methods,* edited by Rosanna Hertz and Jonathan B. Imber, vii–xi. Thousand Oaks, Calif.: Sage, 1995.

Heymann, Jody. *The Widening Gap: Why America's Working Families Are in Jeopardy and What Can Be Done about It.* New York: Basic Books, 2000.

Hochschild, Arlie Russell. *The Commercialization of Intimate Life: Notes from Home and Work.* Berkeley and Los Angeles: University of California Press, 2003.

———. "Inside the Clockwork of Male Careers." In *The Commercialization of Intimate Life: Notes from Home and Work,* edited by Arlie Russell Hochschild, 227–254. Berkeley and Los Angeles: University of California Press, 2003.

———. *The Managed Heart.* Berkeley and Los Angeles: University of California Press, 1983.

———. *The Time Bind.* New York: Metropolitan, 1997.

Hochschild, Arlie Russell, with Anne Machung. *The Second Shift: Working Parents and the Revolution at Home.* New York: Viking, 1989.

Hofferth, Sandra L. "Kin Networks, Race, and Family Structure." *Journal of Marriage and the Family* 46, no. 4 (1984): 791–806.

Hofferth, Sandra L., April Brayfield, Sharon Deich, and Pamela Holcomb. "National Child Care Survey, 1990." Washington, D.C.: Urban Institute Press, 1991.

Hogan, Dennis P., David J. Eggebeen, and Clifford C. Clogg. "The Structure of Intergenerational Exchanges in American Families." *American Journal of Sociology* 98, no. 6 (1993): 1428–1458.

Hogan, Dennis P., Ling-Xin Hao, and William L. Parish. "Race, Kin Networks, and Assistance to Mother-Headed Families." *Social Forces* 68, no. 3 (1990): 797–812.

Holloway, Sarah L., and Gill Valentine, eds. *Children's Geographies: Playing, Living, Learning*. New York: Routledge, 2000.

Homans, George. "Social Behavior as Exchange." *American Journal of Sociology* 63, no. 6 (1958): 597–606.

Hondagneu-Sotelo, Pierrette. *Doméstica: Immigrant Workers Cleaning and Caring in the Shadows of Affluence*. Berkeley and Los Angeles: University of California Press, 2001.

hooks, bell. "Revolutionary Parenting." In *Families in the U.S.: Kinship and Domestic Politics*, edited by Karen V. Hansen and Anita Ilta Garey, 587–596. Philadelphia: Temple University Press, 1998.

Hughes, Robert. "The Informal Help-Giving of Home and Center Childcare Providers." *Family Relations* 34, no. 3 (1985): 359–366.

Hunter, Andrea. "Counting on Grandmothers: Black Mothers' and Fathers' Reliance on Grandmothers for Parenting Support." *Journal of Family Issues* 18, no. 3 (1997): 251–269.

Hunts, Holly Jo, and Rosemary Avery. "Relatives as Child Care Givers: After Hours Support for Nontraditional Workers." *Journal of Family and Economic Issues* 19, no. 4 (1998): 315–341.

Jacobs, Jerry, and Kathleen Gerson. "Who Are the Overworked Americans?" *Review of Social Economy* 56, no. 4 (1998): 443–460.

Jones, Jacqueline. *Labor of Love, Labor of Sorrow: Black Women, Work, and the Family from Slavery to the Present*. New York: Basic Books, 1985.

Kaplan, Elaine Bell. *Not Our Kind of Girl: Unraveling the Myths of Black Teenage Motherhood*. Berkeley and Los Angeles: University of California Press, 1997.

Keister, Lisa A. *Wealth in America: Trends in Wealth Inequality*. New York: Cambridge University Press, 2000.

Kendall, Diana. *The Power of Good Deeds: Privileged Women and the Social Reproduction of Class*. Lanham, Md.: Rowman and Littlefield, 2002.

Kibria, Nazli. *Family Tightrope: The Changing Lives of Vietnamese Americans*. Princeton, N.J.: Princeton University Press, 1992.

King, Valerie. "Nonresident Father Involvement and Child Well-Being: Can Dads Make a Difference?" *Journal of Family Issues* 15 (1993): 78–96.

Kittay, Eva Feder. *Love's Labor. Essays on Women, Equality, and Dependency*. New York: Routledge, 1999.

Kittay, Eva Feder, and Ellen K. Feder, eds. *The Subject of Care: Feminist Perspectives on Dependency*. Lanham, Md.: Rowman and Littlefield, 2002.

Kivett, Vira R. "Grandfathers and Grandchildren: Patterns of Association, Helping, and Psychological Closeness." *Family Relations* 34, no. 4 (1985): 565–571.

Kurz, Demie. *For Richer, for Poorer: Mothers Confront Divorce*. New York: Routledge, 1995.

Lajewski, Henry C. "Working Mothers and Their Arrangements for Care of Their Children." *Social Security Bulletin* (1959): 8–13.

Lamb, Michael E., ed. *The Father's Role: Cross-Cultural Perspectives*. Hillsdale, N.J.: Lawrence Erlbaum Associates, 1987.

Lamont, Michele. *The Dignity of Working Men: Morality and the Boundaries of Race, Class, and Immigration*. Cambridge: Harvard University Press, 2000.

Lan, Pei-Cha. "Subcontracting Filial Piety." *Journal of Family Issues* 23, no. 7 (2002): 812–835.

Lareau, Annette. "Invisible Inequality: Social Class and Childrearing in Black Families and White Families." *American Sociological Review* 67, no. 5 (2002): 747–776.

———. "My Wife Can Tell Me Who I Know: Methodological and Conceptual Problems in Studying Fathers." *Qualitative Sociology* 23, no. 4 (2000): 407–433.

————. *Unequal Childhoods: The Importance of Social Class in Family Life*. Berkeley and Los Angeles: University of California Press, 2003.

Larner, Mary B., Lorraine Zippiroli, and Richard E. Behrman. "When School Is Out: Analysis and Recommendations." *Future of Children* 9, no. 2 (1999): 4–20.

LaRossa, Ralph. *The Modernization of Fatherhood: A Social and Political History*. Chicago: University of Chicago Press, 1997.

LaRossa, Ralph, and Maureen LaRossa. *Transition to Parenthood: How Infants Change Families*. Beverly Hills, Calif.: Sage, 1981.

Laslett, Peter. *Household and Family in Past Time*. Cambridge: Cambridge University Press, 1972.

Lehr, Valerie. *Queer Family Values: Debunking the Myth of the Nuclear Family*. Philadelphia: Temple University Press, 1999.

Levin, Diane E., and Nancy Carlsson-Paige. "Developmentally Appropriate Television: Putting Children First." *Young Children* 49, no. 5 (1994): 38–44.

Levi-Strauss, Claude. *The Elementary Structures of Kinship*. London: Eyre and Spottiswoode, 1949.

Logan, John R., and Glenna D. Spitze. *Family Ties: Enduring Relations between Parents and Their Grown Children*. Philadelphia: Temple University Press, 1997.

Macdonald, Cameron. "Working Mothers and Mother-Workers: Nannies, Au Pairs, and the Social Construction of Motherhood." Ph.D. diss., Brandeis University, 1998.

Malinowski, Bronislaw. *Argonauts of the Western Pacific*. 3d imprint ed. London: Routledge and Kegan Paul, 1922.

Marshall, Nancy L., Anne E. Noonan, Kathleen McCartney, Fern Marx, and Nancy Keefe. "It Takes an Urban Village: Parenting Networks of Urban Families." *Journal of Family Issues* 22, no. 2 (2001): 163–182.

Marsiglio, William. "Contemporary Scholarship on Fatherhood." *Journal of Family Issues* 14, no. 4 (1993): 484–509.

Maus, Marcel. *The Gift*. New York: W.W. Norton, 1990.

Mayer, Susan E. *What Money Can't Buy: Family Income and Children's Chances*. Cambridge: Harvard University Press, 1997.

McAdoo, Harriet. "Black Mothers and the Extended Family Support Network." In *The Black Woman*, edited by La Frances Rodgers-Rose, 125–144. Beverly Hills, Calif.: Sage, 1980.

McCall, Leslie. *Complex Inequality: Gender, Race, and Class in the New Economy*. New York: Routledge, 2001.

McCallister, Lynne, and Claude S. Fischer. "A Procedure for Surveying Personal Networks." *Sociological Methods and Research* 7 (1978): 131–148.

McLanahan, Sara S., and Gary Sandefur. *Growing Up with a Single Parent*. Cambridge: Harvard University Press, 1994.

Meiksins, Peter, and Peter Whalley. *Putting Work in Its Place: A Quiet Revolution*. Ithaca, N.Y.: Cornell University Press, 2002.

Menjivar, Cecilia. "Kinship Networks among Immigrants: Lessons from a Qualitative Comparative Approach." *International Journal of Comparative Sociology* 36 (1996): 219–232.

Messner, Michael. "Changing Men and Feminist Politics in the United States." *Theory and Society* 22, no. 5 (1993): 723–737.

Meyer, Madonna Harrington, ed. *Care Work: Gender, Labor, and the Welfare State*. New York: Routledge, 2000.

Michel, Sonya. *Children's Interests/Mothers' Rights: The Shaping of America's Child Care Policy*. New Haven, Conn.: Yale University Press, 1999.

Miles, Matthew B., and A. Michael Huberman. *Qualitative Data Analysis*. 2d ed. Thousand Oaks, Calif.: Sage, 1994.

Miller, Beth M., Susan O'Conner, Sylvia W. Sirignano, and Pamela Joshi. "I Wish the Kids Didn't Watch So Much TV": Out-of-School Time in Three Low Income Communities." Wellesley, Mass.: Wellesley Center for Research on Women, 1996.

Mills, C. Wright. *The Power Elite*. New York: Oxford University Press, 1956.

———. *The Sociological Imagination*. New York: Oxford University Press, 1959.

Minow, Martha. "Who's In and Who's Out." In *Families in the U.S.: Kinship and Domestic Politics*, edited by Karen V. Hansen and Anita Ilta Garey, 7–19. Philadelphia: Temple University Press, 1998.

Mishel, Lawrence, Jared Bernstein, and Heather Boushey. *The State of Working America, 2002/2003*. Ithaca, N.Y.: ILR Press, 2003.

Moore, Barrington, Jr. *Injustice: The Social Bases of Obedience and Revolt*. White Plains, N.Y.: M. E. Sharpe, 1978.

Naples, Nancy A. "A Feminist Revisiting of the Insider/Outsider Debate: The 'Outsider Phenomenon' in Rural Iowa." In *Reflexivity and Voice*, edited by Rosanna Hertz, 70–94. Thousand Oaks, Calif.: Sage, 1997.

Nelson, Julie A. *Beyond Economic Man: Feminist Theory and Economics*. Chicago: University of Chicago Press, 1993.

Nelson, Margaret. "How Men Matter: Housework and Self-Provisioning among Rural Single-Mother and Married-Couple Families in Vermont, U.S." *Feminist Economics* 10, no. 2 (2004): 9–36.

———. *Negotiated Care: The Experience of Family Day Care Providers*. Philadelphia: Temple University Press, 1990.

———. "Single Mothers and Social Support: The Commitment to, and Retreat from, Reciprocity." *Qualitative Sociology* 23 (2000): 291–317.

Nelson, Margaret, and Joan Smith. *Working Hard and Making Do*. Berkeley and Los Angeles: University of California Press, 1999.

Nelson, Robert L. "The Futures of American Lawyers: A Demographic Profile of a Changing Profession in a Changing Society." *Case Western Reserve Law Review* 44, no. 2 (1994): 345–406.

Neufeld, Anne, and Margaret J. Harrison. "Reciprocity and Social Support in Caregivers' Relationships: Variations and Consequences." *Qualitative Health Research* 5 (1995): 348–365.

Newman, Katherine S. *Falling from Grace: Downward Mobility in the Age of Affluence*. Berkeley and Los Angeles: University of California Press, 1999.

Oakley, Ann. *The Sociology of Housework*. New York: Pantheon, 1974.

Oliker, Stacey J. *Best Friends and Marriage*. Berkeley and Los Angeles: University of California Press, 1989.

———. "Examining Care at Welfare's End." In *Care Work: Gender, Labor, and the Welfare State*, edited by Madonna Harrington Meyer, 167–185. New York: Routledge, 2000.

Osnowitz, Debra. "Constructing Opportunity and Choice: Contract Professionals in Comparative Context." Paper presented at the Society for the Study of Social Problems, Chicago, August 2002.

———. "Marketing Expertise: The Contingent Experience of Contract Professionals." Ph.D. diss., Brandeis University, forthcoming.

Ostrander, Susan. *Money for Change: Social Movement Philanthropy at Haymarket People's Fund*. Philadelphia: Temple University Press, 1995.

———. "'Surely You're Not in This Just to Be Helpful': Access, Rapport, and Interviews in Three Studies of Elites." In *Studying Elites Using Qualitative Methods*, edited by Rosanna Hertz and Jonathan B. Ember, 133–150. Thousand Oaks, Calif.: Sage, 1995.

———. *Women of the Upper Class*. Philadelphia: Temple University Press, 1984.

Parreñas, Rhacel Salazar. "The Care Crisis in the Philippines: Children and Transnational Families in the New Global Economy." In *Global Woman: Nannies, Maids, and Sex Workers in the New Economy*, edited by Barbara Ehrenreich and Arlie Russell Hochschild, 39–54. New York: Metropolitan Books, 2003.

Parsons, Talcott, and Robert F. Bales. *Family, Socialization, and Interaction Process*. New York: Free Press, 1955.

Perlow, Leslie A. *Finding Time: How Corporations, Individuals, and Families Can Benefit from New Work Practices*. Ithaca, N.Y.: Cornell University Press, 1997.

Philipson, Ilene J. *Married to the Job*. New York: New Press, 2002.

Pierce, Jennifer L. *Gender Trials: Emotional Lives in Contemporary Law Firms*. Berkeley and Los Angeles: University of California Press, 1995.

Popenoe, David. *Life without Father*. New York: Free Press, 1996.

Potuchek, Jeanne. *Gender and Breadwinning in Dual-Earner Marriages: Who Supports the Family?* Stanford, Calif.: Stanford University Press, 1997.

Presser, Harriet B. "Shift Work and Child Care among Young Dual-Earner American Parents." *Journal of Marriage and the Family* 50, no. 1 (1988): 133–148.

———. "Some Economic Complexities of Child Care Provided by Grandmothers." *Journal of Marriage and the Family* 51, no. 3 (1989): 581–591.

Pryor, Frederic L., and Nelson H. H. Graburn. "The Myth of Reciprocity." In *Social Exchange: Advances in Theory and Research*, edited by Kenneth J. Bergen, Martin S. Greenberg, and Richard H. Willis, 215–237. New York: Plenum Press, 1980.

Putnam, Robert D. *Bowling Alone: The Collapse and Revival of American Community*. New York: Simon and Schuster, 2000.

Pyke, Karen. "'The Normal American Family' as an Interpretive Structure of Family Life among Grown Children of Korean and Vietnamese Immigrants." *Journal of Marriage and the Family* 62 (2000): 1014–1029.

Reinharz, Shula. "Who Am I? The Need for a Variety of Selves in the Field." In *Reflexivity and Voice*, edited by Rosanna Hertz, 3–20. Thousand Oaks, Calif.: Sage, 1997.

Risman, Barbara, and Kristen Myers. "As the Twig Is Bent: Children Reared in Feminist Households." *Qualitative Sociology* 20, no. 2 (1997): 229–252.

Rivas, Lynn May. "Invisible Labors: Caring for the Independent Person." In *Global Woman: Nannies, Maids, and Sex Workers in the New Economy*, edited by Barbara Ehrenreich and Arlie Russell Hochschild, 70–84. New York: Metropolitan Books, 2003.

Rogers, Jackie Krasas. *Temps: The Many Faces of the Changing Workplace*. Ithaca, N.Y.: Cornell University Press, 2000.

Romero, Mary. *Maid in the U.S.A.* New York: Routledge, 2002.

Roschelle, Anne R. *No More Kin: Exploring Race, Class, and Gender in Family Networks*. Thousand Oaks, Calif.: Sage, 1997.

Rubin, Gayle. "The Traffic in Women: Notes on the 'Political Economy' of Sex." In *Women, Class, and the Feminist Imagination*, edited by Karen V. Hansen and Ilene J. Philipson, 74–113. Philadelphia: Temple University Press, 1990.

Rubin, Lillian. *Just Friends: The Role of Friendship in Our Lives*. New York: Harper and Row, 1985.

———. *Worlds of Pain: Life in the Working-Class Family*. New York: Basic Books, 1992.

Ruddick, Sara. "Care as Labor and Relationship." In *Norms and Values: Essays on the Work of Virginia Held*, edited by Joram G. Haber and Mark S. Halfon, 3–25. Lanham, Md.: Rowman and Littlefield, 1998.

Russell, Graeme. *The Changing Role of Fathers*. St. Lucia, Queensland: University of Queensland Press, 1982.

Russell, Graeme, and Norma Radin. "Increased Paternal Participation: The Fathers' Perspective." In *Fatherhood and Family Policy*, edited by Michael E. Lamb and Abraham Sagi, 139–165. Hillsdale, N.J.: Lawrence Erlbaum Associates, 1983.

Sahlins, Marshall. *Stone Age Economics*. Chicago: Aldine, 1972.

Salmon, Marylynn. *Women and the Law of Property in Early America*. Chapel Hill: University of North Carolina Press, 1986.

Schaffer, Diane M., and Roland M. Wagner. "Mexican American and Anglo Single Mothers: The Influence of Ethnicity, Generation, and Socioeconomic Status on Social Support Networks." *Hispanic Journal of Behavioral Sciences* 18, no. 1 (1996): 74–86.

Schneider, David. *American Kinship: A Cultural Account*. Chicago: University of Chicago Press, 1980.

Schneider, David, and Raymond T. Smith. *Class Differences in American Kinship*. Detroit: University of Michigan Press, 1978.

Schnitzer, Phoebe Kazdin. "He Needs His Father: The Clinical Discourse and Politics of Single Mothering." In *Mothering against the Odds: Diverse Voices of Contemporary Mothers*, edited by Cynthia Garcia Coll, Janet L. Surrey, and Kathy Weingarten, 151–172. New York: Guilford Press, 1998.

Schor, Juliet B. *The Overworked American: The Unexpected Decline of Leisure*. New York: Basic Books, 1992.

Simmel, Georg. *The Sociology of Georg Simmel*. Translated by Kurt H. Wolff. Glencoe, Ill.: Free Press, 1950.

Sirianni, Carmen, and Lewis Friedland. *Civic Innovation in America: Community Empowerment, Public Policy, and the Movement for Civic Renewal*. Berkeley and Los Angeles: University of California Press, 2001.

Smith, Dorothy. "The Standard North American Family: SNAF as an Ideological Code." *Journal of Family Issues* 14 (1993): 50–65.

Smith, Kristin. "Who's Minding the Kids? Child Care Arrangements: Spring 1997." Washington, D.C.: U.S. Census Bureau, 2002.

Sonenstein, Freya L., Gary Gates, Stefanie R. Schmidt, and Natalya Bolshun. *Primary Child Care Arrangements of Employed Parents: Findings from the 1999 National Survey of America's Families*. Washington, D.C.: Urban Institute, 2002.

Stacey, Judith. *Brave New Families: Stories of Domestic Upheaval in Late-Twentieth-Century America*. New York: Basic Books, 1998.

———. *In the Name of the Family: Rethinking Family Values in the Postmodern Age*. Boston: Beacon Press, 1996.

Stack, Carol. *All Our Kin: Strategies for Survival in a Black Community*. New York: Harper and Row, 1974.

Stack, Carol, and Linda M. Burton. "Kinscripts." In *Families in the U.S.: Kinship and Domestic Politics*, edited by Karen V. Hansen and Anita Ilta Garey, 405–417. Philadelphia: Temple University Press, 1998.

Steedman, Carolyn Kay. *Landscape for a Good Woman: A Story of Two Lives*. New Brunswick, N.J.: Rutgers University Press, 1987.

Steinbeck, John. *The Grapes of Wrath*. New York: Viking, 1939.

Stewart, Abigail J., David G. Winter, Donna Henderson-King, and Eaaron Henderson-King. "Staying and Leaving Home: The Impact of Close Encounters with the Fifties in Midwestern Families." Paper presented at "Dutiful Occasions: Working Families, Everyday Lives," Ann Arbor, Mich., May 2001.

Stone, Deborah. "Caring by the Book." In *Care Work: Gender, Labor, and the Welfare State*, edited by Madonna Harrington Meyer, 89–111. New York: Routledge, 2000.

Thorne, Barrie. "Feminism and the Family." In *Rethinking the Family: Some Feminist*

Questions, edited by Barrie Thorne, with Marilyn Yalom, 3–30. Boston: Northeastern University Press, 1992.

———. "Pick-up Time at Oakdale Elementary School: Work and Family from the Vantage Points of Children." In *Working Families: The Transformation of the American Home*, edited by Rosanna Hertz and Nancy L. Marshall, 354–376. Berkeley and Los Angeles: University of California Press, 2001.

Townsend, Nicholas. *The Package Deal: Marriage, Work, and Fatherhood in Men's Lives*. Philadelphia: Temple University Press, 2002.

Trimberger, E. Kay. "Friendship Networks and Care." Working Paper 31, Berkeley Center for Working Families, University of California, Berkeley, 2002.

Tronto, Joan C. *Moral Boundaries: A Political Argument for an Ethic of Care*. New York: Routledge, 1993.

Trotter, Robert T., II. "Ethnography and Network Analysis: The Study of Social Context in Cultures and Societies." In *Social Studies in Health and Medicine*, edited by Gary L. Albrecht, Ray Fitzpatrick, and Susan C. Scrimshaw, 210–229. Thousand Oaks, Calif.: Sage, 2000.

Tuominen, Mary C. *We Are Not Babysitters: Family Child Care Providers Redefine Work and Care*. New Brunswick, N.J.: Rutgers University Press, 2003.

Uehara, Edwina S. "Reciprocity Reconsidered: Gouldner's 'Moral Norm of Reciprocity' and Social Support." *Journal of Social and Personal Relationships* 12, no. 4 (1995): 483–502.

Ulrich, Laurel Thatcher. "Housewife and Gadder: Themes of Self-Sufficiency and Community in Eighteenth Century New England." In *"To Toil the Livelong Day": America's Women at Work, 1780–1980*, edited by Carol Groneman and Mary Beth Norton, 21–34. Ithaca, N.Y.: Cornell University Press, 1987.

Ungerson, Clare. "Cash in Care." In *Care Work: Gender, Labor, and the Welfare State*, edited by Madonna Harrington Meyer, 68–88. New York: Routledge, 2000.

———. "Why Do Women Care?" In *A Labour of Love: Women, Work, and Caring*, edited by Janet Finch and Dulcie Groves, 31–49. Boston: Routledge and Kegan Paul, 1983.

U.S. Census Bureau. *Statistical Abstract of the United States*. U.S. Bureau of Labor Statistics, Bulletin 2307, 2001. Cited 2001, 2003.

———. "Who's Minding the Kids? Child Care Arrangements: Spring 1999." Detailed Tables (PPL–168). Washington, D.C.: U.S. Census Bureau, 2003.

Uttal, Lynet. *Making Care Work: Employed Mothers in the New Childcare Market*. New Brunswick, N.J.: Rutgers University Press, 2002.

Waldrop, Deborah P., Joseph A. Weber, Shondel L. Herald, Julie Pruett, Kathy Cooper, and Kevin Juozapavicius. "Wisdom and Life Experience: How Grandfathers Mentor Their Grandchildren." *Journal of Aging and Identity* 4, no. 1 (1999): 33–46.

Walker, Karen. "Always There for Me: Friendship Patterns and Expectations among Middle-Class and Working-Class Men and Women." *Sociological Forum* 10, no. 2 (1995): 273–296.

———. "Men, Women, and Friendship: What They Say, What They Do." *Gender and Society* 8, no. 2 (1994): 246–265.

Warren, Elizabeth, and Amelia Warren Tyagi. *The Two-Income Trap: Why Middle-Class Mothers and Fathers Are Going Broke*. New York: Basic Books, 2003.

Waters, Mary. *Ethnic Options: Choosing Identities in America*. Berkeley and Los Angeles: University of California Press, 1990.

Weinberg, Davida Jean. "Reciprocity Reconsidered: Motivations to Give and Return in the Everyday Exchange of Favors." Ph.D. diss., University of California, 1994.

Wellman, Barry. "Are Personal Communities Local? A Dumptarian Reconsideration." *Social Networks* 18, no. 4 (1996): 347–354.

———. "The Network Community: An Introduction." In *Networks in the Global Village: Life in Contemporary Communities*, edited by Barry Wellman, 1–47. Boulder, Colo.: Westview Press, 1999.

———, ed. *Networks in the Global Village: Life in Contemporary Communities*. Boulder, Colo.: Westview Press, 1999.

———. "The Place of Kinfolk in Personal Community Networks." *Marriage and Family Review* 15 (1990): 195–228.

Wellman, Barry, and Scot Wortley. "Different Strokes from Different Folks: Community Ties and Social Support." *American Journal of Sociology* 96, no. 3 (1990): 558–588.

Weston, Kath. *Families We Choose: Lesbians, Gays, Kinship*. New York: Columbia University Press, 1991.

White, Lynn K., and Agnes Riedmann. "Ties among Adult Siblings." *Social Forces* 71, no. 1 (1992): 85–102.

Williams, Joan. *Unbending Gender: Why Family and Work Conflict and What to Do about It*. New York: Oxford University Press, 2000.

Wilson, William Julius. *The Truly Disadvantaged*. Chicago: University of Chicago Press, 1987.

Wolfe, Alan. *One Nation, after All*. New York: Viking, 1998.

Wolff, Edward N. "Recent Trends in Wealth Ownership, 1983–1998." Working Paper 300, Levy Economics Institute, Annandale-on-Hudson, N.Y., 2000.

Wright, Erik Olin. *Classes*. New York: Verso, 1987.

Wrigley, Julia. *Other People's Children*. New York: Basic Books, 1995.

Young, Michael, and Peter Willmott. *Family and Kinship in East London*. 2d ed. Berkeley and Los Angeles: University of California Press, 1992.

Zandy, Janet, ed. *Liberating Memory: Our Work and Our Working-Class Consciousness*. New Brunswick, N.J.: Rutgers University Press, 1995.

Zaretsky, Eli. *Capitalism, the Family and Personal Life*. New York: Perennial Library, 1986.

Zavella, Patricia. *Women's Work and Chicano Families: Cannery Workers of the Santa Clara Valley*. Ithaca, N.Y.: Cornell University Press, 1987.

Zelizer, Vivianna. *Pricing the Priceless Child*. New York: Basic Books, 1985.

Zweig, Michael. *The Working Class Majority: America's Best Kept Secret*. Ithaca, N.Y.: ILR Press, 2000.

Zweigenhaft, Richard, and G. William Domhoff. *Diversity in the Power Elite: Have Women and Minorities Reached the Top?* New Haven, Conn.: Yale University Press, 1998.

Index

affirmative action, 12
Aldrich, Jane, 48, 51, 52, 54, 55, 60, 62–63, 139
Aldrich, Sarah, 47, 49, 50, 51, 53, 54, 56–57, 60, 65, 129, 132, 135, 139, 149, 168, 176, 177, 186, 193, 194
Aldrich network, 20, 47–71; authoritative anchor in, 48; background, 50–56; balanced reciprocity in, 176; characteristics of members of, 18tab; delegation of primary child care to skilled workers, 47; effect of parental separation on, 55; enrichment activities available, 53; executive style of, 67–69; expectation that help be paid for, 129; extended kin network in, 54; family participation in, 47; gender/marital status of members, 19tab; grandfather in, 186; member exclusion issues, 149, 150; members, 48, 48tab, 49, 57–67; need/capacity assessment and, 168–169; philanthropic activities in, 52, 70; public service obligations in, 67–69; reliance on nonkin, 69; role of men in, 193–194; sense of family in, 54; transportation needs, 61–62; view of nonkin in, 129
anchors: backgrounds, 48, 49, 50–56, 78, 80; centrality of, 14; characteristics of, 29, 78, 79, 103–106; child care arrangements made, 31–32, 56–57, 104–105; child rearing philosophy shared with members, 17; education, 29; employment experience, 29–30,

49, 50, 79; establishment of primary child care arrangements by, 18; exclusion of individuals from networks, 148–154; family relationships, 30–32, 56–57; as gatekeepers, 21; identifying and screening network members, 127–154, 234n25; interviews with, 29–32, 56–57, 78–81, 103–106; management style, 48, 56–57; need for confidence in other caretakers, 68; need to determine trustworthiness of members, 143; recruitment tactics, 21; screening for network, 21, 234n25; seeking to establish stability in network, 143; stability and, 14; use of inclusion principles, 133–147

Baltzell, E. Digby, 71
Becker, Barbara, 100, 142
Becker, Dina, 98, 103–106, 135, 138, 142, 149, 151, 162, 163, 167, 169, 170, 174, 188, 194–196
Becker, Kent, 100, 108–109, 129, 134, 136, 140, 142, 147, 151, 152, 174, 175, 187, 212
Becker, Michaela, 100, 101, 103, 116, 129, 142, 144, 152, 153, 165
Becker, Peter, 100, 101, 109–110, 130, 167, 202, 203
Becker, Ryan, 99, 100, 102, 113–114, 134, 140, 142, 151, 187
Becker, Shannon, 100, 111–112, 140, 142, 152, 178

Becker, Susan, 100, 101, 104, 110–111, 130, 147, 171

Becker network, 20, 98–123, 100*tab*; background, 99–103; balanced reciprocity in, 173–175; centrality of children in, 118–121; characteristics of members of, 18*tab*; culture of helping in, 118–121; family-first approach, 129, 130; gender/marital status of members, 19*tab*; kinship obligation in, 165–166; labor supply in, 121–123; member exclusion issues, 149; need/capacity assessment and, 169–172; reciprocity in, 162–164; role of men in, 194–196; split-shift child care strategy, 98–99; television issues in, 146–147; traditions of care in, 99–103; uncles in, 186, 187, 188; view of nonkin, 129

Becker-Walde, Aaron, 114–116

Becker-Walde, Donalyn, 114–116

Bergman, Ruth, 74, 86–88, 155, 170, 178

Blair-Loy, Mary, 94

Brennan, Amanda, 92, 170

Brennan, Jack, 72, 79–81, 135, 137, 142, 145, 146, 155, 156, 169, 170, 177, 189, 201, 207

Brennan, Tom, 77, 82–84, 142, 146, 155

Brolin, Alex, 47, 52, 54, 57–58, 60, 70, 135, 136, 139, 168, 193, 194, 200, 201

Brolin, Jacob, 47, 49, 59–62, 186

Brolin, Kimberly, 47, 59–62

Burton, Linda, 45

capital, social, 15

Carter, Teresa, 77, 82–84

child care: advice from others on, 139; crisis of, 2; division of labor in, 107, 108; emergency, 45, 77, 89, 155–156; factors shaping, 19; formal, 6; gaps in, 10; gender and, 182–208; income spectrum and, 233n1; increase in demand for, 10; informal, 3; institutional, 72, 73, 76, 97; by kin, 3; lack of adults for, 2; mobilization of help

for, 7; nannies and, 47, 49; need for, 2; 'out of school time,' 9; patchwork arrangements of, 3; preference for kin in, 6; for school-age children, 9–10; sufficiency of arrangements, 18

child rearing: class differences, 144; 'concerted cultivation' approach to, 144; demographic trends and, 8; gender divisions of labor in, 6; gender strategies of, 7; mothers in paid labor force and, 8, 9; proportion of employed mothers in full time work and, 8, 9; shared values, 17, 21; shared values and, 27, 85, 142–147

children: continuation of legacy of family by, 4; 'latch-key,' 226n62; parental responsibilities for, 1; perception of fewer people caring for, 9–10; self-care by, 226n62; with working mothers, 8, 9

class: assets and, 14; child rearing approaches and, 231n18; child rearing variations, 144; contingencies of, 14; defining, 229n89; dynamics of, 14; effect on network composition, 128; home ownership and, 14; kinship and, 211–215; location, 14, 211, 221n12; myths of, 3; of network members, 17; privilege, 61; values and practices shaped by, 17

Coltrane, Scott, 203

Crane, Ben, 26, 35–36, 134, 136, 186, 190, 201–202

Crane, Brendan, 30

Crane, Fran, 25, 26, 31, 32–35, 141, 150, 166, 179, 189, 235n26

Crane, Patricia, 25, 130, 131, 132, 134, 142, 143, 149, 150, 173, 175, 188, 190, 192, 210

Crane, Robbie, 25, 40–41, 186, 189, 190

Crane network, 20, 25–46, 134, 135; balanced reciprocity in, 173, 175; characteristics of members of, 18*tab*; charitable caretaking behavior in, 44; child care arrangements made, 31–32; commodification of exchanges in, 46; competence issues in, 150, 151;

culture of helping others in, 42–45; employment experience, 29–30; employment flexibility in, 46; family-first approach, 42–45, 129; family relationships, 30–32; family resourcefulness in, 45; financial resources, 26; gender/marital status of members, 19*tab*; kin as care providers in, 27; kinship obligation in, 166; labor power in, 45–46; member exclusion issues, 149, 150; members, 26*tab*, 32–42; need/capacity assessment and, 168–172; neighborhood characteristics, 27–29; preference for family members as providers, 42, 43; role of men in, 189–193; scheduling, 26; shared responsibilities in, 25; uncles in, 186, 188; uneven resources available to, 45; view of nonkin, 129; vulnerability to health emergencies, 45

cultural expectations, 6

culture: of helping, 118–121; individualism and, 5; mainstream beliefs, 5; values and practices shaped by, 17

Cumming, Elaine, 185

Daly, Kerry, 200

day care, 73, 226n62. *See also* child care

divorce/separation, 47, 54, 55

drugs, 12

Dunn, Lydia, 55, 63–65, 132, 136, 139, 141, 193

Duvall, Maggie, 72, 78–79, 137–138, 145, 146, 154, 155, 156, 170, 177

Duvall-Brennan, Danielle, 76, 77, 81–82

Duvall-Brennan network, 20, 72–97, 73*tab*; balanced reciprocity in, 173; before/after-school arrangements, 77; challenge of reciprocity in, 155–157; characteristics of members of, 18*tab*; child-care strategies, 74–77; effect of geographical change on, 74–77; gender/marital status of members, 19*tab*; impact of careers on, 138; members, 73, 81–92; primary caregivers not in network, 97;

reciprocal obligations in, 170; resentments in, 81, 82; at risk for emergency care, 77, 155–156; role of men in, 197–200; share-care tactics, 76; substantial but brittle ties in, 73; television issues in, 145–146; view of nonkin in, 129

Duvall-Brennan, Scott, 76

emergencies, 45, 77, 89, 155–156

Emerson, Brenda, 90–92, 199

employment: affirmative action and, 12; anxiety over, 95, 137; changing to accommodate child care needs, 138; class location and, 213; constraint by structures of, 137; constraints on women in, 212; decisions on child care and, 127; family-friendly, 74–77; female-dominated occupations, 8; flexibility as factor in ability to be in networks, 137; flexibility in, 46, 76; government policies and, 12; household labor shortage and, 2, 8–9; inclusion in networks and, 136–139; lack of family-supportive conditions in, 8, 92–96; less flexibility in for women, 8; limiting demands of, 136; mothers and, 2; need for family-friendly places of, 136; scheduling for split-shift child care, 99; structural constraints of, 212–215

Eriksen, Shelly, 185

exclusion, network, 21, 148–154; affinity issues, 149–150; by anchor, 149–151; competence issues, 150–151; expense factors, 149–150; reasons for, 148–149; role model factors, 151; self-exclusion/opting-out, 151–154

familism, 5, 118–121

family: alternative structures, 210; assumptions on, 1; beliefs/traditions about, 4; cohesiveness, 101; coming first, 27, 118–121; conflict in, 131; cultural expectations in, 1; doctrine of privacy in defining, 4, 75, 121; effect of economic/social change on,

family (*continued*)
2; effect of structural forces on, 212; functionalist approach to ideology of, 222n11; intentional proximity of, 133–139; interdependence and, 5; members as property of head of household, 223n18; modern, 223n12; monolothic, 223n12; privacy and, 5, 121, 223n19; sense of lineage in, 119; solidarity, 99. *See also* kin

family, extended, 4, 5; changes imposed by industrialization, 222n11; primacy of family over individuals in, 5

family first, 27, 118–121

family, middle-class: contradictory images of, 5; cultural expectations and, 6; earnings decline for, 7; image of self-reliance and, 5; likelihood of use of networks for, 11; networks as normative asset for, 11; presentation as less familistic, 5

family, nuclear, 4; autonomy in negotiation of relationships in, 5; as heterosexual, two-parent, 4; ideology of, 2, 4–7; 'proper' configuration of, 2

family, upper-class: background characteristics of, 50–56; isolation of, 51; philanthropic obligations of, 52, 70

family, working-class: cultural expectations and, 6; economic change and, 11, 12; government policies and, 12; seen as aberrant for reliance on networks, 11; traditional use of networks in, 11

Farnsworth, Kate, 51, 55, 65–66, 68, 132, 137, 153, 177

fathers: becoming involved in care, 200–204; as breadwinners, 1, 4; cultural constructs of appropriateness of, 7; in networks, 183*tab*, 188–200; non-reliance on friends, 132

Feagin, Joe, 20

Fischer, Claude, 5

Fox, Robin, 185

friend(ship), 26, 36–38, 43, 131;

voluntary nature of, 131. *See also individual network members*

functionalism, 222n11

Garey, Antia Ilta, 14

gender: of caregiving, 182–208; division of labor, 4, 6, 182; networks of care and, 182–208; perspectives on kinship, 6; role-modeling, 190; social construction of, 6; strategies, 7

Gerson, Kathleen, 200

Gerstel, Naomi, 185

Gouldner, Alvin, 161, 165, 166, 167, 175

grandparents: in network, 184–188. *See also individual networks*

Hackstaff, Karla, 171

Hartsock, Nancy, 161

Hertz, Rosanna, 138

Heymann, Jody, 8

Hochschild, Arlie, 7, 169

Hoffman, Rebecca, 74, 76, 84–85, 145, 155, 166, 170, 171, 173

Holcomb, Robert, 1, 25, 38–40, 100, 101, 130, 135–136, 189–193, 203, 206, 207

Homans, George, 161

household labor shortage, 2, 8–9, 209, 225n57

ideology: child-rearing, 2; conflict with practice, 96–97; in everyday life, 4–7; of independence, 3; of individualism, 5; of intensive mothering, 6; of nuclear family, 4–7; power of, 4–7; of small/independent families, 2

imposition, 169–170

inclusion, network, 21, 133–147; availability and, 133; construction of place in, 133–136; individual expertise/specialization and, 133, 139–142; interpretation of time and employment in, 136–139; job flexibility as factor in, 137; need to assess members' time uses in, 137; principles of, 133–147; proximity of time/place, 133–139; sharing child rearing values and, 133, 142–147; use of television as defining issue in, 144–145

independence, 1, 2, 210; ideology of, 3

individualism: belief in, 5, 224n22; ideology of, 5; types of, 224n21

insurance, 26, 32

interdependence: beliefs on, 5; importance of, 162; informal networks of, 6; kinship and, 212; networks and, 14; reciprocity and, 162

James, Caitlin Becker, 112–113, 140, 143, 145, 169, 173, 174

Johnson, Tracy, 26, 36–38, 43, 130, 131, 132, 143, 150, 170, 173, 175, 190

kin: alienation from, 95–96; availability of, 6; constitution of, 6; dysfunction and, 6, 80; marginalization of, 147; preference for in child care, 6; rejection and, 6; restructuring relationships of, 4; trust of, 130

kinscription, 45

kinship: beliefs about, 4; class contingencies and, 211–215; constructing, 130; gender perspectives on, 6; obligations of, 6, 21, 130, 165–166, 235n26; reciprocity and, 159

labor: class division of, 6; conflict in division of, 90; gendered division of, 4, 21, 225n58, 237n15; household shortage of, 2, 8–9, 209, 225n57; itinerant, 45–46; market, 203–204; racial/ethnic division of, 6; racialized division of, 228n83; supply, 121–123; unequal division of, 107, 108

Lareau, Annette, 49, 119, 143, 144, 145, 182, 188

Macleod, Aidan, 54, 66–67, 176

Marx, Karl, 20

McKendrick, Lila Becker, 100, 101, 117–118, 130, 135

men, 184–200; becoming involved in care, 200–204; concrete assistance from, 186; contributions of, 21; in Crane network, 189–193; feelings about involvement in networks, 183; impact of being with children on lives of, 188–189; impact of involvement on women in networks, 183, 189; involvement in child care, 182–208; involvement in networks, 21; in networks, 183*tab*; rejection of own father's child rearing philosophy, 200–203; relation to labor market, 203–204; responsibilities in networks, 183; 'watching' children, 185. *See also* fathers; uncles

Miller, April, 47, 49, 51, 54, 55, 58 59, 61, 141, 176

mobilization: social logics of, 21

mothers: cultural constructs of appropriateness of, 7; in full-time work, 8, 9, 98; reliance on friends, 132; stay-at-home, 1, 5

Nelson, Margaret, 159, 161, 177, 212

network members: affinity issues, 149–150; Aldrich network, 57–67; Becker network, 106–118; competence issues, 150–151; Crane network, 32–42; defining 'availability' of, 137; Duvall-Brennan network, 81–92; exclusion principles, 148–154; friends as, 131, 132; having networks of their own, 20, 88–90, 91; household structures of, 17; identifying and screening for, 127–154, 234n25; impact of network on lives of, 226n65; importance of time and employment for, 136–139; inclusion principles in recruiting, 133–147; individual expertise/specialization and, 133, 139–142; interchangeable, 101–102; navigation of structural constraints by, 21; need/capacity assessment and, 167–172; need to determine trustworthiness of, 143; proximity of, 133–139; role model factors, 151; sharing child rearing

network members (*continued*)
　values, 133, 142–147; social construc-
　　tion of candidacy for, 128–132
networks, middle-class, 72–123;
　'concerted cultivation' in, 144;
　employment and, 72; inclusion of
　more friends than kin, 128; other
　commitments of, 73; work arrange-
　ments and, 138–139; work-related
　demands and, 137
networks, upper-class, 47–71; impor-
　tance of friends in, 132; inclusion of
　more friends than kin, 128; manage-
　ment styles, 67–69; privacy and, 67;
　resources available, 50; transmission
　of privilege in, 671; work arrange-
　ments and, 138–139
networks, working-class, 25–46;
　activities of members, 32–42;
　importance of friends in, 132;
　multigenerational environments in,
　144; scheduling, 26; work arrange-
　ments, 139
networks of care: active kinship and,
　130; asking rules and, 169; character-
　istics of, 17; class and, 3;
　commodification of exchanges in, 46;
　conscious construction of, 3;
　constellations of resources in, 45–46;
　construction of balance in, 172–176;
　construction of place in, 133–136;
　defining, 228n86; demands of careers
　and, 92–96; economic restructuring
　and, 209–211; effect of class on, 128;
　exchanges in, 27; exclusion from, 21,
　148–154; family proximity and, 99;
　family reliance on, 10–12; fathers in,
　188–200; feeling rules and, 169;
　formal, 6; gender and, 6, 182–208;
　gender/marital status of members/
　anchors, 19*tab*; grandfathers in, 184–
　188; hierarchy of legitimacy in asking
　for help in, 167–172; impact of
　culture/immigrant status on forma-
　tion of, 227n69; impact of differential
　resources on formation of, 11;
　imposition and, 169–170; inclusion

in, 21, 133–147; informal, 6, 228n83;
　interdependence in, 3, 14; internal
　processes of, 13; involvement of
　extended kin in, 129; job flexibility
　as factor in inclusion in, 137;
　male involvement in, 21;
　marginalization of kin in, 147;
　member characteristics, 18*tab*;
　members' employment schedules
　and, 136–139; member specializa-
　tion/expertise in, 133, 139–142;
　need/capacity assessment and, 167–
　172; nonfamily members, 27;
　obligations of, 27, 165–166; opting
　out of obligations to, 21; partici-
　pant contributions in, 15; processes
　involved in assembling, 21;
　reciprocity in, 21, 155–181;
　research and, 12–19; shared child
　rearing values and, 142–147; social
　construction of candidacy for, 128–
　132; social policy and, 215–217;
　sorting mechanisms in, 17; staging,
　21, 127–154; time/place proximity
　in, 133–139; uncles in, 184–188;
　value of multiple caregivers in, 129
networks of interdependence, 74;
　development of, 21; purposeful
　construction of, 127; recruitment/
　screening for, 21
Newman, Katherine, 7, 137

Ostrander, Susan, 143

parents/parenting: demands of, 72;
　intensive, 72; need for assistance in
　child rearing, 5; responsibilities for
　children, 1; shared, 72, 97; working, 2
Pollyanna Fallacy, 167
proximity of members, 133–139;
　construction of place, 133–136;
　interpretation of time and employ-
　ment and, 136–139

Ramsey, Lee, 27, 34, 41–42, 143
reciprocity, 155–181; asking rules and,
　169; balanced, 158, 158*fig*, 159*fig*,

160*fig*, 162–164, 172–176; conceptualization of, 157–164; as continuum, 157, 158*fig*; cultural context, 160; defining, 156–157; feeling rules and, 169; generalized, 157, 158, 158*fig*, 159, 159*fig*, 160, 160*fig*; incurring of obligation in, 161, 165–166; interdependence and, 162; kinship and, 159, 160, 162–166; longevity of relationship and, 174; market-based model, 156, 158, 158*fig*; market factors in, 161; need/capacity assessment and, 167–172; negative, 158, 158*fig*, 160*fig*; negotiating, 164–179; norms of, 165, 166–167; obligation and, 165–166; perceptions of value in, 176–179; relationships with children as reward of, 177–179; rewards from, 176–179; social distance and, 159; social exchange theory and, 161; support gained from, 176–177

relationships: with children as reward, 177–179; interdependent, 1; kin, 4; lesbian, 17; network, 13; of network members, 17, 18; reciprocal, 21; restructuring, 4
religion, 51–52, 75, 95, 119
resources: constellations of, 14, 15
Roschelle, Anne, 10, 12, 184
Rubin, Gayle, 6
Russell, Byron, 74, 76, 85–86, 143, 145, 155, 166, 168, 171, 173

Sahlins, Marshall, 157, 158, 159, 160, 161
Schneider, David, 185
schools: before/after programs in, 2, 6, 9, 72, 226n63; as factor in networks, 74–77; structural inflexibility of, 9
self-reliance, 1
self-sufficiency, 1, 73, 210, 224n20; belief in, 5
Smith, Joan, 212
SNAF. *See* Standard North American Family
social: capital, 15; connections, 135; constructions, 21; mobility, 221n12

social security, 26
society: divisions of labor in, 6; myths of middle class in, 7; as sum of connections and relationships of individuals, 20; wealth disparities in, 7
Stack, Carol, 45
staging, 21, 127–154; dimensions of, 21; identifying and screening network members in, 127–154; inclusion principles, 133–147; phases, 127; process of, 127, 128
Standard North American Family, 4, 223n14; feminist discussion of, 223n12
Stanley, Lucia, 88–90, 177, 198
support groups: for men, 184; for mothers, 78, 88, 89, 90, 132, 177
support systems: dimensions of, 1

Townsend, Nicholas, 188, 189, 200
trust, 130, 143

Uehara, Edwina, 162, 172
uncles: in networks, 183*tab*, 184–188

values: child rearing, 17, 21, 142–147; class variation in, 143–144; commonality of perspectives as, 143; hard work, 143; independence, 143, public service, 143, 144; respect, 143; shared, 143; trust, 130, 143
Van Ausdale, Debra, 20

Walde, Mark, 98, 104, 106–108, 138, 149, 167, 171, 189, 194–196, 203, 207
Walker, Karen, 131, 132
workplace: assumptions on independence of workers in, 8; family-friendly, 136; lack of family-supportive conditions in, 8; lack of structural transformation in, 8; less flexibility in for women, 8

About the Author

KAREN V. HANSEN studies the intersections of gender, class, and race in the context of families and communities in the nineteenth-, twentieth-, and twenty-first-century United States. Author of *A Very Social Time: Crafting Community in Antebellum New England*, she also coedited *Families in the U.S.: Kinship and Domestic Politics* and *Women, Class, and the Feminist Imagination*. She is working on a study of the intercultural experiences of the Native Americans and Scandinavian immigrants to North Dakota in the early 1900s. Hansen is associate professor of sociology and women's studies at Brandeis University.